T0210824

Investigative Journalism, Democracy and the Digital Age

Investigative Journalism, Democracy and the Digital Age explores watchdog reporting in the digital age. Mapping new forms of global collaborative investigative journalism, the book debunks the myth that traditional newsrooms and investigative journalism are dying, and shows how journalists are adapting and experimenting.

The book brings together expert analysis and lively examples of investigative journalism in developed economies, with a close focus on the United States, United Kingdom, and Australia. Combining decades of investigative journalism analyses with expert interviews with watchdog reporters from across the globe, the author shows us how investigative journalism thrives despite significant challenges, and explores why investigative journalism is integral to democratic accountability and public trust in the news in a fake news era.

Offering an original contribution to media theory and providing a new methodology for defining and evaluating investigative journalism, this book will be an essential volume for scholars, media professionals, and academics in the fields of media and communications and postgraduate students of journalism.

Andrea Carson is a political scientist and an Associate Professor in the Department of Politics, Media, and Philosophy at La Trobe University in Melbourne, Australia. She has authored numerous articles on investigative journalism, Australian politics, election campaigns, and digital media. Her most recent co-authored book is *Australian Politics in the Twenty-First Century: Old Institutions, New Challenges* (2018). She was awarded Australian Research Council (2018–21) funding as part of a team using big data to understand the media's role in political debate and policy decisions. She holds a PhD in Political Science and a Master of Arts in International Politics. She has taught courses on journalism, political communication, women in politics, and campaigns and elections. She worked as a newspaper journalist and section editor at *The Age* in Melbourne from 1997 to 2001 and as a radio broadcaster (RRR) and radio and television producer (Australian Broadcasting Corporation) from 2001 to 2010. She is a regular media commentator and examines the latest media trends and issues for *The Conversation*'s 'Media Files' with colleagues, available on iTunes.

Routledge Research in Journalism

News of Baltimore
Race, Rage and the City
Edited by Linda Steiner and Silvio Waisbord

The Trump Presidency, Journalism, and Democracy
Edited by Robert E. Gutsche, Jr.

Russia's Liberal Media
Handcuffed but Free
Vera Slavtcheva-Petkova

Critical Perspectives on Journalistic Beliefs and Actions
Global Experiences
Edited by Eric Freedman, Robyn S. Goodman, and Elanie Steyn

Economic News
Informing the Inattentive Audience
*Arjen van Dalen, Helle Svensson, Anotinus Kalogeropoulos,
Erik Albæk, Claes H. de Vreese*

Reporting Humanitarian Disasters in a Social Media Age
Glenda Cooper

The Rise of Nonprofit Investigative Journalism in the United States
Bill Birnbauer

Tech Giants, Artificial Intelligence, and the Future of Journalism
Jason Whittaker

Investigative Journalism, Democracy and the Digital Age
Andrea Carson

For more information about this series, please visit: www.routledge.com/
Routledge-Research-in-Journalism/book-series/RRJ

Investigative Journalism,
Democracy and the
Digital Age

Andrea Carson

NEW YORK AND LONDON

First published 2020
by Routledge
605 Third Avenue, New York, NY 10017

and by Routledge
2 Park Square, Milton Park, Abingdon, Oxon, OX14 4RN

First issued in paperback 2021

Routledge is an imprint of the Taylor & Francis Group, an informa business

© 2020 Taylor & Francis

Publisher's Note
The publisher has gone to great lengths to ensure the quality of
this reprint but points out that some imperfections in the original
copies may be apparent.

Library of Congress Cataloging-in-Publication Data
A catalog record for this book has been requested

ISBN 13: 978-1-03-209168-6 (pbk)
ISBN 13: 978-1-138-20052-4 (hbk)

Typeset in Sabon
by Apex CoVantage, LLC

For my wise and supportive parents,
Vonda and Stewart Carson

Contents

List of Figures   viii
List of Tables   x
List of Boxes   xi
Acknowledgements   xii

Introduction: Studying Investigative Journalism   1

1   From 'Rivers of Gold' to the Digital Economy   21

2   What Is Investigative Journalism?   53

3   Why Watchdog Reporting Endures: Theories About
    the Public Sphere, Media Power, and Democracy   83

4   Six Decades of Investigative Journalism: The 1950s
    to the 2000s   107

5   The Rise of Collaborative Investigative Journalism   144

6   New Frontiers: Big Data, Leaks, and Large-Scale
    Investigative Journalism   171

7   Bankrolling Journalism to Support Investigative Reporting   194

    Conclusion: The Future of Investigative Journalism:
    Reasons for Optimism   223

Appendix: Tools for Defining Investigative Journalism
(Operative Definition)   238
Index   241

Figures

1.1   Number of Australian Daily Metropolitan Newspapers,
1901–2017   24

1.2   Comparing Australian Print Walkley Award Winners,
1956–2011   30

1.3   Fairfax Media (FXJ) Share Price Over a Decade
Compared to the ASX200 Index (XJO)   33

1.4   News Corp Australia (NWS) Share Price Since the
Company Changed Its Structure Compared to
the ASX200 Index (XJO)   33

1.5   US Newspaper Advertising Revenue Growth
Compared to GDP, 1990–2016   34

1.6   Australian Newspaper Revenue (% Change) Compared
to Australian GDP   35

1.7   Losses in Paid Sales of Australian Print Newspapers,
2000–17   40

1.8   Selected Australian Daily Print Newspaper Circulations,
1984–2017   41

1.9   Decline in Paid Circulations of Daily Newspapers in
OECD States, 2007–09   42

1.10   Falling Levels of Trust in the Australian News Media
2010–17   46

2.1   The Traffic Light Scale Used to Define Investigative
Journalism   79

3.1   A Venn Representation of Conceptual Common Space
Between the Chaos and Control Models, Where
Investigative Journalism Is Likely to Endure in
the Digital Age   102

4.1a   Amount of Australian Broadsheet Investigative
Journalism, 1971–2011   110

4.1b   Amount of Australian Newspaper Investigative
Journalism Winning Walkley Awards, 1950s–2000s   110

4.2   'Golden Eras' for Australian Print Award-Winning
Investigative Journalism, 1956–2011   111

4.3   Australian Paid Print Circulation (per 1,000 Population)
        Compared to Amount of Investigative Journalism
        (Number of Broadsheet Stories per Month)   113
4.4   Percentage Comparison of Australian Walkley and
        Broadsheet Investigative Stories Defined as
        'Green Zone' Stories, 1970–2011   115
4.5   Percentage of Australian Print Investigations That
        Are Part of an Investigative Series, 1970–2011   128
4.6   Promotion of Investigative Stories (Australian Broadsheets)
        Over Time, 1971–2011   133
4.7   Press Walkley Awards: Amount of Australian
        Broadsheets Versus Tabloid Investigative Stories,
        1956–2011   135
4.8   The Medium That Produced the Most Australian
        Walkley Award-Winning Investigative Journalism   138
5.1   British Publishers of Award-Winning Watchdog
        Reporting, 2007–16   152
5.2   Number of Stories Passing the Definition of Investigative
        Reporting in Three Countries, 2007–16   153
5.3   Investigative Story Targets in Three Countries, 2007–16   154
5.4   Australian Walkley-Winning Investigative Stories:
        Systemic Issue Versus Single Issue, 1960s–2000s   156
5.5   Australian Publishers of Award-Winning Watchdog
        Reporting, 2007–16   159
5.6   US Publishers of Award-Winning Watchdog Reporting,
        2007–16   160

Tables

1.1 Australian Advertising Market Share by Platform, 2006–21   36

2.1 Criteria for Identifying Investigative Journalism in Content
Analysis   78

3.1 Comparison of Chaos and Control Media Models With
Reference to Investigative Journalism   96

5.1 The Award Categories and Number of Investigative Stories
Identified Across Three Countries From 2007 to 2016   150

Boxes

3.1 The Essential Elements Informing Herman and Chomsky's
Propaganda Model   92
3.2 Six Reasons Why Media Outlets Would Pursue Investigative
Reporting   99
4.1 The 1950s Investigative Reporting: The Melbourne *Herald*   120
4.2 The 1970s Investigative Reporting: *The National Times*
and *The West Australian*   122
4.3 The 1980s Investigative Reporting: *The Age*   123
4.4 The 2000s Corporate Investigative Reporting: *The
Australian Financial Review*   125
7.1 Types of Native Advertising   207
7.2 Examples of UK Philanthropists Funding Journalism in the
Digital Age   212
7.3 Examples of Billionaire Buyers 'Rescuing' News Media
Companies in the Digital Age   216

Acknowledgements

This book was many years in the making. My early impressions about investigative journalism formed during profitable times for newspapers in the 1990s. I was working as a journalist at *The Age* in Melbourne, Australia, and had a front row view of the painstaking work undertaken by practitioners like Gerard Ryle (now head of the International Consortium of Investigative Journalism). By 2004, I had moved to producing radio, television, and online content for Australia's public broadcaster, the Australian Broadcasting Corporation (ABC). What followed were more austere times for Australian media.

By 2010, I had returned to study, focusing my doctoral thesis on an analysis of what was happening to Australia's investigative reporting amid deepening economic uncertainty for the traditional journalism models. My interest in the media's watchdog role led to further studies in the United Kingdom and United States. The result of these multi-nation endeavours is this new comparative study: *Investigative Journalism, Democracy and the Digital Age*.

This monograph would not have been possible were it not for the selfless assistance and time of many wonderful people whom I would like to thank here. I begin with the investigative journalists, editors, proprietors, media equity analysts, and other media experts who agreed to be interviewed so that I could advance the story of what has happening to investigative journalism in the first decades of the 21st century.

I sincerely thank Wendy Bacon, Mark Baker, Richard Baker, David Barstow, Eric Beecher, Emily Bell, Helena Bengtsson, Linton Besser, Hamish Boland-Rudder, Tim Burrowes, Louise Connor, Sheila Coronel, Ross Coulthart, Mike Dobbie, Tim Duggan, Rafael Epstein, Jon Faine, Robin Fields, Michael Gawenda, Ray Gill, Ross Gittins, the late Michael Gordon, Christian Guerra, Bruce Guthrie, Jonathan Holmes, Brant Houston, Michael Isikoff, Andrew Jaspan, David Kaplan, Alan Kohler, Jeff Leen, Charles Lewis, Tory Maguire, Chris Masters, Kate McClymont, Nick McKenzie, Anna Nemtsova, Michael Parks, Paul Robinson, Walter 'Robby' Robinson, Gerard Ryle, Mark Scott, Fergus Shiel, Margaret Simons, Lenore Taylor, Hedley Thomas, the late Evan Whitton, and Marian Wilkinson. All gave generously of their time and expert knowledge about journalism and the media for no reward other than assisting me with my research. I also add the usual but sincere disclaimer that any errors are my own.

To my academic colleagues who have offered valuable assistance along the way, I also extend my heartfelt gratitude. These include Emeritus Professor Graeme Gill and Professor Sally Young who guided me when I decided to begin this project. My sincere thanks also to Emeritus Professor Rodney Tiffen, Professor Darren Halpin, Dr Denis Muller, and Dr Andrew Gibbons for commenting on earlier versions of this text and providing their constructive advice.

I am indebted to Tom Ormonde, whose passion for clarity and knowledge of journalism contributed to making this a better read. I also note the help of Dr Kate Farhall and Leon Gettler during the information gathering process. I have great appreciation for Hamish Wallace for his efforts in helping me in the final stages of this demanding project.

The team at my publisher, Routledge, have been a pleasure to work with. I acknowledge that sections of Chapters 5 and 7 draw on my published journal articles 'Behind the Newspaper Paywall—Lessons in Charging for Online Content: A Comparative Analysis of Why Australian Newspapers Are Stuck in the Purgatorial Space Between Digital and Print' in *Media, Culture & Society*, and 'Understanding Collaborative Investigative Journalism in a "Post-Truth" Age' in *Journalism Studies*. A section of Chapter 7 on new digital entrants is informed by Facebook-funded research *The Future Newsroom* published online at the University of Melbourne (https://arts.unimelb.edu.au/__data/assets/pdf_file/0003/2517726/20913_FNReport_Sept2017_Web-Final.pdf).

I want to further acknowledge my alma mater, the University of Melbourne's School of Social and Political Sciences, for providing me with opportunities to teach and research journalism and political science. A visit to Nepal for the Global Investigative Journalism Network (GIJN) conference in 2016 gave me the pathway to interview some of the experts quoted in the chapters ahead, and I thank the University of Melbourne Arts Faculty for the research grant that supported this travel.

Importantly, I must thank my current employer, La Trobe University, and especially Professor Lawrie Zion, Dr Kevin Brianton, and Professor Nick Bisley for their first-class welcome and for allowing me time to finish this work.

Of course, this is not an exhaustive list, and I appreciate my friends and family who have made life enjoyable during the more challenging stages of writing, including Farah Farouque and fellow *Media Files* (iTunes) podcasters, Associate Professor Andrew Dodd, and Professor Matthew Ricketson.

Finally, but never lastly, thank you to Andrew, my supportive husband, and our children, Alex, Lilly, and Emma, for your love, humour, and everyday acts of kindness.

Introduction
Studying Investigative Journalism

When one of Australia's leading newspaper companies announced in 2006 that its flagship city headquarters would move to an upmarket district overlooking Sydney's Darling Harbour, it was hailed as a 'Darling deal' (*Sydney Morning Herald* 2006).

John Fairfax Holdings occupied all five floors of the purpose-built building from the outset. Executives were on the top, with commanding views of city skyscrapers and the harbour, while the group's *Sydney Morning Herald, Australian Financial Review*, and *Sun-Herald* reporters filled the floors below.

The journalists had barely settled in to their swish new open plan office when the global financial crisis (GFC) struck, dealing a heavy financial blow to an already ailing global newspaper industry. Suddenly, Fairfax's new fancy harbourside building was taking on the appearance of a badly timed indulgence. Across North America and Europe, the GFC led to masthead closures, newsroom cutbacks, and thousands of job losses (Wunsch-Vincent and Vickery 2010). While Australia initially appeared to escape the worst of it (Young 2010), the combined effects of the GFC and the rise of the internet soon engulfed the local newspaper industry. In 2012, facing collapsing advertising revenue and falling newspaper circulations, Fairfax shed 1,900 staff, sold its main broadsheet printing presses at Chullora (Sydney) and Tullamarine (Melbourne), and converted its premium mastheads—*The Age, The Sydney Morning Herald*, and *The Canberra Times*—to tabloid size. It then erected paywalls to try to stem the revenue decline as audiences continued shifting online.

As reporters were made redundant, newly empty floor space in the Darling Harbour building was sublet to internet giant Google. As Google's business kept expanding, and as Fairfax's kept contracting, the global tech company took over the lower three floors, leaving remaining journalists to share desks on levels four and five. Then in January 2018, four years after Google moved in, Fairfax confirmed it was turning over the remainder of the building to the internet company and looking for a new home.

The symbolism was hard to miss. Google, having effectively conquered newspaper companies in the global battle for online advertising, was now physically taking over Fairfax's Sydney HQ. Although not the only online company to have been sucking ad and subscriber revenue away from traditional media companies, Google had certainly been among the main players. By 2019, the online giants known collectively as the FAANG—Facebook, Amazon, Apple, Netflix, and Google (trading as Alphabet)—had risen to achieve a collective market value just under US$3 trillion (Nasdaq 2019). By contrast, many of the legacy media companies at whose expense some of the FAANG group have prospered were struggling to stay alive.

Fairfax's mastheads have (so far) survived the digital revolution, but revenue and profits are a fraction of what they were in the boom times of the late 20th century, and the company no longer exists as a separate trading entity. Like so many other struggling newspaper companies in mature markets this century, Fairfax was taken over—in this case by an Australian commercial television network, Nine, at the end of 2018.

It is not an unfamiliar story. For many years, staff of the *Miami Herald* enjoyed some of the best views overlooking Biscayne Bay. In 2011, facing financial difficulties and needing to raise funds, its parent company Knight Ridder attached a huge billboard to its prized building, advertising Apple's iPad. At the time both companies were valued at just under US$4 billion (Grueskin, Saeve and Graves 2012, p. 1). By 2019, Apple was valued at US$787 billion while the struggling Knight Ridder, like Fairfax, had been taken over and had ceased to operate as an independent company.

The financial predicament of traditional media companies—particularly those involved in print, radio, and free-to-air television—has enormous consequences for journalism. Yet the future of journalism is not necessarily synonymous with that of the traditional media companies. Numerous academic studies this century have sought to shed light on how the collapse of the business model that supported mainstream media in the 20th century has impacted on journalism (Collins 2011; Nielsen 2012; Newman and Levy 2014; Picard 2011, 2014). Clearly, there are negative consequences for news reporting. As newsrooms have lost revenue, some areas of journalism have declined, including local reporting (Kurpius et al. 2010; Hayes and Lawless 2015; Nielsen 2015, 2012) and specialised areas such as courts (Graber and Dunaway 2017). Other studies have identified a widespread trend to a downmarket news approach, with concerns that this means less emphasis on investigative reporting (Sparks and Tulloch 2000; Street 2011; Dahlgren 2009) and a growing appetite for 'clickbait'. These are stories of high entertainment value but questionable wider public benefit that attract mass audience attention online (Bazaco, Redondo and Sánchez-García 2019).

Fears of an existential threat to investigative journalism have accompanied the closure of many mainstream media mastheads and the shrinking of newsrooms where mastheads continue to survive (Schultz 1998; Franklin 2008a; Curran 2005; O'Neill 2009, Kelley 2009; Beecher 2007). In the first decade of the new millennium there were predictions of 'a retreat from investigative journalism and hard news to the preferred territory of "softer" or "lighter" stories' (Franklin 2008a, p. 15). James Curran (2005, p. 225) reasoned that market pressures would lead to the 'downgrading of investigative journalism in favour of entertainment, while corporate ties [could] subdue critical surveillance of corporate power'. By the start of the second decade, Street (2011) observed that the narrative of decline of investigative journalism was widely accepted in scholarly circles. Yet he cautioned that it should not be embraced uncritically, but that 'a decline in investigative journalism' was context specific (2011, pp. 194–5). In this volume I take up that challenge to critically assess investigative journalism's prospects as the digital era enters its next phase.

What This Book Is About

This book is about investigative journalism and its monitorial role in a democracy in the digital age. It examines the changes to the operating environment of the news media from the 20th century and into the 21st, and the effects of the digital age on watchdog reporting. It takes the somewhat controversial view that investigative journalism is a distinct genre of reporting that must be considered and measured separately when studying the news media in democracies (for full details, see Chapter 2). As we near the end of the second decade of the third millennium, it is an opportune time to revisit the prevailing narrative of investigative journalism's inevitable decline—a narrative founded in the financial devastation suffered by mainstream media outlets in developed economies since the commercialisation of the internet in the mid-1990s (detailed below). As we move deeper into the century, changes in the practice of investigative journalism have emerged, and with them new opportunities for journalists. These developments warrant a reappraisal of widespread fears for the future of watchdog journalism and offer significant hope that this valuable pillar of modern democratic societies can continue to prosper, albeit in different forms.

Background: The Digital Disruption to 20th-Century Press

At the start of the 21st century, most newspapers in developed economies were experiencing declines in advertising revenue and paid circulation (Schudson 2003; p. 175; Tiffen 2002, p 38). Technological change that enabled new types of competition is the most commonly cited reason for declines in newspaper circulations dating back many decades. In the 20th century the fresh competition came in the form of radio and television, while in the 21st century it was the internet, online search engines, and social media.

The digital revolution has also largely emptied the so-called rivers of gold—classified advertising—over which press companies enjoyed a virtual monopoly throughout much of the 20th century. eBay and Craigslist Inc. were formative examples of non-media companies penetrating the classified advertising market, shifting advertisers' interest and dollars away from analogue and print to digital platforms. Digital competition further exacerbated media companies' revenue collapse by driving down unit costs of advertising. In 2012 the Newspaper Association of America found newspapers were reclaiming only US$1 in digital advertising revenue for every US$25 of print ad revenue lost. Alarmingly, the ratio had escalated from 1:7 just the year before (Brendish 2012).

Shifts in political attitudes in many democracies, including the United States, Australia, and New Zealand, have resulted in relaxation of restrictions on foreign and cross-media ownership, which in turn have led to mergers and acquisitions across the media industry and an increase in concentration of mainstream media ownership generally. In Australia, changes to content and media ownership regulations in the late 1980s, along with the rise of television news, contributed to the demise of *all* of its evening newspapers by 1990 (Tiffen and Gittins 2009, p. 181). Further changes to media ownership laws this century have resulted in a more foreign ownership and further consolidation of ownership of traditional media companies (Carson 2018).

Cultural and societal changes have also contributed to falls in newspapers' hardcopy circulations in developed nations. Faster-paced lifestyles have changed news consumption habits (Franklin 2008a, p. 6), while urban sprawl has altered commuter patterns and led to worsening traffic problems, making distribution of evening papers more difficult. The lack of public transport in outer areas of many cities means reading a newspaper on the way to or from work has ceased to be an option for many people (Franklin 2008b, p. 635). While nightly television news bulletins contributed to the demise of evening newspapers in the late 20th century, free-to-air television as a medium for news and current affairs has in due course become a victim of technology, having lost large numbers of viewers and advertising revenue to the internet in the 21st century. The arrival of on-demand viewing and easy access to an array of viewing platforms including mobile phones, game consoles, tablets, and computers, has spurred the drift of audiences away from scheduled free-to-air television.

Thus, the financial decline of large newsrooms in traditional media outlets in the digital age has been caused by a convergence of potent technological, economic, political, and cultural factors. Conversely, in less developed nations like India and Brazil, as literacy rates have improved so too have the fortunes and numbers of legacy media such as print newspapers (Wunsch-Vincent and Vickery 2010, p. 24). The complexity of these changes is discussed in Chapter 1. The financial challenges for traditional media in mature economies have raised questions about the viability of investigative reporting, which takes more time and money to produce than daily reporting (see Chapter 2). If large newsrooms are unable to fund watchdog journalism, how can it survive in the digital age? This is a key question that is addressed throughout this book.

Why Study Investigative Journalism?

The internet is a contradictory force for news media in the 21st century. On one hand, it has displaced mass media's revenues—advertising and subscription sales—and weakened its monopoly on news; on the other hand, it has expanded the potential aggregate digital audience for traditional media's news provision through links, story sharing, and the reimagination of space and time. No longer are stories limited to a few column inches in the newspaper on one day. The digital age provides new methods for gathering and interpreting information, such as crowdsourcing stories and big data analyses. These provide journalists with new opportunities for greater audience reach and impact, and to engage in unprecedented global collaborations that put the international spotlight on injustices like slavery, environmental destruction, and economic inequality in its various forms.

Investigative or watchdog reporting is an important subject for academic inquiry because of its history of interrogating the use (and misuse) of power in society with outcomes that affect people's lives. This is a normative function of the news media in democracies (McNair 2017). To apply the simplest definition, watchdog reporters uncover information that matters to the public that would otherwise remain hidden were it not for a journalist's inquiries (de Burgh 2000, p. 17). Such revelations can have impacts on society in a number of ways. These include changes to government policies, closure of legislative loopholes, public repercussions such as criminal or civil charges for those who have acted illegally, or removal from public office of those who have breached public trust (the most famous example being the resignation of US President Richard Nixon in 1974 after reporters Bob Woodward and Carl Bernstein broke the Watergate scandal in *The Washington Post*). Investigative reporting can also increase the salience (public attention) of an issue that informs how people vote.

Investigative reporting is a sub-field of journalism studies that has received increased scholarly attention over recent years as concern about its future has intensified. Earlier studies like Jessica Mitford's (1979) *The Making of a Muckraker* were significant for returning credibility to investigative reporting after a period of complacency during the Cold War. Mitford was a pioneering investigative reporter before entering academia.

Her exposés included a book-length investigation into the funeral home industry in the United States, *The American Way of Death* (1963). In post-Watergate America, the decade-long research of Protess et al. (1991) explored different dimensions of investigative reporting to conclude that it was important for raising issue salience in the media, and for heightening the awareness of the public and elites to a level necessary to bring about policy reforms. They termed this 'agenda-building' (1991, p. 6).

Other seminal work about investigative journalism from the late 20th century included the research of James Ettema and Theodore Glasser, which differentiated investigative journalism from daily news reporting. Ettema and Glasser also focused on the moral dimensions of investigative work and its role in marking out the boundaries of social norms. Arguably, their most notable contribution was the 1998 book-length study *Custodians of Conscience*.

Julianne Schultz's (1998) assessment of the Australian media's role in providing democratic accountability raised questions about the autonomy of reporters and their capacity to investigate as media businesses became more revenue focused. David McKnight (1999) also traced the peaks and troughs of Australian investigative reporting and, like Schultz, concluded that the best days of reporting were probably in the past. British academic Hugo de Burgh's (2000) *Investigative Journalism: Context and Practice* provides case studies showing the societal impact of investigative reporting. Michael Schudson's books (2003; 2008) explain investigative reporting's unique accountability role in democracies.

Schudson (2008, pp. 14–15) provides two related reasons for why investigative journalism is important. The first is that it strikes a fear of negative publicity in the minds of public officials, and therefore cautions them away from wrongdoing. The second is that, unlike daily news reporting, which is targeted at a general audience, investigative reporting targets society's elites and decision makers and can trigger public debate about issues of democratic governance and corporate behaviour.

Notable accounts of investigative journalism practice in the 2000s include Mark Feldstein's (2010) historical analysis of Watergate and James Aucoin's (2007) *The Evolution of American Investigative Journalism*. Aucoin's social-moral development theory helps account for how the group Investigative Reporters and Editors (IRE) developed American investigative journalism, with a case study on the murder of founding member and reporter Don Bolles. More recent book-length studies of investigative journalism include James T. Hamilton's *Democracy's Detectives* (2016), Bill Birnbauer's *The Rise of Nonprofit Investigative Journalism in the United States* (2018), and Beth Knobel's *The Watchdog Still Barks* (2018). All these studies focus on investigative reporting in the United States and provide evidence to reappraise earlier pessimism about investigative journalism's prospects. This volume, while drawing similar conclusions, differs markedly in approach from these other studies by providing a systematic analysis of investigative journalism from an international perspective.

The findings in this book contest the view that investigative journalism is 'dying a death', as one British documentary maker stated (Toolis cited in Halliday 2010). Rather, I demonstrate how digital technology has opened up new opportunities for investigative journalism, including through access to large-scale data and new techniques and tools such as machine learning and free software for 'big data' analyses. Contrary to earlier predictions, watchdog reporting is also being sustained and nurtured by traditional media organisations, which have adapted and innovated to suit their tighter present-day editorial budgets. The changes include more focused selection of story targets and a trend towards collaborations—including with rival media outlets and with non-media organisations such as academia.

Of course, the normative aims of investigative journalism do not always match the reality, and there are limitations to the potential for investigative journalism this century. These themes are critically considered throughout this volume. However, while the broad conclusions of this book might be counter-intuitive for many, the theoretical framework (see below and Chapter 3) helps explain *why* investigative journalism endures in the digital age, and the empirical evidence accounts for *how* it does so.

The Book's Methods

In making the argument for a more optimistic view about investigative journalism's future, *Investigative Journalism, Democracy and the Digital Age* builds upon the empirical research of my PhD inquiry into Australian investigative journalism (Carson 2013), which developed a coding frame to examine six decades of newspaper investigative journalism (1956–2011). To achieve a more comprehensive picture, I conducted extensive interviews with investigative reporters and other media specialists, and content analyses of investigative journalism from the peer-reviewed Australian journalism awards, the Walkley Awards. This book builds on that foundational study, and on my subsequent studies on media payment models published in *Media, Culture & Society* (Carson 2015) and journalism research appearing in *Journalism Studies* (Carson and Farhall 2018; Simons et al. 2017; Young and Carson 2018). It incorporates valuable feedback on my research presented at international conferences, including Cardiff University's biennial 'Future of Journalism' (2013, 2015, 2017) and annual meetings of the European Consortium for Political Research (ECPR 2015, 2018) and American Political Science Association (2015, 2016).

The book's central argument is developed and further substantiated through international fieldwork interviewing investigative journalists in 2016 and 2017, with a particular focus on the United Kingdom, United

States, and Australia for comparative analysis. Further fieldwork was undertaken in Australia exploring the state of digital-only newsrooms and their funding models (Carson and Muller 2017). I also undertook desktop studies of industry and academic reports from specialist research institutions including the European Journalism Centre, Oxford University's Reuters Institute, and the US Pew Research Center, as well as government and intergovernmental agencies such as the Organisation for Economic Co-operation and Development (OECD) and Britain's Ofcom. Given the rapid pace of change in the media, reports by consulting firms and trade unions have provided useful up-to-date accounts of media trends. These have included PricewaterhouseCoopers' annual *Global Entertainment & Media Outlook* and publications by the Newspaper Data Exchange and Australia's Media Arts and Entertainment Alliance (MEAA), among others. By gathering this international data from industry and academia, cautious comparisons can be made within and between news organisations and countries about the state of investigative journalism this century.

Scope

This book traces changes in newsrooms since the late 20th century after the collapse in the historical business model and revenue bases of traditional media companies in Europe, Australia, Britain, and North America. To gain a specific understanding of what has happened to investigative journalism in democracies in the internet era, I undertake a comparative analysis focused on original data gathered from the United States, the United Kingdom, and Australia. For a more granular assessment, a single country case study approach is applied to Australian investigative journalism (see Chapter 4).

The study comprises mixed research methods including almost 50 original interviews with media experts, content analysis of Australian daily newspapers (1971–2011), and longitudinal examination of the comparator countries' award-winning journalism sourced from national journalism awards. To befit the theoretical framework, I focused on similar countries with mature economies to test the health and role of watchdog reporting this century. The study does not explore investigative journalism in non-democratic or democratically transitioning countries. While this would be a useful area of inquiry, these countries do not easily fit within the theoretical framework, and to do so was beyond the reach and expertise of this volume.

Investigative journalism is examined across various media platforms including analogue and digital-only, as well as outlets with varied funding models. Where detailed analysis is required, the focus is on newspapers because, notwithstanding significant cutbacks, they (and their online iterations) remain central to original news provision in democracies. Collectively, newspapers still employ very large numbers of professional journalists and remain important providers of investigative journalism (Knobel 2018).

Theories Used in the Book

This book brings together theories from disciplines of political science, journalism, media, and communication studies. Journalism and media power, democratic governance, and politics cut across research disciplines just as they intersect in the living world. Therefore, media theories of liberal democracy, political economy, critical studies, and the public sphere are drawn upon to interrogate the relationship between liberal democracy, the public sphere, and investigative journalism (see Chapter 3).

These different traditions offer dialogic insights about media historically. They provide useful normative frames to direct inquiries about what drives the technological and regulatory environments for journalism in contemporary liberal democracies. The different approaches also offer a multifocal lens for understanding how the dynamic reporting environment impacts upon investigative journalism and the organisations and people undertaking it.

However, the main framework applied in the book for understanding the endurance of investigative journalism is a chaos-and-control model arising from the 20th-century mass media theories of dominance and pluralism. Looking at its components separately for a moment, theories that best fit within the chaos paradigm are liberal democratic theory and McNair's (2006) revision of Max Horkheimer and Theodor Adorno's use of the term 'cultural chaos'. Dominance or control theories include the Frankfurt School's Critical Theory, other Marxist perspectives, and political economic approaches to the mass media.

Before considering the main framework, a useful starting point for understanding the role of the media in political discourse and democratic accountability is Jürgen Habermas' theorisation of the public sphere—which across its lifespan influenced both chaos and control paradigms. Habermas also outlines a special role for the press in formulating the public sphere. As the public sphere is referred to throughout this book, I briefly touch on Habermas' account here to show the relationships between the 'ideal' of the public sphere, the media, and democratic accountability.

The Public Sphere

While Habermas' writings have evolved since his 1962 text *The Structural Transformation of the Public Sphere*, his original thesis has continued to heavily influence media scholarship. The public sphere's enduring appeal is as a conception of a public communal space, free of the state, where public opinion can be formed.

Defined as the communal, communicative space in which 'private people come together as a public' (Habermas 1992, p. 27), the public sphere emerged because increased trade activity required regular information, free of state interference, to prosper with the rise of mercantilism (p. 36). Coffee houses in Britain, tea salons in France, and 'blossoming journals' in Germany provided public spaces for the bourgeoisie to exchange information (p. 72). This spread to the United States through political pamphlets such as Thomas Paine's famous *Common Sense*. But the public sphere was more than a space for regular information exchange; it enabled the visible transfer of ideas beyond state control, forming a 'private domain carved off from public authority' (p. 25). It was a place to critique the state and compel public authority to 'legitimate itself before public opinion' (p. 25).

Newspapers spread information further than any public gathering and provided a key means, beyond the coffee houses and journals, to communicate and facilitate political discourse. The newspaper, in the words of Habermas, had become the 'public sphere's pre-eminent institution' (Habermas 1992, p. 181). By 1834, a significant milestone in the development of public opinion occurred, when England's House of Commons overturned its ban on reporters taking notes in the London gallery and finally acknowledged the role of the press by providing physical space for reporters (Vice and Farrell 2017, p. 15).

The Fourth Estate

Half a century earlier, in 1787, the term 'fourth estate' was coined by the Scottish philosopher and writer Thomas Carlyle. Noting the reference by the Irish statesman Edmund Burke to the existence of three estates, or powers, in the British Parliament—the commons (House of Commons), the nobility, and the clergy (House of Lords), Carlyle reported: 'Burke said there were Three Estates in Parliament; but, in the Reporters' Gallery yonder, there sat a *Fourth Estate* more important far than they all' (Carlyle [1908] 1948, p. 392). While scholars note that the fourth estate is a mutable term that has represented different things in different country contexts, it has become a short form for the 'ideal' of the news media providing democratic accountability.

Meanwhile, across the Atlantic, the United States welded journalism to democracy in the First Amendment to the US Constitution: 'Congress shall make no law abridging freedom of speech, or of the press' (Schudson 2003, p. 200). While Australia has not explicitly enshrined freedom of the press in its constitution, its highest court, like Britain's, has interpreted an implicit right to freedom of expression to make the system of democratic government work. For the press, however, this freedom has been qualified in common law and refined from time to time in case law.

Transformation and Degeneration of the Public Sphere

For all its promise, the role of the press in connecting people to one another in an 'imagined community' to actively participate as citizens outside state control was not to last, according to Habermas. The successful commerce that engendered the public sphere became the instrument of its failure. Media organisations, which Habermas described as 'public organs' evolving out of the public's use of its own reason, were transformed by the late 19th century into 'a medium for culture as an object of consumption' (Habermas 1992, p. 183). Capitalism enabled successful profit-seeking news organisations to concentrate power and cultural authority, thus interrupting the free flow of ideas. Habermas stated that newspapers succumbed to the needs of their publishers, rather than their editors, arguing that 'they will do as they are told in the private interest of a profit-oriented enterprise' (p. 186). Habermas' criticism of the modern mass media was blunt and scathing: 'The world fashioned by the mass media is a public sphere in appearance only' (p. 171). Here, Habermas' disillusioned perception of 20th-century media usefully links us to Marxist critiques that underpin 'control' theories of the media, which conceive of media owners prioritising profits above all else. While it is true that Habermas ultimately reconsidered his fatal conclusions about the public sphere, determining that deliberative democracy was still possible in the digital age, he attached significant qualifications.[1]

Habermas' original theory, while compelling, as the number of texts dedicated to it testify, is critiqued on many fronts, including for its lack of inclusivity (mainly of class, race, and gender), its singularity (overlooking the coexistence of multiple public spheres), and its historical amnesia. Rather than elaborating on these issues here, it should suffice to acknowledge the detailed appraisals of the theory by others (see Calhoun 1992).

For all its shortcomings, the conception of the public sphere has endured, and liberal democratic theory of the media was reinvigorated from the Habermasian framework. As media scholar Michael Schudson (2003, p. 67) stated, it has 'been held up as a normative model of exemplary civic life'.

Liberal Democratic Theory of the Media

Democracy literally means rule by the 'demos', or the people. The liberal tradition emphasises the virtues of freedom and liberty of the citizenry. Representative democracy is therefore predicated on the idea that the representatives of the 'demos' are accountable to those they represent.[2] Thus 'democracy is about an autonomous demos governing itself as a collective, which entails that rulers who control the coercive power of the state need to be constrained' (Hendriks and Karsten 2014, p. 42).

This book is concerned with the *liberal* aspect of democracy and the media's role in facilitating democracy. This includes providing quality information so that citizens are informed and able to meaningfully participate in the democratic process. Citizens should be able to encounter diverse and multiple viewpoints in the public sphere, including those of dissenting and critical voices of the state. According to Brian McNair (2003, p. 18), a well-functioning democracy requires at least three key elements: *participation, rationality* of choice, and *constitutionality*. Italian political philosopher Norberto Bobbio (1987, p. 19) combines the concepts of participation and rationality, saying the role of the media is to inform citizens so that they can ideally 'vote for the wisest, the most honest, the most enlightened of their fellow citizens'.

Important also are the constraints on public representatives to ensure they do not abuse their legislative powers or take undue advantage of the spoils of office by acting outside the rules. For McNair, *constitutionality* encompasses the agreed set of procedures and laws governing the conduct of elections. It oversees the behaviours of those who win them, and the legitimate activities of those who dissent (McNair 2017, p. 18). Therefore, a well-functioning democracy depends on the public being able to monitor its representatives and on the state accepting criticism of its own exercise of power. The media plays a role in both of these functions.

Investigative journalism goes a step further by exposing concealments in democratic governance. Nick Davies, a reporter for Britain's *The Guardian*, made an important observation about democracies compared to autocracies: 'In an established democracy, abuse of power cannot afford to be visible' (2014, p. xiv). In other words, if the rule of law in a democracy is deliberately broken, concealment becomes necessary to avoid consequences.

Direct democracy—a pure, idealistic form of democracy in which people would decide on policy initiatives directly—would be impractical for everyday national governance. Therefore, the relationship between the democratic representatives who govern and the governed has largely been facilitated by the mass media in the 20th century. The monitorial role is the domain of investigative journalism.

In the 21st century, however, this intermediary role is changing as social media allows direct engagement between legislators and the people. Different forms of monitoring power are also possible in the digital age. Political theorist John Keane (2010) observed that the digital age was a time of 'communicative abundance' (p. 739). The new century has provided new mechanisms for observing and reporting abuses of power, in an extension of what he calls 'monitory democracy'. Keane noted: 'Power-monitoring and power-controlling devices have begun to extend sideways and downward through the whole political order' (p. xxvii). But he also observed that monitory democracy's future 'has not yet been determined' (p. xxxiii). This book aims to show that investigative journalists remain part of that future, finding new ways to observe and report abuses of power on an unprecedented scale.

The Chaos-and-Control Framework

The relationship between media and power in democracies is often understood through the theoretical lenses of 'chaos' and 'control'. The control (or dominance) paradigm broadly includes critical approaches to media that view it as upholding the interests of dominant elites in capitalist societies. This approach largely assumes that audiences are passive and unable to rebuff media influence, and are disempowered by top-down economic and political forces. It is a pessimistic assessment of modern news media, and is often referred to by critics when trying to make sense of rising infotainment, tabloidisation of content, and clickbait, which are all generally considered to be undermining journalism's civic role of accurately informing the public.

The chaos paradigm generally includes approaches that embrace technological developments such as the internet and, as Keane sees it, that allow for pluralism of media content, sources, and audiences. Its emphasis is on mechanisms for 'dissent, openness and diversity rather than closure, exclusivity and ideological homogeneity' (McNair 2006, p. vii). In the modern news environment, the digital age tends to be viewed optimistically and media technologies are seen as liberating, providing citizens with greater opportunities for participation and engagement and enabling greater political accountability and transparency in society. Yet it also has a darker side, one that enables the fast, viral spread of false information from anywhere at any time that can confuse the public about what is factual and what is not.

I propose a conceptual reorientation of these different approaches for the study of investigative journalism. While each of these streams is useful for understanding aspects of media power and its functionality in society, they are usually regarded as binaries, as oppositional. Instead, I propose that these two paradigms are not mutually exclusive but can coexist in relation to investigative reporting. Applying an overarching chaos-and-control theoretical framework helps explain the empirical evidence indicating that investigative journalism continues to prosper despite the uncertain economic future of many newsrooms. To do this I conceptualise the chaos and control paradigms as occupying two spaces on a continuum, with the possibility of overlap. This provides a theoretical space, however narrow, where a shared objective is possible (to undertake investigative journalism), even though media outlets' motivations for doing so may be disparate. Within this shared space, investigative journalism endures.

Philip Meyer and Kim Koang-Hyub (2003, p. 1) and other scholars have previously described this space in varying terms such as the 'profit controversy' and the 'sweet spot' (O'Donnell et al. 2012, p. 7). In essence, this space is where the imperatives for commercial news media to remain profitable *and* to maintain a public interest role can coexist. Chapter 3 explains the book's theoretical framework in detail.

The Chapters Ahead

To answer the primary question about the role and capacity of investigative journalism to survive in the digital age, the first three chapters of the book outline the background to the study, provide a working definition of investigative journalism, and describe my methods for measurement and the theoretical framework. The remaining chapters (Chapters 4–7) provide empirical evidence and multilevel analysis to show how investigative journalism has survived and adapted from the 20th century and into the 21st century. Together, these chapters bring together various strands of an important, timely international debate about the viability of investigative journalism and its relationships with the public sphere and democracy in the digital age. In doing so, the book rejects the view that investigative journalism is in perilous decline and argues, by contrast, the case for optimism about its future.

Chapter 1 outlines the major global trends in developed liberal democracies for the news media since the analogue era of the late 20th century through to the digital age. It includes a sobering account of the more recent financial hardships experienced by the press in developed economies, with a focus on the United Kingdom, the United States, and Australia. The chapter introduces the Australian mastheads to be analysed in Chapter 4 to empirically test the assertion that investigative journalism is in decline.

Chapter 2 examines what is meant by investigative journalism. Through a review of investigative reporting's antecedents, and drawing on the work of scholars who have researched this question to date, combined with my own interviews with investigative journalists from different countries, I identify key elements that are commonly thought to constitute investigative reporting. An original working definition of investigation journalism is advanced here based on nine traits, including five mandatory elements. In this chapter, concepts such as 'public interest', morality, objectivity, and journalistic ethics are brought into focus to further probe contemporary understandings of what constitutes investigative journalism.

Having established what investigative journalism is (and is not), Chapter 3 critically examines why investigative journalism matters to democracies and describes in detail the main theoretical framework outlined in this introduction. The chapter compares and contrasts the positive appraisal of investigative journalism that largely falls within liberal democratic theory with political economic theorists' negative assessments of the role of mass media in democratic societies, which also resonates with Habermas' conclusions in *The Structural Transformation of the Public Sphere*. In doing so, the chapter discusses limitations and common criticisms of investigative journalism. Importantly, while tensions exist between the two streams, the theoretical framework is employed to show why they are not entirely mutually exclusive and why neither theoretical space can fully explain modern mass media. It concludes by conceptualising an overlapping space between the 'control' and 'chaos' theories of mass media, where investigative journalism's economic viability and contribution to democratic accountability coexist.

In order to evaluate the state of investigative journalism today, it is important to understand its past practices and norms. Chapter 4 uses Australia as its case study to trace six decades of investigative reporting. It addresses two questions: How has investigative reporting developed and changed since the mid-20th century? And how has it fared since the arrival of the digital revolution? I address (and contest) the widely held romantic view that investigative journalism's 'golden age' is behind us. I demonstrate that there is no simple linear relationship between falling print media revenues and the state of quality newspapers' investigative journalism. Rather, I find that through experimentation and adaptation by newspapers, investigative journalism continues to endure and thrive in the 21st century.

Chapter 5 applies the working definition established in Chapter 2 in its content analyses of national journalism awards in the United States, Britain, and Australia. It aims to track the practice of investigative journalism over recent decades and to identify key changes in the transition from print and analogue to the digital era. I find that earlier adaptations and experimentations are paying off, with cross-media collaborations starting to win major awards and data journalism in watchdog reporting becoming more prevalent, while traditional media outlets continue to play an important role. However, these positive developments are occurring against a backdrop of the 'fake news' phenomenon and falling public trust in media. I argue that traditional media's evidence-based storytelling through investigative reporting provides a critical counterpoint and refuge for the public as confidence in the media is shaken by the virulent spread of fake news.

Chapter 6 uses original interviews and a comparative case study approach to expand on the implications of transnational cross-media collaboration and use of big data in investigative reporting. It examines the value of connecting large-scale data with unprecedented large-scale collaborations to critique global power and its injustices. I also consider negative impacts of the data age, including breaches of privacy through mass data surveillance, which can lead to pressure to reduce press freedom. The chapter begins with a short history of data journalism, including its roots in computer-assisted reporting (CAR), and progresses to the comparative study of the three most famous mega data leaks in recent journalism history: *WikiLeaks*, Edward Snowden's National Security Agency (NSA) revelations, and the International Consortium of Investigative Journalism's (ICIJ) Panama Papers. These examples reveal different models of transnational investigative collaborations and use of social science

methods in parsing data. I highlight mainstream media's role in supporting (and criticising) these large-scale investigations during a transformative period for news media.

Underpinning each of the chapters is the important question of how
investigative reporting is financed. Chapter 7 examines revenue-raising
options being employed by news media outlets in developed countries.
Among the models investigated are digital paywalls, native advertising,
crowdsourcing, philanthropy, micropayments, and 'white knight' proprietors. I find there is no single solution for funding news this century.
Rather, what has emerged is experimentation, adaptation, and flexibility
in the continuing search for new ways to fund journalism and, by extension, investigative reporting. While erecting paywalls has become the most
common adaptive mechanism employed by print mastheads in the second
decade of this century to get online readers to pay for content, this option
is largely shunned by digital-only newsrooms.

The concluding chapter brings together the earlier findings and provides an assessment about the future of investigative reporting and its
role in democratic accountability in the digital age. It offers a relatively
positive appraisal about how technology can regenerate the public sphere
on a global scale, offering new ways to critique power and injustices
through investigative journalism. It shows how reorienting the relationship between political economy and liberal democratic theories can
explain investigative journalism's endurance and its ongoing capacity to
inform the public sphere. While there are challenges and problems ahead
for investigative reporting, which are not ignored, the book concludes
there is considerable cause for optimism about this essential component
of modern democratic society.

A Final Note

This book uses a number of terms interchangeably. References to 'media'
and 'news media' are assumed to have the same meaning, as are 'reporter'
and 'journalist'. Although 'online' and 'digital' are not precise synonyms,
they are also used interchangeably here in reference to media.

My hope is that readers will find this book a useful guide for navigat-
ing recent dynamic changes to the media landscape and the consequences
of these changes for investigative journalism from one century to the
next. To my academic colleagues, the book presents a reappraisal of some
of the main theoretical frameworks used in their teaching and research
areas. I offer what I hope is a useful working definition for detecting
and measuring investigative journalism. My goal in writing this book
is to contribute useful empirical evidence and theoretical insights about
investigative journalism in the digital age to the existing scholarship. In
doing so, I offer an alternative narrative to the pessimistic predictions for
investigative journalism.

I have another, more personal reason for writing this book. As a political scientist, I have a keen interest in the intersection between media and politics, and I seek to acquire a better understanding of journalism's role in informing the public and safeguarding democracy. As a former journalist with almost 15 years' experience in newspapers, radio, television, and online reporting, I am concerned about the quality of information in the public sphere and the deleterious effects of fake news and falling public trust on civic discourse. For these reasons I am curious about the practice of investigative journalism in all its forms, its role in fact-based storytelling, and its impacts on society. Thus this book aims to engage various types of readers with academic, professional, or personal interests in journalism and its contribution to democracy. I hope you enjoy it.

Notes

1. The qualifications were that a self-regulating media system must maintain its independence in relation to its environments while also connecting political discourse with both civil society and the institutionalised political centre. The second condition was that an inclusive civil society must 'empower citizens to participate in, and to respond to, a public discourse which, in turn, must not degenerate into a colonising mode of communication' (Habermas 2009, p. 173).
2. Important elements of representative democracy include popular, periodic elections; competitive political parties; a free mass media; and parliamentary representative assemblies (Almond et al. 2010, p. 23).

References

Almond, GA, Powell, GB, Dalton, RJ & Strom, K 2010, *Comparative Politics Today: A World View*, 9th edn, Longman, New York.

Aucoin, J 2007, *The Evolution of American Investigative Journalism*, University of Missouri Press, Columbia.

Bazaco, A, Redondo, M & Sánchez-García, P 2019, 'Clickbait as a strategy of viral journalism: Conceptualisation and methods', *Revista Latina de Comunicación Social*, 74, 94–115.

Beecher, E 2007, 'War of words: The future of journalism as public trust', *The Monthly*, accessed 5 May 2018, from www.themonthly.com.au/issue/2007/june/1283826117/eric-beecher/war-words.

Birnbauer, B 2018, *The Rise of Nonprofit Investigative Journalism in the United States*, Routledge, New York.

Bobbio, N 1987, *The Future of Democracy*, Polity Press, Cambridge.

Brendish L 2012, 'Death by a thousand cuts?', *NZ Marketing Magazine*, November/December, 28–31.

Calhoun, C 1992, *Habermas and the Public Sphere*, The MIT Press, Baskerville.

Carlyle, T [1908] 1948, *Sartor Resartus, and On Heroes, Hero-Worship, and the Heroic in History*, J. M. Dent & Sons, London.

Carson, AL 2013, *Investigative Journalism, the Public Sphere and Democracy: The Watchdog Role of Australian Broadsheets in the Digital Age*, PhD thesis, School of Social and Political Sciences, Faculty of Arts, The University of Melbourne, Melbourne.

Carson, A 2015, 'Behind the newspaper paywall: Lessons in charging for online content: A comparative analysis of why Australian newspapers are stuck in the purgatorial space between digital and print', *Media, Culture & Society*, 37(7), 1022–1041.

Carson, A 2018, 'Nine-Fairfax merger rings warning bells for investigative journalism and Australian democracy', *The Conversation* 1 August, accessed 1 August 2018, from https://theconversation.com/nine-fairfax-merger-rings-warning-bells-for-investigative-journalism-and-australian-democracy-100747.

Carson A & Farhall, K 2018, 'Understanding collaborative investigative journalism in a "post-truth" age', *Journalism Studies*, 19(13), 1899–1911.

Carson, A & Muller, D 2017, *The Future Newsroom*, University of Melbourne, Melbourne, accessed 12 September 2017, from https://arts.unimelb.edu.au/__data/assets/pdf_file/0003/2517726/20913_FNReport_Sept2017_Web-Final.pdf.

Collins, R 2011, 'Content online and the end of public media? The UK, a canary in the coal mine?', *Media, Culture & Society*, 33(8), 1202–19.

Curran, J 2005, *Media and Power*, Routledge, London.

De Burgh, H 2000, *Investigative Journalism*, Routledge, London.

Dahlgren, P 2009, *Media and Political Engagement: Citizens, Communication and Democracy*, Cambridge University Press, New York.

Davies, N 2014, *Hack Attack: The inside story of how the truth caught up with Rupert Murdoch*, Faber and Faber Inc, New York.

Ettema, J & Glasser, T 1998, *Custodians of Conscience: Investigative Journalism and Public Virtue*, Columbia University Press, New York.

Feldstein, M 2010, *Poisoning the Press: Richard Nixon, Jack Anderson, and the Rise of Washington's Scandal Culture*, Farrar, Straus and Giroux, New York.

Franklin, B 2008a, *Pulling Newspapers Apart: Analysing Print Journalism*, Routledge, Abingdon.

Franklin, B 2008b, 'The future of newspapers', *Journalism Studies*, 9(5), 630–41.

Graber, DA & Dunaway J 2017, *Mass Media and American Politics*, CQ Press, Washington DC.

Grueskin, B, Saeve, A & Graves, L 2012, 'They story so far: What we know about the business of digital journalism', in *Tow Center for Digital Journalism*, Columbia Journalism School, New York.

Habermas, J 1992, *The Structural Transformation of the Public Sphere*, The MIT Press, Cambridge, MA.

Habermas, J 2009, *Europe: The Faltering Project*, Polity Press, Cambridge, UK.

Halliday, J 2010, 'Investigative journalism "dying a death"', *The Guardian*, 5 November, accessed 1 May 2018, from www.theguardian.com/media/2010/nov/04/investigative-reporting-sheffield-docfest.

Hamilton, J 2016, *Democracy's Detectives: The Economics of Investigative Journalism*, Harvard University Press, Cambridge, MA.

Hayes, D & Lawless, JL 2015, 'As local news goes, so goes citizen engagement: Media, knowledge, and participation in US House Elections', *The Journal of Politics*, 77(2), 447–62.

Hendriks, F & Karsten, N 2014, 'Theory of democratic leadership', in PT Hart & R Rhodes (eds), *Oxford Handbook of Political Leadership*, pp. 41–56, Oxford University Press, Oxford.

Keane, J 2010, *The Life and Death of Democracy*, Pocket Books, London.

Kelley, S 2009, 'Investigative reporting, democracy, and the crisis in journalism', in *Centre Blog*, 21 May, The Canadian Centre for Investigative Reporting, Ottawa.

Knobel, B 2018, *The Watchdog Still Barks: How Accountability Reporting Evolved for the Digital Age: How Accountability Reporting Evolved for the Digital Age*, Fordham University Press, New York.

Kurpius, DD, Metzgar, ET & Rowley, KM 2010, 'Sustaining hyperlocal media', *Journalism Studies*, 11(3), 359–76.

McKnight, D 1999, 'The investigative tradition in Australian journalism 1945–1965', in A Curthoys & J Schultz (eds), *Journalism: Print, Politics and Popular Culture*, University of Queensland Press, St Lucia.

McNair, B 2003, *An Introduction to Political Communication*, (3rd edn), Routledge, London.

McNair, B 2006, *Cultural Chaos: Journalism, News and Power in a Globalised World*, Routledge, London.

McNair, B 2017, *An Introduction to Political Communication*, (6th edn), Routledge, London.

Meyer, P & Koang-Hyub, K 2003, 'Quantifying newspaper quality: "I know it when I see it"', *Newspaper Division for Education in Journalism and Mass Communication*, conference paper, Kansas City, July 30, p. 1.

Mitford, J 1963, *The American Way of Death*, Quartet, London.

Mitford, J 1979, *The Making of a Muckraker*, Michael Joseph, London.

Nasdaq 2019, 'Will FAANG stocks remain the market's heartbeat in 2019', *Nasdaq*, 2 January, accessed 4 February, from www.nasdaq.com/article/will-faang-stocks-remain-the-markets-heartbeat-in-2019-cm1076395.

Newman N & Levy D 2014, *Reuters Institute Digital News Report 2014: Tracking the Future of News*, Oxford University Press, Oxford.

Nielsen, RK 2012, *Ten Years that Shook the Media World*, accessed 1 May 2014, from reutersinstitute.politics.ox.ac.uk.

Nielsen, RK 2015, *Local Journalism: The Decline of Newspapers and the Rise of Digital Media*, I. B. Tauris, London.

O'Donnell, P, McKnight, D & Este, J 2012, *Journalism at the Speed of Bytes*, The University of New South Wales, Sydney.

O'Neill, E 2009, 'Media: A duty to the wrongly accused: Miscarriage of justice investigations have fallen out of fashion with editors, but the cases keep piling up', *The Guardian*, p. 7.

Picard, RG. 2011, *Economies and Financing Media Companies*, Fordham University Press, Bronx.

Picard, R 2014, 'The future of the political economy for press freedom', *Communication Law & Policy* 19(1), 97–107.

Protess, D, Cook, F, Doppelt, J, Ettema, J, Gordon, M, Leff, D & Miller, P 1991, *The Journalism of Outrage: Investigative Reporting and Agenda Building in America*, Guilford, New York, NY.

Schudson, M 2003, *The Sociology of News*, W.W. Norton & Company, San Diego.

Schudson, M 2008, *Why Democracies Need an Unlovable Press*, Polity Press, Cambridge, UK.

Schultz, J 1998, *Reviving the Fourth Estate: Democracy, Accountability and the Media*, Cambridge University Press, Melbourne.

Simons, M, Tiffen, R, Hendrie, D, Carson, A, Sullivan, H, Muller, D & McNair, B 2017, 'Understanding the civic impact of journalism: A realistic evaluation perspective', *Journalism Studies*, 18(11), 1400–1414.

Sparks, C & Tulloch, J 2000, *Tabloid Tales: Global Debates Over Media Standards*, Rowman & Littlefield Publishers Inc, Lanham.

Street, J 2011, *Mass Media, Politics and Democracy*, Palgrave Macmillan, London.

Sydney Morning Herald 2006, 'Fairfax HQ move's a Darling deal', *Sydney Morning Herald*, 8 September, accessed 1 February 2019, from www.smh.com.au/business/fairfax-hq-moves-a-darling-deal-20060908-gdocm3.html.

Tiffen, R 2002, 'Political economy and news', in S Cunningham & G Turner (eds), *The Media and Communications in Australia*, Allen & Unwin, Sydney.

Tiffen, R & Gittins, R 2009, *How Australia Compares*, Cambridge University Press, Melbourne.

Vice, J & Farrell, S 2017, 'The history of Hansard', *Parliament UK*, accessed 7 February 2018, from www.parliament.uk/documents/lords-library/History-of-Hansard.pdf.

Wunsch-Vincent, S & Vickery, G 2010, 'The evolution of news and the internet', *Organization for Economic Co-operation and Development, Working Party on the Information Economy* (Report No. DSTI/ICCP/IE (2009) 14/FINAL), http://www. oecd. org/officialdocuments/displaydocumentpdf.

Young, S 2010, 'The journalism "crisis"', *Journalism Studies*, 11(4), 610–24.

Young, S & Carson, A 2018, 'What is a journalist? The view from employers as revealed by their job vacancy advertisements', *Journalism Studies*, 19(3), 452–72.

1 From 'Rivers of Gold' to the Digital Economy

> At the beginning of the twenty-first century, by any criterion the press has a far less central role among the mass media, and by all the most tangible measures newspapers are in relative and, increasingly, in absolute decline.
>
> (Tiffen 2010a, p. 127)

Introduction

This chapter examines dramatic political and economic changes to the landscape of traditional mainstream news media since the late 20th century with the arrival of the digital era. It identifies international trends in the financial underpinnings of the press in developed economies with a focus on the United Kingdom, the United States, and Australia. It traces the days from when print newspaper advertising revenue flowed like 'rivers of gold' to the digital age, in which advertising revenue has largely evaporated, resulting in industry-wide financial duress and concerns about the future of investigative reporting.

The chapter charts the economic decline of print newspapers in developed economies and uses Australia as a case study for more detailed analyses. Although Australia's print media sector is smaller than those of the United States, Britain, and some of the larger economies of Europe, it has similar attributes in its historical reliance on display and classified advertising for the majority of its revenue and in its long tradition of investigative journalism. Australia has also experienced almost identical effects to other developed economies from the arrival of the digital age, particularly since the global financial crisis of 2007–09. As in the United States, Britain, and Europe, collapsing advertising revenue across the Australian print media sector has led to cost-cutting, extensive journalism job losses, masthead closures (mainly regional), and plummeting company share prices. The financial plight of newspaper publishers in these countries has given rise to fears about the future of journalism, and in particular investigative journalism (Franklin 2008; Sampson 1996). This chapter presents evidence to support these concerns, particularly in relation to elite and broadsheet newspapers that have been leaders in investigative journalism since the mid-20th century. Yet while it is likely many legacy news titles across developed economies will ultimately not survive the digital revolution, it is argued in later chapters that fears of investigative journalism's demise are unfounded. It will be shown that the way that media outlets have responded to their new economic (and global) media landscape has seen investigative journalism escape the deepest cutbacks, and that newsrooms have adapted in ways so that watchdog reporting endures in the 21st century.

In charting the financial trajectory of the press from one century to the next, this chapter is divided into two sections. The first provides an overview of prominent Australian newspaper titles that have historically been local leaders in investigative journalism. These are mainly newspapers in the broadsheet tradition, which have won the most national peer-reviewed Walkley Awards for their investigative journalism (see Chapter 4). While the next chapter examines in detail how investigative journalism can be defined, for the purposes of this chapter, in its simplest expression it is often regarded as the pursuit of a truth that someone wants hidden, which is in the public interest (de Burgh 2000). The second section traces the decline of the print newspaper market in Australia, Britain, and the United States, using various indices to understand the basis of concern for investigative reporting's future. It tracks newspaper revenues and circulations from the heady days of the 20th century through to the arrival of the digital age in the 1990s, the GFC of 2007–09, and up to 2018. The chapter concludes with some observations and conclusions about the implications of the changed news media landscape for investigative journalism in Australia and other developed countries.

A Brief History of the Australian Newspaper Market

Australia's first newspaper, *The Sydney Gazette and NSW Advertiser*, was launched as a weekly on 5 March 1803 under government control (Walker 1980, p. 1). Following the lifting of government censorship in 1824, the first independent newspapers emerged (Mayer 1964, p. 10), among them the *Sydney Morning Herald* (known as the *Sydney Herald* from 1831 to 1841) (Walker 1980, p. 4) and *The Age* in Melbourne in 1854 (Mayer 1964, p. 10). Both were launched as broadsheets, in the British tradition of the time, and both went on to prosper and become leaders in Australian investigative journalism.

The Australian newspaper industry expanded for more than 100 years from about the middle of the 19th century. Between 1848 and 1886, the number of daily titles grew from 11 to 48, including regional dailies (Mayer 1964, p. 44). Expansion of daily titles slowed in the 20th century, with the total number hitting 54 by 1958 and peaking at 57 in 1984 (Tiffen 2015, p. 69). The 1980s was also the industry's financial peak, with historically large profits built on advertising revenue flows characterised in the industry as 'rivers of gold' (Hills 2010, p. 505).

The first significant signs of declining fortunes appeared towards the end of the 1980s; by 1990 the last of Australia's daily evening newspapers, *The Herald*, had ceased publication (Tiffen and Gittins 2009, p. 9; Tiffen 2015, p. 69). This coincided with broad destabilisation in the industry, with changes to cross-media ownership laws leading to a rush of acquisitions and mergers that resulted in an increase in print media ownership concentration across Australia.

In the 1990s came the biggest disrupter of all for newspapers across the developed world: commercialisation of the internet and the dawn of the digital media age. Until then, and for much of the 20th century, Australian newspapers had prospered financially by utilising their market power to sell display and classified advertising at premium prices, with journalism used as the lure to attract what the advertisers wanted: readers. The rise of digital media from the mid-1990s quickly eroded the monopoly position of newspapers in their advertising segments, particularly for classified ads. Competing online advertising platforms with low cost bases (and no journalism) had emerged, undercutting newspapers by offering vastly cheaper rates. In just a few years, news publishers lost much of the lucrative classified advertising revenue streams that had previously underpinned their businesses—and supported their journalism—particularly in the real estate, auto and job ad markets. The subsequent rise of global online behemoths Google and Facebook in the 2000s wreaked yet more havoc, attracting large volumes of newspapers' remaining advertising and reader bases away from their online sites and print products. By the start of 2016, it was estimated that Google, Facebook, and other digital companies had secured between A$4 billion and A$5 billion of a A$13.9 billion Australian advertising pool, or 35–40 per cent of the total (Morgan Stanley Research 2016).

The mass migration of ad revenue to the digital giants has resulted in extensive cuts in journalism jobs and other austerity measures by newspaper publishers. In this context, it may be surprising that more newspaper mastheads have not totally disappeared. By mid-2018, the number of Australian daily papers—including regionals—had slipped below its 1980s peak of 54, to 45 (Audit Bureau of Circulations 2017). But of the remaining titles, only 12 were metropolitan dailies—half the number that existed at the turn of the 20th century. Figure 1.1 shows the number of metropolitan dailies and number of owners in Australia from their peak of 26 (*not* including daily regionals) published by 21 different proprietors in 1923 (Walker 1980, p. 225), compared to 12 daily papers published by just three owners in 2018.

The Australian experience is mirrored in varying degrees internationally. In 1940 the United States had 1,878 daily weekday newspapers (Pew Research Center's Project for Excellence in Journalism [PRCPEJ] 2011). By 2016 their numbers had fallen by one third, to 1,286. As in Australia, the first wave of closures in the United States from the 1970s involved

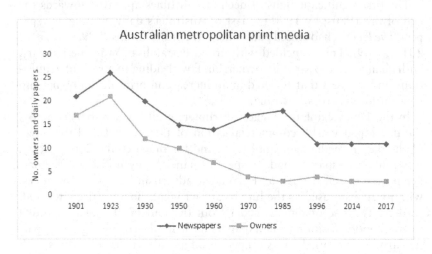

Figure 1.1 Number of Australian Daily Metropolitan Newspapers, 1901–2017

Source: *Author*, analysis of data from: Tiffen (2015, p. 66); Audit Bureau of Circulations. (2017). ABC Paid Media Audit (June 2017).

evening papers. In this century we are now increasingly seeing the demise of morning dailies.

With masthead closures, news media diversity has suffered. In 1909, 689 American cities had two or more competing daily paid newspapers. By 2011, diversity had declined dramatically, with just 11 cities having competing daily mastheads (Schulhofer-Wohl and Garrido 2013). In comparison, Australia has just two cities with competing mastheads: Melbourne and Sydney. Since the GFC, many surviving single-town newspapers in the United States have struggled financially.

A feature of the decline of the newspaper industry in Australia over recent decades has been a simultaneous reduction in the number of newspaper owners. Australia now has the highest newspaper ownership concentration of any developed economy, with more than 90 per cent of its daily papers owned by two proprietors: News Corp Australia and Fairfax Media (Tiffen 2010a, p. 87; IBISWorld 2017, p. 16). The potentially negative implications for society and democracy from a lack of media diversity are discussed in Chapter 3.

In early 2018 there were three major metropolitan print media owners in Australia. By the end of 2018, the second-largest newspaper company, Fairfax Media—owner of *The Age* in Melbourne and *The Sydney Morning Herald*, among other quality titles—had merged with free-to-air television network Channel Nine, further consolidating Australian media ownership. The deal ended the 177-year-old Fairfax brand. Fairfax's media assets included magazines, radio, the online real estate site Domain, streaming service Stan (already co-owned with Nine), and metropolitan and regional newspapers. At the time of writing, the future of Fairfax's regional mastheads such as the *Newcastle Herald* was unclear, as Channel Nine indicated during the merger talks that it had little interest in keeping them. Since the merger they have been purchased by former Fairfax manager Antony Catalano and billionaire Alex Waislitz's Thorney Investment Group. They purchased 170 regional and country newspapers from Nine Entertainment Co in April 2019. It is too early to predict what this purchase will mean for their journalism. This is of concern for investigative journalism because Fairfax has a long history of producing investigative reporting, as does its Newcastle paper. Of note was the *Newcastle Herald*'s standout investigation by reporter Joanne McCarthy into child sex abuse in the Catholic Church. McCarthy's investigation began in 2006 and led to the establishment in 2012 of a Royal Commission into Institutional Responses to Child Sex Abuse.

Australia's third-largest newspaper owner is Seven West Media, controlled by self-made billionaire Kerry Stokes. Among Seven West's diverse media businesses (television, magazines, radio, online, and regional newspapers) is Perth's only hardcopy daily, the *West Australian* (Seven West Media 2017).

The largest of Australia's print proprietors is News Corp Australia (Finkelstein and Ricketson 2012, p. 58). It is the local subsidiary of Rupert Murdoch's international News Corporation. News Corp Australia[1] (henceforth News Corp) is a multi-platform media company with interests in pay television, magazines, online media, and newspapers. To illustrate Australia's concentration of ownership, in 2012 Murdoch's Australian company owned almost 150 national, metropolitan, suburban, regional, and Sunday print titles, including mass audience daily metropolitans, in every state and territory. By 2018, News Corp had extended its ownership to more than 200 metropolitan, suburban, regional and Sunday print titles, including daily metropolitans in each state except Western Australia (News Corporation 2018, p. 5; IBISWorld 2017, p. 23). News Corp owns Australia's only surviving general news national daily broadsheet, *The Australian*. Like its sister broadsheet-style publication in Britain (*The Times*), it tends to be a voice for right-of-centre political perspectives.

Key Australian Broadsheets

The next section gives an overview of four key newspapers owned by the two largest media companies, Fairfax Media and News Corp. The four mastheads—*The Australian, The Sydney Morning Herald, The Age*, and *The National Times*—are selected for analysis because of their long track record for producing award-winning investigative journalism. The empirical evidence derived from analysing the investigative journalism of these mastheads is detailed in Chapter 4. The chapter also uses the example of Australian print investigative journalism to demonstrate the watchdog role newspapers played in holding society's power holders to account in the 20th century.

The Sydney Morning Herald and The Age

The *Sydney Morning Herald* (*SMH*), which was launched as the weekly *Sydney Gazette and NSW Advertiser* in 1803, is the oldest continuously published newspaper in Australia (Sprague 1962, p. 236). It became a daily in 1840 and its title was changed to *The Sydney Morning Herald* shortly thereafter (Sprague 1962, p. 236).[2] In 1841 it was sold for £10,000 to Charles Kemp and John Fairfax, beginning a long era under Fairfax family control. In the 1920s, under the control of two sons of Sir James Fairfax, it was renowned for its conservative character (Sprague 1962, p. 236). Its editors' responsibilities were limited to the editorial page— an arrangement that continued until 1965, when editor John D. Pringle insisted as a condition of his second-term reappointment that he be entitled to editorial authority over the entire newspaper (Walker 1980, p. 1).

Pringle's changes were the beginning of an important transition away from the newspaper's conservative traditions and for an increase in focus on investigative journalism—a focus that has continued to the modern era. In recent decades the *SMH* had developed a centrist editorial and political profile—giving more space to conservative right-wing views than its Fairfax stablemate, *The Age*, but less than its national rival, Murdoch's *The Australian*.

The Age, the oldest surviving daily masthead in the state of Victoria, was launched by brothers John and Henry Cooke during the turmoil of Victoria's gold rush in 1854 (*The Age* 2010). Two years later the paper was sold to the Syme brothers. It became a public company in 1948. A hostile takeover bid in 1972 saw it sold to its minor shareholders, John Fairfax and Sons, owners of the *SMH*. It had a renowned 'golden era' under the editorship of Graham Perkin from 1966 to 1975 (Hills 2010, p. 1), during which it was voted alongside *The Washington Post* and London's *Times* as one of the world's top ten quality newspapers—in part for its commitment to investigative reporting (Hills 2010, p. 1). But measured by circulation, its greatest era came after Perkin under the editorships of Michael Davie and Creighton Burns, when Monday to Friday circulation peaked in 1981 at an average of more than 250,000 sold copies a day. The circulation of its tabloid competitor, *The Sun*, had peaked a decade earlier (Hills 2010, p. 505).

The financial fortunes of both *The Age* and *The Sydney Morning Herald* turned for the worse in the 1990s amid turmoil on the Fairfax company share register. The family lost control of the company in December 1990 after 26-year-old Warwick Fairfax launched an ill-fated private takeover involving a level of debt that proved his undoing. Eventually, after a period of jostling for control by various prominent publishers,

Fairfax and its mastheads ended up in the hands of institutional investors (*The Age* 2010). In 2018 the company merged with the Nine network.

The Australian

The Australian, which began publication on 15 July 1964 under its dynastic owner Rupert Murdoch, was Australia's first national broadsheet newspaper. At the time, Murdoch owned three other Australian tabloid mastheads that had lowbrow reputations for crime stories and tawdry classified advertising, including for brothels (Hills 2010, p. 226).[3] At the time of its launch, it was claimed *The Australian* was created to appease Murdoch's mother, Dame Elizabeth Murdoch, who had urged her son to produce a 'quality' broadsheet newspaper (Hills 2010, p. 226). Its mission statement was to bring readers 'impartial information and independent thinking that are essential to the further advance of our country' (Hills 2010, p. 227). Although *The Australian* rarely turned a profit and was as a result financially subsidised by (the then named) News Limited's other papers, former *Age* editor (1989–92) Mike Smith said the Murdoch broadsheet did what no other Australian paper was doing at the time: it combined the latest overseas design with clever, innovative journalism (Hills 2010, p. 226). *The Australian* is the only national paper for general interest news and the last to retain the broadsheet format. It promotes a commitment to investigative journalism, having launched a dedicated investigative unit in 2010 (Mitchell 2011; *The Australian* 2018). Leading the unit was journalist Hedley Thomas, a six-time national Walkley Awards winner for journalism. Thomas won the prestigious Gold Walkley in 2007 for a story exposing unsubstantiated police and federal government allegations of terrorist activities levelled at Queensland doctor Mohamed Haneef; and in 2018 for investigating the cold case disappearance of Lynette Dawson in 1982 in a podcast series titled *The Teacher's Pet* (see Chapter 2).

The Australian is viewed by academic Robert Manne as the 'country's most important newspaper', though not in his case for good reasons (Manne 2011, p. 3). Other academics, commentators, and politicians at least agree with his assessment of *The Australian*'s power. Beginning with the editorship of Chris Mitchell in 2002, the paper was seen by Manne as pursuing a right-wing agenda and ruthlessly exercising 'power without responsibility' (Manne 2011, p. 5). Himself accused of left-wing bias by News Corp columnists (Young 2011, p. 243), Manne argued that Mitchell, as the *Australian*'s editor-in-chief (2002–15), was committed to 'advancing the causes of neoliberalism in economics and neoconservatism in foreign policy' (Manne 2011, p. 3). Former Greens leader Bob Brown accused the *Australian* and other News Corp newspapers of belonging to the 'hate media', which opposed leftist viewpoints, particularly opposing individuals advocating action over climate change (Cowie 2011). This polemic depiction of News Corp's most 'serious' newspaper fans fears that the loss of Fairfax's rivalry, following the Nine takeover in late 2018, will leave Australians with a news landscape skewed to the right of politics. Until the merger, Fairfax, along with the public broadcaster ABC (which is obliged by its charter to be politically neutral) had provided a counter to the political right (News Corp) in the Australian media landscape.

The National Times

Seven years after *The Australian*'s first edition, Fairfax launched national broadsheet masthead *The National Times* in 1971. Founded by Vic Carroll, previously managing editor of the *Australian Financial Review* (*AFR*), its mission was to uncover 'the news behind the news' and to *analyse* rather than *tell* news stories (Fairfax Media 2011). Despite closing after 16 years of publication, it broke many of the nation's biggest stories through its investigative reporting. Academic David McKnight credited *The National Times* with producing some of Australia's best investigative journalism:

> The 1980s was a 'golden age' of investigative journalism in Australia, of whom the best known outlets were *The National Times* newspaper and ABC TV's *Four Corners* program. The period spawned a number of royal commissions, several ministers of the crown resigned or were sacked, and the issue of corruption in politics and the police force was firmly established in the public mind as never before.
>
> (McKnight 1999, p. 155)

There are degrees of subjectivity in identifying which Australian media organisations have the most impressive record for investigative journalism. McKnight nominates *The National Times*, while former *Age* investigative reporter, the late Ben Hills, a biographer of *The Age*'s most celebrated editor Graham Perkin, argued that *The Age* outshone competitors with its investigative reporting. He wrote: 'At *The Age*, especially, there is an unbroken stream of dedicated—and decorated—investigative reporters dating from the founding of *Insight* [its investigative unit] up until today' (Hills 2010, p. 487).

McKnight identified two peaks for investigative reporting in Australia: immediately post-war, 'when the hopes of a post war "new order" were high', and in the decade of the 1970s and early 1980s responding to the 'cultural and political' revolution of the 1960s (Hills 2010, p. 487). The latter period coincided with the peak for Australia's daily newspaper circulations. Julianne Schultz, researching investigative journalism in the late 1990s, also identified the 1980s as a pinnacle for Australian investigative journalism (Schultz 1998, p. 195).

In retrospect, this period of great profitability for newspapers helped subsidise quality investigative journalism in Australia, particularly by the broadsheets. But as this book will show, investigative journalism can continue, and even thrive, when media companies' economic fortunes wane if there is a commitment to producing it.

The Broadsheet Tradition

The tradition of broadsheet newspapers came from Britain. The word 'broadsheet' defined the size of the newspaper page—typically 22 inches or 56 centimetres deep. The popularity of this large format was encouraged by a 1712 British tax on newspapers, which was levied according to the number of pages (Bloy 2010). Broader sheets meant fewer pages and less tax. In London, *The Times* acquired its own printing press and published daily from 1814. Tabloid newspapers (generally half the size of broadsheets) did not proliferate until the start of the 20th century, long after the tax was repealed. 'Tabloid' was a word said to be coined by London pharmaceutical company Burroughs Wellcome & Co. to describe compressed tablets in the 1880s (Bailey 2010). As in the compressed tablets, tabloid papers were disparagingly seen as easy-to-digest 'compressed' journalism, and they were also the domicile of 'yellow' journalism and the 'penny' press, scorned for its sensationalism in the 19th century (Habermas 2002, p. 168).

Globally, the distinction between the editorial content of the broadsheets compared to the tabloids is rarely any longer simply determined by page size. Previously, the larger format papers were associated with a higher income-earning readership and were considered a mark of style and authority. This divide became increasingly blurred as many large format papers chose to go smaller or 'compact' to make it easier for public transport commuters to read (Cole 2008, p. 182). In Britain, the papers previously labelled broadsheets were now more accurately termed 'elites', referring to their content rather than their size to distinguish them (McNair 2000, p. 16).

In Australia, the symbolic and physical difference between the two varying-sized papers still largely existed until 2012. *The SMH, The Age*, and the *Australian* generally appealed to well-educated and wealthier readers in the so-called AB demographic (Guthrie 2010, interview with the author, 11 February). The *Australian Financial Review* (*AFR*) was the exception—a compact national daily but also with an AB audience (C. Guerra 2010, interview with the author, 12 November). For this reason, the *AFR* is referred to as a financial tabloid and the others as broadsheet-style papers, as are other international mastheads that are imbued with the broadsheet culture, if not its physical size. Studies have found that broadsheet-style newspaper readers in Australia are 'highly interested in politics', and that these newspapers provide more political news than their tabloid rivals (Young 2011, pp. 27–8).

The now defunct *National Times*, a tabloid turned weekly broadsheet, won many Walkley Awards for its investigative journalism. Between them, the four mastheads, whose investigative stories are analysed in Chapter 4, form a comprehensive sample of Australian broadsheets over seven decades. In terms of geographical reach, *The Australian* today is the nation's only national broadsheet. *The Age* and *SMH* cover Australia's two largest cities, Melbourne and Sydney, respectively.

Bruce Guthrie, a former editor of both *The Age* and its Melbourne tabloid rival, the *Herald Sun*, identified investigative journalism as a key point of difference (the other being its political coverage) between the traditional Australian broadsheets and their competitors (Guthrie 2010, interview with the author, 11 February; Young 2011, p. 311).

This book's analysis of print journalism across seven decades from the 1950s until the 2000s of the country's only national peer-reviewed media awards, the Walkley Awards, shows that broadsheets have produced most of Australia's award-winning investigative reporting since the Walkleys originated (see Figure 1.2). Tabloid mastheads have also produced award-winning quality investigative journalism, as has the ABC's *Four Corners* television program. However, in Australia, as in other countries, broadsheet-style newspapers, from *The Washington Post* to London's *Sunday Times* to Melbourne's *Age*, have the strongest record of pursuing and publishing significant investigative stories.

In the selected sample, out of 187 print-media Walkley Award winners, 114 were for broadsheet journalists. Of the winners analysed that passed the operational definition of investigative journalism, 101 print stories were considered investigative, and two thirds of these stories (67) were from broadsheet mastheads. This figure is higher if the compact *AFR* is included in the broadsheet figures, rising to 71 per cent. The significance of size on investigative content is discussed in Chapter 4.

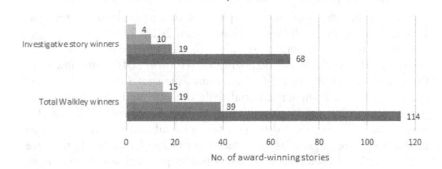

Figure 1.2 Comparing Australian Print Walkley Award Winners, 1956–2011

Source: Author, analysing Australian Walkley awards data from nine select categories; N = 187

Print Revenue Decline and Investigative Journalism

The decline of traditional funding models for print newspapers, arising from the digital media revolution, led many academics and practitioners in the first decade of the third millennium to suggest 'quality' investigative journalism was under threat (Cordell 2009, p. 118). For example, when asked at an editors' international conference about the future of investigative journalism, Mike van Niekerk, then editor-in-chief of online at Fairfax Media, had words of caution:

> The economics of new media make it very difficult to fund investigative journalism in the same way it once was. If you're talking about the kind of journalism that keeps governments and corporations at check, I am concerned about its sustainability in the future.
>
> (Chainon 2010)

Concern about the viability of print investigative reporting is not confined to Australia. Surveyed at an annual US Investigative Reporters and Editors (IRE) conference, journalists were collectively pessimistic about the future of investigative journalism, with one describing publishers' priorities as more about 'profits than Pulitzers' (Aucoin 2007, p. 1). Eamonn O'Neill, a British investigative reporter who spent 11 years investigating the wrongful imprisonment of convicted murderer Robert Brown, among other major stories, lamented how times were changing. He said he had worked for less experienced editors who would not support his efforts to take on miscarriage of justice projects because they 'feared and avoided such stories'. The hassle affected their career prospects (O'Neill 2009, p. 7). O'Neill stated that he had also encountered editors who did support investigative work, but for more shallow reasons: 'They want easy results and clichéd tales instead of the complex truth' (O'Neill 2009, p. 7). On one occasion, his story did not have the conclusion the editor expected of it; it was never published, and the public were left in the dark about its outcome. O'Neill observed that 'investigations aren't as prominent as they once were, but that by no means indicates that the terrible crimes they should be uncovering have gone away' (O'Neill 2009, p. 7).

A 2008 survey of its members by Australia's national journalists' union, the Media, Entertainment and Arts Alliance (MEAA), found reporters' morale was low and pessimism high about the future of quality journalism due to financial pressures on media proprietors. The MEAA survey found falling numbers of journalists in full-time positions, and that those who remained were required to perform broader roles within their news organisation. There was a perception that there was little time for investigative reporting, except among those who belonged to a dedicated investigative unit (Media, Entertainment and Arts Alliance [MEAA] 2008, p. 16). One unnamed respondent wrote: 'Cost cutting has led to reduced staff, while roles have expanded, which is greatly affecting the quality of the paper. Morale in the newsroom is also very low' (MEAA 2008, p. 16).

The Decline of Australian Newspapers

A snapshot of the Australian newspaper market, using a variety of different measures, revealed troubling economic times for the foreseeable future for metropolitan daily newspaper businesses (MEAA 2008, p. 9). Key measures used then included tracking advertising and other revenue, number of full-time employed editorial staff, company share price, annual newspaper sales figures, and reader demographics. On the last point, information about readers included what percentage still read the newspaper each day, compared with other media, and how they might access newspapers (free online or paid print copy). With reference to some of these measurements of newspaper performance, the next section of this chapter independently assesses Australian newspapers' outlooks (financial and other) to provide context to consider newspapers' prospective commitment and capacity to undertake costly journalism, including investigative reporting.

Stock Price

A ten-year analysis of Australia's two major newspaper companies' stocks reveals underperformance compared to the national average. This matters because it reduces the market capitalisation of a media company and limits its capacity to borrow funds to take on new ventures. Figures 1.3 and 1.4 show that between 2000 and 2010, compared to the top 200 Australian publicly listed companies on the S&P/ASX 200 indices,[4] which trended upwards, the stocks of Australia's two largest newspaper companies, Fairfax Media (FXJ) and News Corp (NWS), fell. Fairfax was harder hit. Its 20-year high was a stock price of A$4.80 during a peak in the market just before the global financial crisis (GFC) began in 2007. It fell dramatically thereafter, and by 2012 was down to A$0.46 (Australian Securities Exchange 2012). In 2018, just before the announcement of a merger with the free-to-air television station Channel Nine, it had steadied at A$0.68 (see Figure 1.3) (Australian Securities Exchange 2018). Stock prices, like other indicators, suggests 2012 was a nadir for print media in Australia, and that legacy media's lowest point in Australia lagged a few years behind the hard times for newspapers in Europe and North America.

The picture for News Corp shares is less bleak than for Fairfax. Until 2013, the financial performance of News Corp's newspapers was partly obscured by its very profitable global entertainment holdings in film and television. This changed when the global company announced in 2012 plans to separate its lucrative entertainment assets from its publishing arm. The profitable Australian newspapers were bundled in to the new

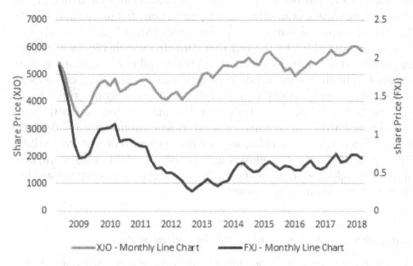

Figure 1.3 Fairfax Media (FXJ) Share Price Over a Decade Compared to the ASX200 Index (XJO)

Source: Prices and Research: FXJ Fairfax Media Limited (2018).

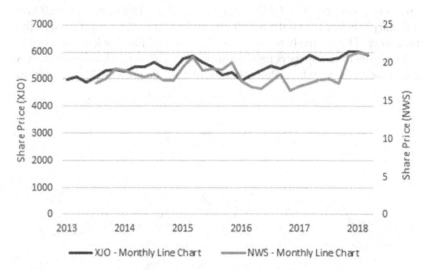

Figure 1.4 News Corp Australia (NWS) Share Price Since the Company Changed Its Structure Compared to the ASX200 Index (XJO)

Source: Author using data from Prices and Research: NWS News Corporation (2018). Retrieved from https://www.asx.com.au/asx/share-price-research/company/NWS

publishing group, News Corp Australia (News Corporation 2012). For this reason, the graph begins at 2013, when the new entity formed.

The share prices of Australia's two biggest newspaper companies plummeted in early 2009, coming out of the GFC. Fairfax fell below A$1 and News Corp fell below A$11 (Australian Securities Exchange 2010). However, news stocks in other developed nations fell more sharply than Australian securities during the global crisis (MEAA 2008, p. 6). This may be accounted for by the fact that Australia weathered the GFC better than most developed nations; its economy did not technically go into recession. The high concentration of newspaper ownership served as an added protection because the market was relatively uncompetitive. Emily Bell, formerly the UK *Guardian*'s digital media director, said at the time that the global fall in newspaper share prices would be no short-term trend: 'This is systematic collapse—not just a cyclical downturn' (MEAA 2008, p. 6). Evidence to follow suggests she was right. Yet the implications of the decline in print media for investigative journalism are less clear, as discussed in later chapters.

Newspaper Revenue: Australia and the United States

Of newspapers' total revenue, advertising revenue has historically been a key measure of the health of newspaper businesses. Figure 1.5 compares annual changes in US newspaper advertising revenue since 1990 with annual growth in gross domestic product (GDP). Print advertising revenue grew more strongly than GDP during much of the 1990s, but after 2000 it fell sharply below the GDP growth rate and has stayed there for most of the time since. The relatively recent rise of Google and Facebook as formidable competitors to newspapers for revenue is starkly illustrated in figures for US digital advertising, which show that almost all the growth (99 per cent) in

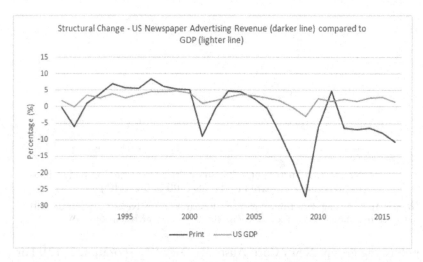

Figure 1.5 US Newspaper Advertising Revenue Growth Compared to GDP, 1990–2016

Source: Author developed using data from Pew Research Center (2017).

digital advertising revenue went to Google or Facebook between the third quarter of 2015 and the same period in 2016 (Newman 2017).

Australian total newspaper revenue has followed a similar pattern of decline as the United States compared to national changes in GDP since 1994, just prior to the commercialisation of the internet in Australia. As shown in Figure 1.6, the decline accelerated after the GFC between 2010 and 2012, by which time annual falls in revenue exceeded 10 per cent. Although the rate of revenue decline has slowed since 2012, the trend has remained downward.

The continued erosion of newspaper revenue has raised concerns about the future of journalism and, by extension, the functioning and accountability of political democracy and its institutions. Falling revenue potentially affects the capacity of newspaper organisations to commit to expensive, time-consuming journalism, including investigative journalism, which historically has played a critical role in holding powerful individuals and institutions in Western democracies to account. However, as will be shown in Chapters 4 and 5, innovation and adaptation by Australian newspaper organisations to their chastened circumstances has not only enabled the survival of investigative journalism, but in some cases it has resulted in its dissemination to a wider audience through collaborations with other media and non-media outlets.

Advertising Revenue in Australia

Research from economists and media industry specialists shows that, on all measures, Australian newspapers have been losing ground to other media

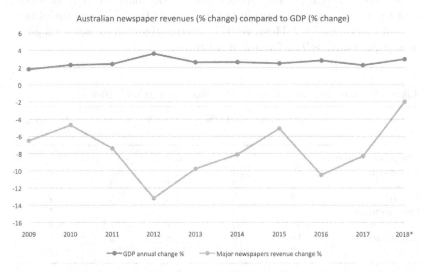

Figure 1.6 Australian Newspaper Revenue (% Change) Compared to Australian GDP

Source: Author using data from Reserve Bank (GDP) and newspaper data from IBISWorld (June 2018).

as the migration of advertising to online platforms, including pay TV and M-commerce (advertising on mobile phones) continues apace. Growth in online advertising expenditure—including search and display ads, banner and pop-up ads, and classifieds—accelerated after the GFC, increasing by 18.5 per cent in 2009 alone (Budde 2010, p. 1). In the same year, metropolitan print newspaper advertising revenue fell 9.8 per cent. Figures for subsequent years confirm that newspapers are not recovering nearly as much revenue from online advertising as they are losing from print.

A broader view of how Australian media advertising revenue is distributed confirms that the post-GFC period has been a difficult one for print media, with online and pay TV revenue growing at the expense of others in the sector. Newspapers and magazines have been hardest hit.

According to a 2017 PricewaterhouseCoopers' (PWC) report (Pash 2017), Australia's total advertising market was worth A$15.7 billion in 2016, with newspapers' share of that just 14.5 per cent (A$2.3 billion). In comparison, 45 per cent of advertising revenue (A$7.1 billion) was earned online. This represented a dramatic change from 2010, when online advertising was worth just A$2 billion, or less than a third of the 2016 figure. PWC forecast that by 2021 the Australian advertising market would be worth A$17.3 billion, with online advertising accounting for 58 per cent of the market (A$10 billion). By then, newspapers were predicted to have just 8.3 per cent of the market (A$1.4 billion). By comparison, in 2010 newspapers had the lion's share of advertising, then worth A$4 billion.

In the decade to 2016, newspapers' share of the advertising market collapsed from a dominant 35 per cent to just 14.5 per cent. Most of the damage occurred in the five years from 2011 to 2016, as Table 1.1 shows. In the same ten-year period, online's share of the market rose from 9 per cent to 36 per cent and is projected to account for 57.9 per cent of the overall market in 2012. However, this internet figure does include digital newspapers such as *The Guardian* Australia.

Table 1.1 Australian Advertising Market Share by Platform, 2006–21*

Sector	2006 (%)	2011(%)	2016 (%)	Change (2006–16)	*Projected for 2021
Filmed entertainment	1	1	0.7	−0.3	0.7
Free-to-air TV	30	28	23.5	−6.5	16.9
Subscription TV	2	3	3.4	+1.4	3.6
Radio	9	8	8.2	−0.8	8.4
Out-of-home	4	4	5.7	+1.7	7.2
Newspapers	35	30	14.5	−20.5	8.3
Magazines	10	10	2.8	−7.2	1.7
Internet	9	16	45	+36	57.9

Source: Author, analysis of data supplied by Paul Budde (2010, pp. 6–7); Business Insider (2017); Price Waterhouse Coopers (2018); ASNE (2015).

The downward trend for newspaper advertising share has been experienced across the developed world. According to one report, expenditure on global print advertising was forecast to be just 8.1 per cent of the total market by the end of 2018, down from 12.4 per cent in 2015. This suggests the Australian print industry (at 14 per cent) has fared slightly better than print markets in comparator countries (Dentsu Aegis Network n.d.).

In comparison, digital advertising's global market share of all advertising expenditure has increased from 24.6 per cent in 2015 to a predicted 38.3 per cent in 2018. Using these figures, Australia's digital advertising share (at 45 per cent, see Table 1.1) as a proportion of its overall advertising market is slightly above the international level (Dentsu Aegis Network n.d.). This might be explained by the high public penetration rate of digital technologies in Australia, and Australians' use of these, that might be attracting digital advertisers (Park et al. 2018). In Australia, online video is the fastest growing area of internet advertising (Pash 2017).

Online advertising is not without its own set of problems in Australia, including relatively slow broadband speeds, click fraud (false reporting of website visits), and the absence of a standardised measuring system, which makes it difficult to compare the impact of online advertising campaigns (Budde 2010, p. 2). But as the national broadband network (NBN) improves, greater convergence of audio and visual advertising is expected. Eventually TV and internet advertising are expected to become the same thing, which will exacerbate economic hardship for traditional media like free-to-air (FTA) television and print (Budde 2010, p. 2). FTA television has lost viewers in recent years due to pay television (Foxtel), time shifting of programs, and internet streaming and downloads of favourite series (Carson 2012a).

An obvious advantage for online platforms over print is that is that the audience for every story online can be individually measured and categorised, giving advertisers more information on which to target ads to audiences. Digital marketers can charge a significant premium for this service (A. Kohler 2010, interview with the author, 5 October).

Newspaper publishers can and do take advantage of these technologies by publishing their stories online, tracking their appeal, and selling online advertising to match their readership. Australian newspaper companies, like counterparts abroad, have identified the need to adapt and 'colonise the web' with their own online products, and since 1998 have successfully developed news and other websites.

As of February 2019, both News Corp (ranked no. 1) and Nine-Fairfax (ranked nos. 3, 4, 8, and 9) have newspapers in the top ten online news rankings (Nielsen 2019). Fairfax's major papers, *The Age* and *SMH* (the only outlets in the top ten with a subscriber paywall), and News Corp's News.com.au rank in the top ten. The greatest performers are News.com at number one (News Corp), the public broadcaster's website for ABC

News (ranked no. 2), and television channels such as Nine (ranked no. 3) and Yahoo! (ranked no. 6).

The difficulty for newspapers is that in the highly competitive environment for online advertising, they can charge only a fraction of what they used to charge for print advertising, resulting in an overall loss of revenue for these legacy businesses. Adding to their challenge has been a wave of international news media competitors entering the Australian market since 2012. These include the youth news site *Junkee* (2012), *Daily Mail* (2015), *HuffPost* (2015), *The Guardian* Australia (2013), *BuzzFeed, Vice* (2014) and its digital TV station, SBS *Viceland* (2016), and an Australian version of *The New York Times* (2017). *The Guardian* Australia, the local *Daily Mail*, and the BBC quickly entered this top ten 'most visited news sites' ranking. None has a paywall to charge readers for content.

Both News Corp and Fairfax have attempted to diversify their product and regain market share by buying and developing online classified websites, and other popular websites to attract advertising, such as dating and social networking sites. These are cross-promoted in their print and online pages.

Yet these online successes do not overcome the challenges facing print newspapers. Specialist online advertisers have presented a formidable challenge, gaining majority share of key advertising segments (vehicle sales, real estate, and employment) that were formerly dominated by newspapers, and underpinned large newspaper profits. Non-newspaper websites that have taken classified advertising share away from newspapers include Carsales.com.au, Realestate.com.au, and employment website Seek.com.au (in which News Corp has acquired a minority stake). These three sites had an aggregate of more than 37.5 million unique browsers a month in 2018 (up from ten million in 2010),[5] and each is listed in the top 300 Australian companies on the stock exchange (Market Index 2018).

Further, the newspaper company websites are *not* in the top ten most popular Australian websites. In mid-2018, the most popular sites overall were Google, with almost a billion monthly visits, YouTube, Facebook, Wikipedia, Ebay.com.au, Live.com, Reddit, Netflix, and Twitter. The first news website in Australia's most post popular sites is News Corp's News.com, which ranks 14th overall. The next most popular is ABC.net.au, which ranks 18th (Alexa 2019).

Consistent with the rankings, sector analysts identify the growth areas in online advertising not as classified or display ads but rather the search and directories market, mobile phone advertising, and online video advertising (Budde 2010, Pash 2017). Further, it has proved difficult in Australia, as it has in other parts of the world, for newcomers to break into these advertising areas to compete with Google, which has a 90 per cent share of online-search-related spending in Australia (Budde 2010, p. 4).

The relationship between news organisations and content aggregators, such as Google, is problematic yet increasingly necessary. News organisations have protested over the flight of advertising to the internet to search indexes that use their content as a lure. Rupert Murdoch has called it 'stealing' (Speers 2009). Sites such as Google index news content, without permission, to attract huge volumes of viewers and advertisers. But news media are also becoming dependent on aggregators such as Google, and social networks like Facebook, to reach a larger audience (PRCPEJ 2011).

The 2011 US Pew Research Center's *State of the News Media* report found that as news consumption became more mobile, news organisations were increasingly subjected to the rules of device makers, such as Apple, and software developers (Google) to deliver their content. It concluded: 'In the 20th century, the news media thrived by being the intermediary others needed to reach customers. In the 21st [century], increasingly there is a new intermediary: Software programmers, content aggregators and device makers' (PRCPEJ 2011). This is the nub of the problem for traditional media outlets: loss of cultural power—as articulated in this chapter's opening quote by media academic Rodney Tiffen.

Australia's two major newspaper companies have experimented with different online strategies to try to regain cultural power and market share. Many have failed. News Corp invested heavily in its acquisition of social networking site MySpace, for which it paid a premium. Market analysts expected News Corp's strategy was to develop MySpace to include job classifieds powered by its CareerOne site (Budde 2010). But MySpace had already peaked with its audience, and News Corp subsequently sold it for US$35million, resulting in a loss on the investment of US$545 million (Vascarello 2011). Fairfax's online division, Fairfax Digital, sought to challenge television for the online video advertising market. It launched FDTV to provide TV-quality online advertisements that autoplay within its online stories. Fairfax, for a time, abandoned the autoplay after advertisers stopped buying the advertising space because it was slowing viewers' internet speed and 'having a negative impact on brands being advertised' (Sear 2011).

These examples demonstrate that the major print media companies in Australia, as elsewhere, have struggled to find the future revenue sources to sustain their journalism. Alternative revenue sources that might go some way to subsidising investigative journalism are examined in Chapter 7.

Australian Newspaper Sales: Circulation

As with advertising revenue, sales of Australia's daily newspapers over the past two decades show a long-term downward trend (Tiffen 2010b, p. 1). While online readership of the main mastheads is high—and in many cases, the highest it has ever been—large proportions of these readers do not pay to read stories as they once did (see Chapter 7). This has potentially negative implications for investigative journalism for several reasons. Not only has the capacity to fund expensive journalism been potentially reduced, but also the paying print audience share of total readership is falling. A shrinking paying readership puts pressure on editors to prioritise popular, often easy-to-digest stories to appeal to as broad an audience as possible. The online versions of even the most serious broadsheet Australian newspapers have thus tended to have a more tabloid, downmarket tone than their print counterparts—both in content and presentation—as the companies chase additional 'clicks' to attract advertisers.

Falling circulation of Australian newspapers is consistent with the experience in other OECD economies, with few exceptions.[6] Between 1980 and 2007, the rate at which Australians bought hard copies of newspapers virtually halved, from 323 people per 1,000 population to 166 (Tiffen 2010b, p. 1). Despite strong Australian population growth, circulations have also plummeted in absolute terms. *The Age, SMH,* and *The Australian* each shed tens of thousands of paying readers between 1992 and 2017. Most of the losses have occurred since 2000, when the companies were strategically shifting their readers to online subscriptions (or 'bundled' digital and print subscriptions), with a view to pursuing a 'digital only' model, as can be seen in Figure 1.7.

When these paid circulation figures are broken down to show movements in four-year periods during the past 34 years, a more complex picture emerges, as can be seen in Figure 1.8. The long-term hardcopy circulation trend is downward since 1992, before the internet's ascension, for News Corp's *The Australian*, but even earlier for Fairfax's *The Age.* This confirms the early observations of this chapter that a range of factors, not just the disruption of the digital age, have contributed to the decline of print newspapers.

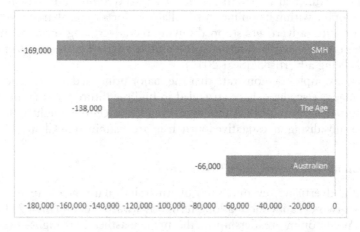

Figure 1.7 Losses in Paid Sales of Australian Print Newspapers, 2000–17

Source: Author, analysis of data from Tiffen (2015, p. 76); Audit Bureau of Circulations (2017). ABC Paid Media Audit (2017).

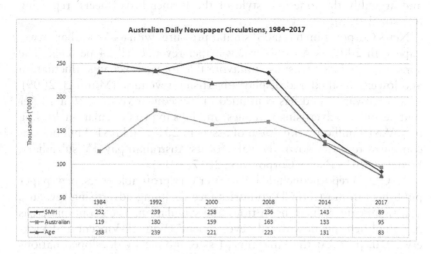

Figure 1.8 Selected Australian Daily Print Newspaper Circulations, 1984–2017

Source: Author, analysis of data from Tiffen (2015, p. 76); Audit Bureau of Circulations (2017). ABC Paid Media Audit (June 2017).

The GFC may have accelerated the decline, with most developed nations experiencing declines in paid-for daily newspaper markets during this period. A 2010 OECD report found that in developed economies, the newspaper publishing market made on average 57 per cent of its revenues from print advertising (this proportion was higher in Australia), with online advertising comprising just 4 per cent of total newspaper revenues (Wunsch-Vincent and Vickery 2010, p. 8). Over time, this print advertising revenue proportion has declined. WAN-IFRA's World Press Trends estimated in 2016 that, overall, the newspaper publishing market made 44 per cent of its revenue from print advertising. The difficulty for newspapers is that overall online advertising had only lifted slightly to constitute 6 per cent of total newspaper revenues (WAN-IFRA 2017). There are exceptions where digital ad share is much higher; these are discussed in Chapter 7.

Australian newspapers were hit particularly hard in the post-GFC years because of their relatively high reliance on classified and display advertising, which has migrated online at an increased rate since 2009 (Fairfax Media 2009). This was a significant factor in Fairfax declaring a A$2.7 billion loss and a write-down of A$2.8 billion on its value in 2012 (Williams 2013, p. 294). Its CEO, Greg Hywood, responded with 1,900 job cuts and converted its three metropolitan daily broadsheets (*The Age*, the *SMH*, and later *The Canberra Times*) to tabloids and closed its expensive nine-year-old broadsheet printing presses on the outskirts of Melbourne (IBISWorld 2017, p. 25).[7] The conversion to tabloid and increased syndication of stories between the mastheads were significant changes for the legacy brands that changed the amount of local coverage and arguably the tone and style of the former broadsheets' reporting (Carson 2012b).

News Corporation has faced similar pressures with its Australian newspapers. In 2009 its Australian newspaper revenue fell 24 per cent. The company cited two reasons: 'unfavourable foreign exchange fluctuation and lower classified and display advertising revenues' (Murdoch 2009). The downward trend has continued in subsequent years, with a 16 per cent decline in advertising revenues, and falls in print circulation, leading to a A$310 million write-down of assets in 2017, and A$1.9 billion as it continued to write down the value of its Australian pay TV subsidiary, Foxtel, in 2018 (News Corporation 2017, 2018).

An OECD report concluded that 'after very profitable years, newspaper publishers in most OECD countries face declining advertising revenues and significant reductions in titles and circulation. The economic crisis has amplified this downward development' (Wunsch-Vincent and Vickery 2010, p. 6). At the same time, less economically developed nations such as India experienced growth in their newspaper markets, and therefore the number of titles worldwide actually increased during the first decade of the new century. Thus, the case for the 'death of the newspaper' could not be successfully argued at a global level at this time (Wunsch-Vincent and Vickery 2010, p. 6).[8]

Figure 1.9 shows percentage declines in newspaper circulations in OECD countries from 2007 to 2009. As can be seen, Australian newspaper circulations were among the least affected at this time. Globally, the newspaper market has continued to slow since 2004, and its growth was almost zero by 2007. Since 2007, newspaper print circulations have shrunk in most developed nations (Wunsch-Vincent and Vickery 2010, p. 7).

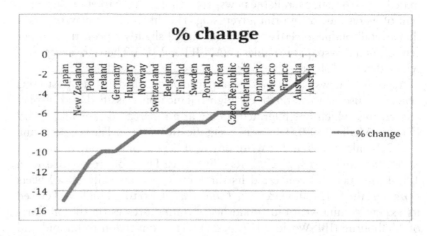

Figure 1.9 Decline in Paid Circulations of Daily Newspapers in OECD States, 2007–09

Source: Author, analysis of from OECD (2010, p. 18).

Cutting Costs in the 21st Century

The collapse in the advertising revenue of old media empires has triggered widespread and deep cost-cutting across the industry in developed economies. While the main cuts have been to full-time editorial staff numbers, there have also been cuts targeted at high-cost journalism, including the closure of foreign bureaus, and hundreds of masthead closures. There are no official Australian figures for print journalism job losses since the millennium. However, the journalists' union, the MEAA, has estimated that the number of full-time Australian journalists fell by 13 per cent between 2001 and 2009, to 7,500 positions. Massive job losses have occurred since then. In 2012, News Corp, Fairfax, and Channel 10 collectively shed about 3,000 media staff, many of them journalists (Carson 2012b). Further extensive job cuts have occurred in more recent years across free-to-air television, Fairfax Media, News Corp Australia, and the ABC. These have included some forced redundancies and mass sackings due to closures of regional mastheads.

The turmoil in Australia mirrored developments in other developed economies, where job shedding in the print sector took off during the GFC (Wunsch-Vincent and Vickery 2010, p. 21). In the United States, soaring debt levels coupled with falling property and share prices and diminished revenues resulted in an estimated 166 mastheads closing between 2008 and 2010, and significant cost-cutting at surviving mastheads (Smith 2011; Greenslade 2010). In 2015 the American Society of News Editors said the number of American print journalism jobs had dropped more than 20 per cent in five years, from 41,500 in 2010 to 32,900.

The OECD report concluded that 2009 was the worst year on record for journalism job losses in most developed nations, accelerating a trend that began in the late 1990s. However, the effects varied between countries or regions, such as Germany (–25 per cent), Korea (–30 per cent), Scandinavia (–30 per cent), the United States (–12 per cent), Netherlands (–41 per cent), and Japan (–18 per cent) (Wunsch-Vincent and Vickery 2010, p. 21).

Other Legacy Media Responses to the Digital Age

In addition to mass staff cuts, newspaper businesses have tried other ways to adjust to the digital media age. Some have cut down on print frequency to fewer editions each week, such as at *The Ann Arbor News* in Michigan. Others like the Pittsburgh *Tribune-Review* have scrapped their printed editions to become digital-only publications. Others have tried to keep their print advertising and combine it with digital subscriptions by locking content behind a paywall (see Chapter 7). A consequence of paywalls, which most daily newspapers in Australia now have in place, is that overall revenues have fallen while the proportion of revenue derived from subscription has increased. This is an emerging trend for newspapers in developed economies generally. It means that newspapers can become less reliant on volatile advertising revenue and more reliant on a loyal subscriber base. But it also means that many newspaper newsrooms of the 21st century are smaller and must adapt to living within greatly reduced means. This can mean fewer staff, fewer stories or different types of stories, more collaboration, and less frequent print publishing or moving to digital-only.

Newspaper Consolidation

Another significant contemporary trend has been further consolidation of newspaper ownership through company takeovers. In addition, some outlets such as Australia's News Corp and Fairfax have hived off parts of their businesses, resulting in the effective financial isolation of their newspaper operations.

Worldwide, News Corporation kept its print assets and spun off the rest into 21st Century Fox. In Australia, Fairfax Media established separate classified advertising websites including *MyCareer*, and it purchased the dating website *RSVP*. But its most successful website has been *Domain*, its real estate advertising entity. After a failed takeover bidding war for the entire Fairfax company in 2017 between two private equity giants, TPG and Hellman & Friedman, Fairfax spun off *Domain* and listed it as a separate entity on the stock exchange. The new company's debut market capitalisation was A$2.2 billion while its parent company, even with a 60 per cent share in Domain, was worth A$1.7 billion— meaning that the once grand metropolitan mastheads were valued at only about A$400 million (Mason 2017). The significance of the listing was that Fairfax actively decoupled its main advertising revenue generator from its journalism. What followed was a relaxation of Australia's cross-media ownership laws, which paved the way for the most dramatic change to the media landscape in 30 years: a takeover bid from free-to-air commercial television network Nine. The new company, worth about A$4 billion, epitomises the international trend for consolidation of legacy media businesses in an attempt to achieve economies of synergy and scale.

Commercial Newspaper Attacks on Public Broadcasting

Commercial news providers in Australia, especially print, have clashed with the government-owned broadcaster, the ABC, over its expanding provision of free (taxpayer-funded) digital media services. News companies say the availability of free online news from the government provider amounts to unfair competition in a market where commercial operators are increasingly trying to survive on paid subscriptions. A similar debate has occurred in Britain, where Rupert Murdoch's son James, then CEO of British pay TV channel BSkyB, said in 2009 that the BBC's £9 billion annual cheque from the British government was anti-democratic and a threat to pluralism. He argued that 'dumping free, state-sponsored news on the market makes it incredibly difficult for journalism to flourish on the Internet' (Murdoch cited in Kissane 2010, p. 2).

Successive conservative governments in Australia, Canada, and Britain have imposed budget cuts on their public broadcasters. In Australia, the ABC lost 10 per cent of its workforce in 2014 following a A$254 million cut. In 2018, a freeze on annual indexation of funding cost it another A$84 million. In addition, the government announced an inquiry as part of a package of concessions gained by right-wing political party One Nation to examine the role of the national broadcaster in the modern media environment and its impact on commercial media's viability.

The Audience: Internet as a News Source

As outlined above, newspaper companies' loss of paid audience share to online media has added to the financial woes caused by the evaporation of their advertising revenue. As most general news is now read and viewed for free online, newspaper companies are trying to survive on less revenue, which at least potentially means less funding for investigative journalism.

In a 2017 study by University of Canberra scholars as part of a wider multi-nation Oxford University study, a majority of survey respondents reported using digital platforms (websites, apps, social media, blogs) in preference to traditional platforms (TV, radio, and print) as news sources (Park et al. 2018, p. 60). The findings were most pronounced among younger Australians, with three quarters of 18- to 24-year-olds using social media for news, and a third of this age group nominating social media as their *main* source of news. Print newspapers (excluding online versions) were the least used source of news, accessed by just 36 per cent of respondents (Park et al. 2018, p. 60).

Studies have shown that the time spent consuming news on the internet tends to be more sporadic and ad hoc than traditional print newspaper readership (Wunsch-Vincent and Vickery 2010, p. 9). This raises a question about how investigative journalism, which tends to involve longer stories and requires more of the reader's attention, is received online. Online, readers are empowered to mix and match information and news sources and to participate by compiling their own personalised information through blogs and social media sites such as Facebook. How the various actors in the online environment contribute to the public sphere through citizen engagement and democratic participation is an ongoing question of interest, and obviously one that has implications for both the reception and production of investigative journalism in the future. These issues are discussed in the chapters ahead.

Trust in the News Media

Various studies have contributed to a general perception that news 'quality' is decreasing, while audience concerns about journalism standards, bias in stories, and more recently concerns about 'fake news' are increasing. Australia's Essential Media annual surveys have consistently shown that trust in news media is falling across all platforms, most notably daily print media and local newspapers (see Figure 1.10).

The falling level of public trust over time is particularly striking for print media, which raises questions about the degree to which it can continue to be relied upon by the public in a watchdog role. Fairfax readers who took part in an earlier survey strongly agreed that the media should act as a 'watchdog', but were critical of a perceived fall in journalism standards. These readers were more inclined to read newspapers 'because of quality journalism', and believed that the online sphere could not replace quality journalism. They were especially concerned about the rise in celebrity gossip stories in newspapers and online (MEAA 2010, p. 28). This raises important questions about Fairfax's capacity to continue to produce trustworthy investigative journalism since the television takeover by Nine in late 2018. If the Nine takeover were to lead to a reduction in the quality and quantity of investigative journalism at Fairfax, who or what would be left to fulfil the media watchdog role beyond the besieged ABC?

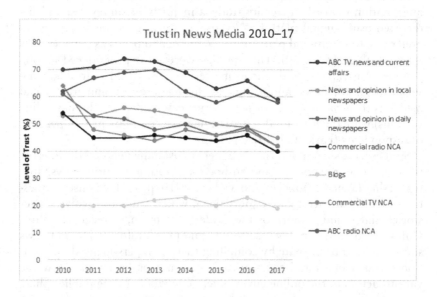

Figure 1.10 Falling Levels of Trust in the Australian News Media 2010–17

Source: Author using Essential Media survey data (2010–17).

Conclusion

Print journalism is at a crossroads in developed countries. Its future depends on finding a new business model to replace the old one, which has been fractured by the digital revolution and the new era of largely free online information. Expensive journalism, and in particular investigative journalism, is vulnerable as news media companies cut deeply into their editorial staff numbers and resources in a bid to survive.

Australia's golden economic era for newspapers was the early 1980s when circulations peaked, advertising revenue flowed, and profits were high. It was an era when investigative journalism was said to have experienced its 'second wave' following the 'muckraking' wave of the early 20th century. Since the 1990s, on almost any measure—from company stock prices to print circulation, advertising revenue, and audience reach—Australian newspapers have been in decline. The rate of decline grew during the 2007–09 GFC and appeared to peak in 2012. While the downward trend has slowed since 2012, there are few indications that Australian newspapers fortunes will reverse in the absence of feasible alternative funding models. There are positive signs for the prospects of some digital-only media companies, and these are discussed in Chapter 7. But for legacy media, the global trend appears to be one of acquisition and further consolidation of these media markets. While paywalls and other forms of monetisation are part of the funding mix in the 21st century for print outlets, it has not yet been demonstrated that paywalls alone (in most instances) can restore newspaper company revenue to anything like the levels of the last century.

Australians' adoption of new technologies is high, and the use of the internet as a primary news source is increasing. As in other countries, younger generations have been the quickest to adapt. This generation has no history of buying print newspapers, and their expectation is for free online news. Yet Australians, when surveyed, appreciated that 'quality' journalism was more likely to come from newspapers, particularly broadsheets, and nominated newspaper journalists for best serving the media's 'watchdog' role (MEAA 2010).

Australian newspaper businesses, like their international counterparts, have recognised and attempted to adapt to the changing online environment, but have yet to find a fully sustainable model to underwrite journalism in the digital era. Their experimentation with the latest technological delivery services, such as tablets and mobile phone apps, has not delivered sufficient revenue to provide a complete solution to their economic conundrum. This financially challenging environment has fuelled the commercial media's hostility toward government-financed journalism, and in particular the ABC, which is perceived as a rival providing 'free' news that makes it difficult for them to charge consumers for general news content online.

The decline of legacy newspaper businesses has implications for print investigative journalism. Compared to others types of journalism, it is expensive and time-consuming. Yet, as this chapter has shown, Australian newspapers, particularly broadsheets, have a long history of producing it. And although the line between news reporting and investigative journalism can sometimes appear blurred, the additional time, expense, and effort required to produce investigative journalism goes part of the way towards defining it and differentiating it from other forms. The next chapter tackles the question of 'what is investigative journalism' by tracing its history and, combined with expert interviews, arrives at a working definition of it. While this chapter has drawn a sobering account of how newspapers have suffered in the late 20th century with the onset of the digital age, subsequent chapters of this book show that investigative journalism is not only withstanding the slow, steady decline of print newspapers, but it potentially has a bright future as journalists and media outlets adapt to a new (global) news environment in the 21st century.

Notes

1. News Limited is now News Australia Holdings Pty Limited, but operates under its parent company News Corp and is referred to as News Corp Australia.
2. Mayer and Walker disagree on the date the *SMH* changed its name. Mayer reports 1842, and Walker reports 1841; see Walker, R. B., *Yesterday's News: A History of the Newspaper Press in New South Wales from 1920 to 1945*, p. 1.
3. They were the *Daily News* in Adelaide, Sydney's *Daily Mirror*, and Melbourne's *Truth*.
4. The S&P/ASX 200 is recognised as the primary investable benchmark in Australia. The index covers approximately 78 per cent of Australian equity market capitalisation.
5. According to company websites: Carsales.com.au, Realestate.com.au, and Seek.com.au, all accessed 1 July 2018.
6. Out of 18 surveyed nations, newspaper circulation has only increased in Japan, Norway, the Netherlands, and Ireland between 1980 and 2007.
7. *The Age* and *SMH* became tabloids in 2013. *The Canberra Times* followed several years later.
8. Ibid.

References

The Age 2010, 'The history of *The Age*', accessed 25 November 2010, from http://about.theage.com.au/cmspage.php?intid=93.

Alexa 2019, 'Top sites in Australia', accessed 18 February 2019, from www.alexa.com/topsites/countries/AU.

ASNE [American Society of News Editors] 2015, *Number of Full Time Daily Newspaper Journalists in United States from 2010 to 2015*, Statista: The Statistics Portal., accessed 10 May 2018, from www-statista-com.ezp.lib.unimelb.edu.au/statistics/315563/number-full-time-journalists-usa/.

Aucoin, J 2007, *The Evolution of American Investigative Journalism*, University of Missouri Press, Columbia.

Audit Bureau of Circulations 2017, *ABC Paid Media Audit: ABC Total Sales Reporting: Period Ending June 2017*, Audited Media Association of Australia.

The Australian 2018, *Investigative Journalism*, accessed 26 April 2018, from www.theaustralian.com.au/news/investigations.

Australian Securities Exchange 2010, *News Corporation (NWS)*, accessed 10 November 2010, from www.asx.com.au/asx/research/companyInfo.do?by=asxCode& asxCode=NWS.

Australian Securities Exchange 2012, *Fairfax Media Limited (FXJ)*, ASX, accessed 28 November 2012, retrieved from iPhone App.

Australian Securities Exchange 2018, *Prices and Research: FXJ Fairfax Media Limited*, accessed 11 June 2018, from www.asx.com.au/asx/share-price-research/company/FXJ.

Bailey, P 2010, 'Henry Wellcome the salesman', *Wellcome Trust*, accessed 22 March 2010, from www.wellcome.ac.uk/About-us/History/WTX051935.htm.

Bloy, M 2010, 'A web of English history', *The Campaign for a Free Press*, accessed 8 April 2010, from http://historyhome.co.uk/peel/social/unstamp.htm.

Budde, P 2010, *Australia: Digital Economy: Advertising, Statistics, Revenues and Forecasts*, Paul Budde Communications Pty Ltd, Sydney.

Carson, A 2012a, 'Debt deal saves channel nine: For now', *The Conversation*, accessed 1 May 2018, from https://theconversation.com/debt-deal-saves-channel-nine-for-now-10214.

Carson, A 2012b, 'Death by 1900 cuts: Will quality journalism thrive under Fairfax's new model', *The Conversation*, 18 June, accessed 1 May 2018, from https://theconversation.com/death-by-1-900-cuts-will-quality-journalism-thrive-under-fairfaxs-new-model-7734.

Chainon, Y 2010, *Future of Journalism Series: Fairfax: Mike Van Niekerk*, World Association of Newspapers and the World Editors Forum, 10 March 2008, Paris, accessed 12 June 2012, from www.editorsweblog.org.

Cole, P 2008, 'Compacts', in B Franklin (ed), *Pulling Newspapers Apart: Analysing Print Journalism*, pp. 183–92, Routledge, Abingdon.

Cordell, M 2009, 'What is happening to investigative journalism? A pilot study of ABC's Four Corners', *Pacific Journalism Review*, 15(2), 118–31.

Cowie, T 2011, 'News' revenge: Editorial pages rain down on brown's crusade', *Crikey*, accessed 2 January 2013, from www.Crikey.com.au/2011/05/19/brown-brands-news-the-hate-media-in-presser-salvo/.

De Burgh, H 2000, *Investigative Journalism*, Routledge, London.

Dentsu Aegis Network n.d., *Distribution of Global Advertising Expenditure from 2015 to 2018, by Media*, Statista: The Statistics Portal, accessed 2 May 2018, from www-statista-com.ezp.lib.unimelb.edu.au/statistics/245440/distributuion-of-global-advertising-expenditure-by-media/.

Fairfax Media 2009, *Annual Report 2009: Building on Our Strengths*, Fairfax Media, Sydney.

Fairfax Media 2011, 'History of the National Times', *Fairfax Media*, accessed 25 February 2011, from http://www.nationaltimes.com.au/aboutnationaltimes.

Finkelstein, R & Ricketson, M 2012, *Independent Inquiry into the Australian Media*, DBCDE, Australian Government, accessed 2 March 2012, from www.dbcde.gov.au/digital_economy/independent_media_inquiry.

Franklin, B 2008, *Pulling Newspapers Apart: Analysing Print Journalism*, Routledge, Abingdon.

Greenslade, R 2010, '166 US newspapers vanish in two years', *The Guardian*, 6 July, accessed 8 May 2018, from www.theguardian.com/media/greenslade/2010/jul/06/us-press-publishing-downturn.

Habermas, J (trans T Burger) 2002, *The Structural Transformation of the Public Sphere*, Polity Press, Cambridge.

Hills, B 2010, *Breaking News: The Golden Age of Graham Perkin*, Scribe, Melbourne.

IBISWorld 2017, *IBISWorld Industry Report: Newspaper Publishing in Australia*, accessed 8 October 2018, from http://clients1.ibisworld.com.au.ezp.lib.unimelb.edu.au/reports/au/industry/default.aspx?entid=169.

Kelley, S 2009, 'Investigative Reporting, Democracy, and the Crisis in Journalism', in *Centre Blog*, 21 May. The Canadian Centre for Investigative Reporting, Ottawa.

Kissane, K 2010, 'The ABC goes forth into a brave new world', *The Age*, p. Insight p. 2.

Manne, R 2011, 'Bad news: Murdoch's Australian and the shaping of the nation', *Quarterly Essay*, 43.

Market Index 2018, *S&P/ASX 300*, accessed 8 October 2018, from www.marketindex.com.au/asx300.

Mason, M 2017, 'Domain hits the ASX with a $2.2 billion valuation', *Australian Financial Review*, accessed 6 June 2018, from www.afr.com/business/media-and-marketing/publishing/domain-hits-the-asx-with-a-22-billion-valuation-20171115-gzltvt.

Mayer, H 1964, *The Press in Australia*, Lansdowne Press, Melbourne.

McKnight, D 1999, 'The investigative tradition in Australian journalism 1945–1965', in A Curthoys & J Schultz (eds), University of Queensland Press, St Lucia.

McNair, B 2000, *Journalism and Democracy: An Evaluation of the Political Public Sphere*, Routledge, London.

Media, Entertainment and Arts Alliance 2008, *Life in the Clickstream: The Future of Journalism*, Printcraft, Brisbane.

MEAA [Media Entertainment and Arts Alliance] 2010, *Life in the Clickstream 2: The Future of Journalism*, MEAA, Sydney.

Mitchell, C 2011, 'Award-winning journalists to undertake special investigations', *The Australian*, accessed 3 March 2011, from www.theaustralian.com.au/national-affairs/award-winning-journalists-to-undertakespecial-investigations/story-fn59niix-1225942450312.

Morgan Stanley Research 2016, *Australian Media, Internet and Technology*, accessed 3 August 2018, from www.comcom.govt.nz/dmsdocument/15024.

Murdoch, R 2009, *News Corporation Annual Report*, News Corporation, New York.

Nielsen 2019, *Nielsen Digital Content Ratings (Monthly) January 2019*, 11 February, accessed 18 February 2019, from https://mumbrella.com.au/daily-mail-unique-audience-hits-6m-for-first-time-while-news-com-au-retains-top-spot-on-nielsen-ratings-564625.

Newman, N 2017, *Journalism, Media, and Technology Trends and Predictions*, Reuters Institute for the Study of Journalism, accessed 1 August 2018, from https://reutersinstitute.politics.ox.ac.uk.

News Corporation 2012, *News Corporation Announces Intent to Pursue Separation of Businesses to Enhance Strategic Alignment and Increase Operational*

Flexibility, News Corporation, accessed 28 November 2012, from www.news corp.com/news/news_535.html.

News Corporation 2017, *News Corp Annual Report 2017*, News Corporation, New York.

News Corporation 2018, *News Corp Annual Report 2017*, News Corporation, New York.

O'Neill, E 2009, 'Media: A duty to the wrongly accused: Miscarriage of justice investigations have fallen out of fashion with editors, but the cases keep piling up', *The Guardian*, p. 7.

Park, S, Fisher, C, Fuller, G & Lee, J 2018, *Digital News Report: Australia 2018*, News and Media Research Centre, University of Canberra, Canberra.

Pash, C 2017, 'PWC: Growth in Australia's advertising industry is shrinking fast but online video has taken off', *Business Insider*, accessed 6 June 2018, from at www.businessinsider.com.au/pwc-growth-in-australias-advertising-industry-is-shrinking-fast-but-online-video-has-taken-off-2017-6.

Pew Research Center 2011, 'Pew's project for excellence in journalism 2011', *2011 State of the News Media*, Pew Research Center, accessed 17 March 2011, from http://stateofthemedia.org/2011/newspapers-essay/data-page-6/.

Sampson, A 1996, 'The crisis at the heart of our media', *British Journalism Review*, 7(3), 42–56.

Schulhofer-Wohl, S & Garrido, M 2013, 'Do newspapers matter? Short-run and long-run evidence from the closure of *The Cincinnati Post*', *Journal of Media Economics*, 26(2), 60–81.

Schultz, J 1998, *Reviving the Fourth Estate: Democracy, Accountability and the Media*, Cambridge University Press, Melbourne.

Sear, J 2011, 'Fairfax's autoplay video ads backfire; will be abandoned', *Crikey*, 18 April, accessed 10 November 2011, from http://Crikey.com.au/purepoison/2011/04/18/fairfaxs-autoplay-video-ads-backfire-will-be-abandoned/.

Seven West Media 2017, *Seven West Media: 2017 Annual Report*, Seven West Media, accessed 1 June 2018, from www.sevenwestmedia.com.au/investors/annual-reports/.

Smith, E 2011, *Paper Cuts*, St Louis, accessed 3 March 2011, from http://news paperlayoffs.com.

Speers, D 2009, 'Interview with Rupert Murdoch', *Sky News Australia*, 7th November.

Sprague, H 1962, *Australia Goes to Press*, Melbourne University Press, Melbourne.

Tiffen, R 2010a 'The press' in S Cunningham & G Turner (eds), *The Media and Communications in Australia*, Allen & Unwin, Crows Nest.

Tiffen, R 2010b, 'Trends in newspaper circulation and ownership', presented at *Communications Policy Research Forum*, 15–16 November 2010, Sydney, pp. 1–8.

Tiffen, R 2015, 'From punctuated equilibrium to threatened species: The evolution of Australian newspaper circulation and ownership', *Australian Journalism Review*, 37(1), 63–80.

Tiffen, R & Gittins, R 2009, *How Australia Compares*, Cambridge University Press, Melbourne.

Vascarello, J 2011, 'Justin Timberlake group buys myspace from News Corp', *The Wall Street Journal*, 30 June, accessed 10 November 2012, from www.the Australian.com.au/business/world/justin-timberlake-group-buys-Myspace-fromNews-Corp/story-e6frg90o-1226084692121.

Walker, RB 1980, *Yesterday's News: A History of the Newspaper Press in New South Wales from 1920 to 1945*, Sydney University Press, Sydney.

Williams, P 2013, *Killing Fairfax: Packer, Murdoch and the Ultimate Revenge*, Harper Collins Publishers, Sydney.

World Press Trends 2017, *Facts and Figures 2017*, accessed 10 June 2018, from www.wptdatabase.org/world-press-trends-2017-facts-and-figures.

Wunsch-Vincent, S & Vickery, G 2010, 'The evolution of news and the internet', *Organization for Economic Co-operation and Development, Working Party on the Information Economy* (Report No. DSTI/ICCP/IE (2009) 14/FINAL), http://www.oecd.org/officialdocuments/displaydocumentpdf.

Young, S 2011, *How Australia Decides: Election Reporting and the Media*, Cambridge University Press, Melbourne.

2   What Is Investigative Journalism?

We don't accept that things just happen, that mistakes were made and it was no one's fault. No! Decisions were made and people made them. What we want to do is to understand who made them and then hold those people accountable for making decisions if they were harmful to people, particularly if those people were voiceless and powerless and can't speak up for themselves.

(Robin Fields, managing editor, *ProPublica*, interview with the author, 6 September 2016)

Introduction

There is no universal definition of investigative journalism. Over time it has been described in various ways: watchdog or reform journalism, muckraking or exposure reporting, the fourth estate, detective reporting, adversarial journalism, advocacy reporting, public interest journalism, and campaign journalism. While some of these labels have appreciably different meanings, others like 'watchdog' and 'investigative' reporting are often used interchangeably.[1] Broadly, there are two distinct ways of thinking about investigative journalism. On one hand, scholars and journalists argue that all quality reporting is in some way investigative. Prominent investigative reporters who subscribe to this view and who were interviewed for this book include Yahoo's chief investigative correspondent Michael Isikoff and award-winning Australian investigative reporters the late Evan Whitton (*The National Times, Truth*) and Kate McClymont (*The Sydney Morning Herald*). The man behind the 2003 'Spotlight' investigation, which exposed systemic child sex abuse by Catholic priests, *Boston Globe* editor-at-large Walter 'Robby' Robinson, put it this way:

I don't like the term investigative reporting. Now, I'm the last person who should be saying that, but I've never liked it. In most people's minds, it means investigative reporters are those who don't have to deal with the daily chores in the newsroom, that they work apart.

And they have time to work on in-depth stories. My view is that there are no investigative reporters. There are good reporters and there are mediocre reporters.

(Robinson 2016, interview with the author, 25 September)

Others who have focused on this definitional question, such as British academic Hugo de Burgh, Australian academic Rodney Tiffen, US scholars James Ettema, Theodore Glasser and Brant Houston, a former executive director of the US Investigative Reporters and Editors, see investigative reporting as a distinct form of reporting, requiring special efforts beyond reporting the daily news. Houston argues: 'It is a different kind of reporting . . . it generally requires more time, more interviews, and more documents than other stories do' (B. Houston 2016, interview with the author, 23 September). *ProPublica's* managing editor Robin Fields also shares this view:

The great privilege of investigative reporting is that you can go deeper and you can explore the 'why' of something. Day-to-day journalism tends to focus almost exclusively on the 'what'. We drill down in to the 'how' and the 'why' and the 'who' is to be held accountable, aspects of things.

(Fields 2016, interview with the author, 6 September)

While acknowledging there is no right or wrong answer to this question, this book classifies investigative journalism as a distinct reporting genre with specific elements that combine to provide audiences with more information than they are likely to get from non-investigative reporting. Not every distinguishing element discussed in the following pages will be found in each example of investigative journalism, but some will be and it is these that set it apart from other types of journalism.

Although investigative journalism lacks a singular broadly accepted definition, a *working* definition is needed to identify it, measure it and make findings about its quantitative and qualitative features over time. As the previous chapter highlighted, the journalistic landscape has changed in the 21st century, with news reporting no longer the exclusive domain of established media institutions. Nor is it a practice confined to single newsrooms or within national boundaries. In this chapter we consider the impact of this changing news landscape and digital technologies on how we think about investigative journalism and its future. The chapter is divided into three sections. First, it examines how investigative reporting has been presented over time. Second, it reviews the scholarly literature and compares it with my primary research—interviews with academics and journalists who have provide contemporary views on the elements they consider essential to investigative reporting. The final section develops a working definition of investigative journalism. It isolates nine key features of investigative journalism, including five essential qualities that I argue need to be present if a story is to be considered investigative reporting. Throughout this chapter, concepts such as truth, morality, objectivity, facts, and journalistic ethics are discussed to enhance understandings of what watchdog reporting endeavours to achieve, its motivations, and the methods used to accomplish its aims.

Muckraking Throughout the Ages

To realise how investigative practices have shifted from the mid-18th century through to the 21st century, we will examine examples of investigative reporting at particular moments in time. This chronological approach is useful for identifying the enduring features of investigative reporting that can inform a working definition. Tracking moments in the history of investigative reporting also helps to inform assumptions about its role in a democracy, and how it is tied to concepts of the 'public interest' or 'public good'. In liberal democracies such as the United States and Australia, investigative reporting is commonly understood to be primarily concerned with probing the use and misuse of power on behalf of the public. Columbia University's Sheila Coronel puts it this way: 'the very notion of investigative reporting is really premised on holding power accountable, holding institutions and individuals accountable for what they do' (Coronel 2016, interview with the author, 24 September). Theoretical debate about the role of investigative reporting, including assumptions about its motivations and functions, is the focus of Chapter 3.

The Antebellum and Gilded Ages

The antecedents of watchdog reporting can be traced back to the tabloid-style newspapers colloquially known as the penny press (costing a penny a day) that emerged on the East Coast of the United States in the 1830s (Canada 2011). While there is scholarly debate about whether these newspapers prefigured a style of journalism different to 20th-century practice and development of mass media markets or, as Nerone argues, marked an evolutionary rather than revolutionary shift in professional reporting and the mass commercialisation of news, they do provide early examples of watchdog reporting (1987, p. 402).

In the early to mid-19th century, as New York's population boomed, local newspapers turned their focus on the city's emerging criminal underbelly. Papers such as the *New York Tribune, New York Times,* and *New York Evening Post* enlisted undercover reporters to masquerade as customers of fortune tellers, matrimonial brokers, and backyard abortionists, to expose examples of 'moral transgressions' and illegal practices blighting the city (Thyer 2016, p. 32). In the 1850s, Mortimer Thomson, using the alias Q. K. Philander Doesticks, P. B., reported on the activities of fortune tellers and astrologists in a series for the *New York Tribune*, warning readers of female 'swindlers' who possessed no unique gifts or insights and who were behaving outside the boundaries of society's norms (Thyer 2016, pp. 39–40).

The 'Gilded Age' of the late 1800s brought fresh approaches and examples of investigative writing. Fiction writers Mark Twain and Charles Dudley Warner, in *The Gilded Age: A Tale of Today*, satirised an American society that appeared on the surface to glitter with prosperity, while underneath lay serious social problems and rank corruption among public officers. Journalism historian Danielle Thyer, studying investigative journalism of this period, observes that New York's newspapers saw it as their duty to expose those who threatened the predominant Protestant religious values of the time: sobriety, thrift, self-discipline, and industriousness (Thyer 2016, p. 2).

American investigative reporter Charles Lewis, among others, argues the first 'golden age' for investigative reporting ran from the Progressive era of the late 1800s up until World War I (Lewis 2016, interview with the author, 1 September). One of the best-known examples of undercover reporting from this era was an exposé by Nellie Bly (born Elizabeth Cochran). Working for Joseph Pulitzer's *New York World*, Bly feigned insanity to get inside New York's Women's Lunatic Asylum and expose the mistreatment of patients. Her work earned her fame and spawned a string of copycats, mostly female reporters, who adopted similar undercover techniques against chosen targets (Banks 1898, cited in Thyer 2016, p. 10). Over time, the focus of watchdog reporting shifted from single targets to examples that suggested systemic corruption and breaches of public trust. An early example of this came in the 1870s, when *The New York Times* investigated the corrupt activities of city alderman turned congressman William Tweed and his so-called Tweed Ring. After three years of investigation by *The New York Times*, Tweed was convicted and jailed in 1873 on charges including larceny and forgery (Strausbaugh 2016, p. xix).

These earliest forms of watchdog reporting, often called detective reporting, had some of the main elements of modern investigative journalism (Aucoin 2006, p. 89). For instance, the stories were exclusive to the newspaper that pursued them, although other mastheads would follow up the stories. The wrongdoing would likely not have been exposed were it not for the journalist's investigative efforts and institutional support from the masthead. The stories involved reporters actively gathering information from primary sources—in many cases putting themselves at physical risk by masquerading as someone else to obtain hidden information. The stories typically had a moral dimension as well, differentiating between victims and villains and, in doing so, giving victims a voice. The investigations took time and required newspaper resources such as reporter's wages, travel expenses, and props for undercover work. Investigations could take weeks, months, or even years, as was the case with the exposure of the Tweed Ring scandals. *The New York Times* was not shy in publicising its role in these convictions, writing:

> The Times was compelled to work single-handed and alone . . . there was honor enough in the service rendered to the city and to public morals to distinguish the newspaper and those who aided it, but the chief honor was earned by the newspaper.
>
> (*The New York Times* 1886)

These elements of exclusivity, unearthing hidden truths, villains, and victims, and operating within a moral dimension, have endured over time and are important for distinguishing investigative reporting from daily news.

Early 20th-Century 'Muckraking'

In 1906, US President Theodore Roosevelt famously coined the term 'muckraker' to shame journalists he considered had crossed the ethical line in their efforts to expose deviance in government and beyond (Mitford 1979, p. 4). Roosevelt linked reporters whose stories caused a stir among the masses to the dirt-digger character from John Bunyan's 17th-century fable, *Pilgrim's Progress*: 'The man with the Muck-rake, the man who could look no way but downward with the muck-rake in his hands' (Feldstein 2006, p. 106).

Television investigative reporter and scholar Mark Feldstein argued that after the American Revolution, muckraking was largely a partisan weapon used by political factions that funded various newspapers. For example, the paper of Thomas Jefferson's Republican Party, *The National Gazette*, exposed insider trading in the office of rival Federalist leader Alexander Hamilton, leading to several convictions of Hamilton's aides at the Treasury Department. In the case of the Tweed exposé, some have argued that *The New York Times*, then a Republican voice, was using its reportage to weaken the Democratic machine (Feldstein 2006, pp. 107–08). Irrespective of the motivation, the public interest was served with the conviction of a fraudster.

Feldstein says the decade between 1902 and 1912 was the heyday of muckraking, which had by then become an international phenomenon. Reporters were celebrated for unearthing corruption, exposing crimes and social injustices. Lincoln Steffens, in a series of articles that became a book, *The Shame of the Cities*, exposed graft and corruption taking hold in major US cities at the hands of big business. Another muckraker, Ida Tarbell, documented the crimes of John D. Rockefeller's Standard Oil in *McClure's Magazine*. And Upton Sinclair went undercover in Chicago meatpacking plants and exposed exploitation of immigrant workers in his muckraking novel *The Jungle*.

In Australia, weekly publications such as *Smith's Weekly, The Bulletin,* and John Norton's *Truth* tended to focus on exposing single targets such as shysters and dodgy doctors. A 1923 *Smith's Weekly* front page proclaimed 'a strong sense of duty and of public responsibility' to expose a surgeon who allegedly left a portion of a pair of forceps inside a patient during an operation. The story included evidence gathered through interviews, the original medical paperwork and the patient's first-hand account of 'years of pain' before another doctor operated to discover the cause (Smith's Weekly 1923, p. 1). With the luxury of seven days between deadlines, weekly papers could set the news agenda independently from the daily newspapers (Lloyd 2002, p. 12).

The Oxford English Dictionary (OED) at the time reflected Roosevelt's derogatory view of watchdog reporting, defining muckraking as 'a depraved interest in what is morally unsavory or scandalous' (Mitford 1979. p. 4). But, as is often the case with language, muckraking's meaning shifted, and later dictionary versions reflected this change. A self-proclaimed muckraker, British journalist Jessica Mitford argued the term had gained respectability by the time she was writing investigative stories in the 1950s and 1960s. In the third millennium, the OED has reverted to a less virtuous view of muckraking, associating it with searching out scandals about famous people (Oxford Dictionary 2018).

The 'Golden Era' for Systemic Investigative Reporting

The period from the late 1960s to the early 1980s is, for several reasons, recalled as a golden era for investigative journalism. It followed a period of reporting complicity with governments in the 1950s and subsequent complacency towards investigative reporting during the early days of the Cold War. Mark Feldstein calls the period between World War I and the Vietnam War the 'dark ages' for investigative reporting. It was a time when the mass media in Australia, as in Europe and the United States, was largely deferential to the idea of anti-Communism as the organising principle of a broader cultural Cold War. The late Australian investigative reporter Evan Whitton observed that 'the collaborating relationship between the press and the political establishment only started to pull apart as social and political movements gained strength, including feminism and Vietnam war protests' (Whitton 2012, interview with the author, 8 February). In 1965, the editor-in-chief of Australia's *The Courier Mail*, Sir Theodor Bray, implored the press to assume its watchdog role:

> It has also to be a watchdog of civil liberties and a protector against the petty tyranny of bureaucrats and all those clothed with or assuming authority against the common man. . . . Newspapers clearly have a function beyond mere reporting and recording—a function of

probing behind the straight news, of interpreting and explaining and sometimes of exposing.

(Schultz 1998, p. 43)

Center for Public Integrity founder Charles Lewis argued the complacency was disrupted in the United States when journalists 'discovered racism' and began reporting on it and covering the civil rights protest marches. Lewis argued that the murder of 14-year-old African American Emmett Till by white men in Mississippi in 1955 was the beginning of a new consciousness of the reporter's role to expose injustice (Lewis 2016, interview with the author, 31 August). The injustice was compounded when the two men charged with the murder were acquitted by an all-white jury, only to confess under the protection of double jeopardy laws in *Look* magazine, for which they were paid. Lewis observed:

> From the period of 1955 to 1968 when Martin Luther King is assassinated; the Civil Rights Act and the Voting Rights Act in 1964/1965, and the march on Washington in 1963, you had all these things happen, but journalists were essential to it because they were filming it. They were filming the dogs attacking people and it was high quality, aggressive, muscular journalism and it was really important journalism. We don't call it investigative and that term wasn't even used till the 70s . . . from the late '50s all the way up to 1975, to me, is the second golden age.
>
> (Lewis 2016, interview with the author, 31 August)

Other developments engendering this so-called golden period were technological advances, particularly television's capacity to visualise a story and distribute it to a mass audience. Media historian James Baughman and *Time* editor Richard Clurman suggest that during this time, print media responded to the competitive challenge from television through increased investigative reporting. Watchdog reporting's focus on 'systemic' rather than 'single-target' stories also made it stand out during this time by drawing attention to areas requiring social reform. These stories, according to Ettema and Glasser, 'call attention to the breakdown of social systems and the disorder within public institutions that cause injury or injustice' (1998, p. 3).

In a similar vein, Australian academic David McKnight agreed that journalists responding to the cultural and political revolution of the late 1960s triggered a golden period for investigative reporting in Australia (1999, p. 150). While Australian muckraking in the earlier part of the 20th century tended to involve single targets, the third wave of watchdog reporting in the 1970s and early 1980s yielded more systemic investigations, such as a series investigating a corrupt health department (McKnight 1999, pp. 150–6). This period coincided with the boom time for Australian daily newspaper circulations and readership (Tiffen 2010, p. 127). Scholar Julianne Schultz argues this 'golden era' for Australian investigative journalism continued into the early 1980s (1998, p. 195). In prosecuting these investigations, Schultz argues the media became 'equal contenders' in the existing power dynamic and not, as previously thought, 'cooperating servants' to authoritative figures (1998 p. 224).

I add a further reason for investigative journalism's resurgence after the mid-20th century: technological advances that improved telecommunications and made international travel easier, enabling journalists to watch and learn from one another in different parts of the world. For example, London's *Sunday Times* 'Insight' team of investigative reporters significantly influenced Australian investigative reporting during the 1960s. The then editor of Melbourne's *The Age*, Graham Perkin, travelled to Britain several times, and he was said to be so impressed with the *Sunday Times'* investigations and its editor Harold Evans that he instituted an exchange program for journalists between the two papers, and he bought the rights to republish its stories in Australia, including the 1963 Kim Philby spy ring story (Hills 2010, p. 294). Australian journalist Phillip Knightley was part of that London investigative team that exposed Philby's treachery almost a decade before investigative journalism gained international prestige because of the Watergate investigation (Evans 2010).

James Aucoin documents how the muckraking tradition in the United States had evolved into 'systemic investigative reporting' by the second half of the 20th century (2006, p. 92). He names the Pulitzer Prize–winning stories by the *Chicago Tribune*, exposing voter fraud (1972), and *Newsday*, exposing the flow of heroin into Long Island from the poppy fields of Turkey (1974), as prime examples of systemic investigative reporting. He also noted that reporters were learning from one another. Journalists at the *Boston Globe* studied the *Newsday* team prior to the establishment of their 'Spotlight' investigative unit in 1970 (Aucoin 2006, p. 94). In addition, the Investigative Reporters and Editors, Inc (Ullman and Honeyman 1983, pp. vii–viii) adopted a definition of investigative journalism in the 1970s that saw it as distinct from daily reporting, and established a community of practice.

In summary, the resurgence of watchdog reporting in the second half of the 20th century had a systemic focus, with the villains more likely to be organisations or governments rather than individuals. Having broken free of the government lines on issues such as Vietnam and racial segregation, and responding to civic movements such as feminism, reporters had become 'equal contenders' with authorities. With newspaper revenues thriving, the press' economic and political power gave reporters institutional clout and the financial means to defend any arising legal actions when exposing wrongdoing in the name of the public interest.

However, the commercial media did not always critique the systemic failings of the corporate world (to which they also belonged), as they should have.

A Decline in Corporate Investigative Reporting

My earlier research has found Australian investigative journalism generally was not strong at uncovering corporate wrongdoing in the lead-up to the GFC of 2007–09 (Carson 2014). Two decades earlier, Jennifer Kitchener, Brian Toohey, Trevor Sykes, and Graeme Turner critiqued Australia's business press in the lead-up to the 1987 global stock market crash with similar findings. They also found an absence of critical reporting of the corporate sector immediately prior to a market crisis. Kitchener argued a central problem was that finance journalists tended to act more as cheerleaders for capitalism than for the public interest, and they missed the signs of impending crisis. Australian ABC television's former *Media Watch* host Jonathan Holmes observed that investigative reporters were also slow to expose corporate wrongdoers after the 1987 stock market crash as further financial dramas unfolded including the collapse of several financial lenders. 'The big bank collapses that happened in Victoria and South Australia went largely unnoticed', observed Holmes. In his view—with some exceptions like investigative journalist Paul Barry's exposé of the financial misdeeds of billionaire Alan Bond—it was not investigative journalism's finest period (Holmes 2011, interview with the author, 19 December).

Internationally, Anya Schiffrin and colleagues found the mainstream US media also failed to anticipate the GFC (2007–09), and the Asian financial crisis (1997) (2011, p. x). The 2001 winner of the Nobel Prize in Economics, Joseph Stiglitz, wrote that 'overall, the press acted more like a cheerleader as the bubble grew than like a check . . . so too, in the aftermath of the [GFC], it has provided both less analysis and less investigative reporting than one might have hoped' (2011, p. 35).

A Lack of Scrutiny of the Doctrine of War

In a similar vein, Charles Lewis has researched the media's general lack of scrutiny (with some commendable exceptions) of the US government's 2003 decision to go to war against Iraq. 'You had the deep silence by the media right after 9/11. They bought, hook, line and sinker, what the President said' (Lewis, interview with the author, 1 September). In 2008, Lewis shone the spotlight on this lack of scrutiny when he and a team of 25 reporters published a 380,000-word report documenting at least 935 false statements of the George W. Bush administration about the national security threat posed by Iraq. Three months later, David Barstow revealed in *The New York Times* how the Pentagon had recruited retired military officers to appear in the media to make the case for war while giving the appearance of being 'independent' analysts (Lewis 2014, p. xiv).

In *935 Lies*, Lewis catalogues how the quest for truth has become more difficult and confusing because government leaders and corporations wilfully lie. There are other factors too, including the sheer volume of information available via the internet and the financial strains on media outlets that led to editorial cutbacks. Together, these factors combine to add difficulty to the task of exposing systemic wrongdoing of the powerful. Lewis' book is important because it heralded— before the rise of fake news and Donald Trump's active reliance on it to delegitimise the mainstream media—the need for evidence-based reporting. This is where data journalism, collaboration, and a cross-national exposure of global injustices can play a countervailing role (see Chapter 6).

The Digital Age: A New Golden Era?

Many factors have influenced changes in investigative journalism practice since the end of the 20th century. Chief among these have been the development of digital technologies and the commercialisation of the internet, which have significantly undermined the economic environment for traditional media, particularly the press, as outlined in the previous chapter. Yet digital disruption has also led to adaptations including unprecedented collaborations and cross-border watchdog reporting. In this section, we touch on some of the features of investigative journalism in the digital age from the perspective of current-day practitioners interviewed for this book.

Investigative editor in charge of *The Washington Post*'s dedicated investigative units, Jeff Leen has found that investigative reporting in the digital age has responded and adapted to these challenges:

> The web has changed the way we display investigative journalism, the way we use video, the way we can link documents, the way we can annotate documents, the way we can create interactive graphics, the way we can create photo galleries and all that can be built around the text.
>
> (Leen 2016, interview with the author, 30 August)

However, Leen added, some aspects of investigative journalism stay the same because 'you still have to use sourcing and documents to break through secrecy to undercover truth', he said. 'There's no algorithm that does that for you. . . . The database gives you a starting point but then you have to use the paper trails and the shoe leather to get to the end point. So, that hasn't changed from 80 years ago', said Leen.

Brant Houston and Sheila Coronel point out that investigative journalism extends beyond state borders:

> We finally have the ability as journalists to better track global corruption where it used to be that people could just jump across the border and they're out of our circulation or we don't have the resources. Now, because of collaborations, because of technology, we're catching up.
>
> (Houston 2016, interview with the author, 23 September)

Coronel adds: 'as we see companies and organisations becoming much more global I think the notion of what investigative reporting is—as being primarily nation-state bound—is also changing and must change' (Coronel 2016, interview with the author, 24 September). She predicted that investigative reporting would remain important at the local level, but that 'there needs to be much more investment in investigative reporting that is transnational'. Obvious examples of this are cross-national collaborations such as the International Consortium of Investigative Journalists (ICIJ) and its work on the Panama Papers and Snowden's NSA leaks. McClymont, Houston, Leen, and Barstow all believe investigative journalism requires the continued support of large, established media organisations that retain institutional and cultural power, and skilled journalists to undertake this work, as well as the capacity to defend legal actions if required. McClymont says:

> The biggest success of the Panama Papers was coordinating the worldwide release so everyone went at once. I just think that had the most amazing effect. But I think that in reverse . . . *WikiLeaks* was at its best when it used mainstream media to analyse, to present, to interpret. If you can get mainstream media onboard to disseminate your material, I just think the overall effect is like a gathering avalanche.
>
> (McClymont 2017, interview with the author, 16 March)

Panama Papers reporter Helena Bengtsson, formerly at *The Guardian*, said the greatest lesson she learned from the Panama Papers was that 'collaboration works' (H. Bengtsson 2016, interview with the author, 24 September). She found that her competitive attitude towards other media organisations like the BBC was transformed and replaced by a community spirit and common purpose.

Since the turn of the millennium, *The Washington Post* has engaged in cross-media collaborations at the national and international level, including the reporting of the NSA Snowden leaks. These collaborations strengthen the impact and reach of stories and add a collective institutional clout when taking on powerful institutions such as the US government. *The Washington Post*'s range of investigative partners has included television and radio networks such as ABC, NBC, CBS, and PBS; non-profits such as *ProPublica*, the Center for Public Integrity, the Center for Investigative Reporting, and the Marshall Project; and academics.

Journalist and Columbia University scholar Emily Bell says now is an exciting time to be an investigative reporter, considering the opportunities and advantages provided to journalists by digital tools, collaborations, big data leaks, encryption methods to encourage whistleblowers, and the various platforms available for telling stories. 'I know it goes against the narrative, but it is a golden age. It feels like a golden age for investigative journalism' (Bell 2017, interview with the author, 14 March).

But she acknowledges that investigative journalists also face additional challenges in the digital age. For example, she says there are fewer investigative reporters than in the past and they have much tougher competition for the attention of audiences in an era of information overflow.

> Once you've actually got the story, how do you make it count? I think this is probably the biggest challenge. It's very hard to get people's attention . . . that in a way is a skill in itself, that sort of story management journalism.
> (Bell 2017, interview with the author, 14 March)

Coronel, while optimistic overall about the future of investigative reporting, is concerned about the dominance of and reliance upon digital platforms such as Facebook and Google. 'If you want to engage with an audience you have to go through Facebook, through Twitter, through Instagram because people won't go to you', she said.

> It's problematic. Whether you're a public broadcaster or a small start-up, you have no control over the platform, but the platform decides what your audience sees, when they see it. So that loss of control is profound and we still don't know what the consequences are; that's where I see the major challenge.
> (Coronel 2016, interview with the author, 24 September)

It is clear that watchdog reporting of the digital age, while quite different in its scope and tools from the past, has maintained many of the elements of its antecedents—moral outrage, prosecuting the case against villains to give voice to victims, uncovering hidden truths, exposing breaches of public trust—and doing all of these things in the public interest. But it has also expanded the story focus beyond national borders, which is made possible by forming collaborations, harnessing data, and advancing its methods of data journalism.

The next section examines features of investigative reporting as identified above, and builds on the work of established scholars and expert interviewees to create an operative definition for the identification of investigative journalism. The purpose here is twofold: to map distinct functions of investigative reporting, and to develop a robust coding frame to identify and evaluate investigative reporting in Australia, Britain, and the United States through the method of content analysis, detailed in later chapters.

Traits of Investigative Journalism

If, from the liberal democratic perspective, the purpose of investigative reporting is to protect the public interest by exposing abuses of power in society, we need to understand how journalists themselves reflect on how they perform this role (their methods) and their expectations of societal outcomes, and how watchdog journalism differs from other reporting genres. The expert interviews and the scholarly literature is used here to identify key recurring themes of watchdog reporting. This is useful to refine the analysis of what are key features of investigative journalism in order to arrive at a working definition of it.

Time and Resources

The US Investigative Reporters and Editors was (IRE) among the first organisations to try to clearly identify and define the role of investigative journalism. Formed in 1975, IRE stated that investigative journalism dealt in matters of public importance, in the production of stories that would not reach the public sphere were it not for the 'investigative' efforts of the reporter, and in uncovering information that others wanted kept secret. It defined investigative journalism thus:

> The reporting through one's own work product and initiative matters of importance, which some persons or organisations wish to keep secret. The three basic elements are that the investigation be the work of the reporter, not the report of an investigation made by someone else; that the subject of the story involves something of reasonable importance to the reader or viewer; and that others are attempting to hide these matters from the public.
> (Ullman and Honeyman 1983, pp. vii–viii)

James Ettema and Theodore Glasser argued that the investigative journalist's job was to 'look beyond what is conventionally acceptable, behind the interpretations of events provided for us by authorities and the authoritative' (1998, p. 3). In other words, investigative journalists must critically assess what is presented by authorities, and not just report opposing accounts of an event. Ettema and Glasser distinguished between daily reporters who 'often don't have to decide what they believe to be true in the same way that investigative reporters have to decide'. Further, they draw a distinction whereby 'daily reporters take responsibility for the accurate transcription of official discourse but not the veracity of that discourse' (Ettema and Glasser 1998, p. 158). Investigating the veracity of information is another dimension of investigative reporting that sets it apart from conventional news reporting.

John Hohenberg wrote about the differences between 'exposure journalism' and 'routine reporting' in the 1960s, saying investigative reporters dug beneath the surface of events. They were 'digging specialists' (Aucoin 2006, p. 86). For Hohenberg, digging had two dimensions.

> First, it implies that the reporting process involved lengthy and persistent efforts to uncover information not generally available to the public. Second, it requires that reporters themselves do the investigation, rather than simply reporting the results of a law-enforcement investigation or the proceedings of congressional investigators.
>
> (Aucoin 2006, p. 88)

The New York Times investigative reporter David Barstow concurs:

> You are trying to deliver not just one fact, but an assessment of a particular problem or a particular organisation or agency. So that's the big difference between investigative reporting and regular reporting. The newspaper or the news organisation is putting itself on the line. It can't simply hide behind . . . 'a grand jury has found . . .' it is actually the *New York Times* that has done this examination and this is what we have concluded.
>
> (Barstow 2016, interview with the author, 5 May)

Limits of Investigative Reporting

Investigative reporting has always required more time, resources, and effort than daily reporting. Thus, the scope for reporters to pursue more difficult, time-consuming, and potentially fruitless investigations becomes more limited when resources are scarce. As the business model for commercial journalism has broken down, the expensive pursuit of investigative stories with uncertain outcomes—previously a given in the golden days of big editorial budgets—is under threat.

Veteran investigative journalist and former executive producer of Australia's *Four Corners* program, Jonathan Holmes, said the time allocated to find and produce investigative stories for television had shortened at the Australian Broadcasting Corporation in the new millennium. Speaking about *Four Corners*, he said:

The program was structured around the idea that you would try once or twice a year to do a big gig, where you would make the time for one team to be off for months and everyone else would have to paddle harder. Now they don't do that anymore. . . . They expect everyone to produce a program in a set time . . . usually seven to eight weeks. You have to produce a program on that day, regardless of what problems you have encountered along the way and whether, in fact, there is a bigger story you could get if you took longer.

(Holmes 2011, interview with the author, 19 December)

Jeff Leen also observed that the economic environment for traditional newsrooms means there were now 'shorter leashes and less fishing expeditions' for investigative journalists.

You work on a story for two to three months with a minimum/maximum strategy. If you hit the minimum you put it in the paper, if you hit the maximum you go longer, and that's generally how we try to do it.

(Leen 2016, interview with the author, 30 August)

Another serious restraint on investigative practice can be the prohibitive legal costs of defending stories in the courts. Editors and proprietors have to weigh up the story's potential for lengthy litigations against the journalist, publisher, or both before publishing (Birnbauer 2012, p. 83).

Verification: Checking the Facts

The high level of scrutiny applied to ostensible facts may not be evident in the casual reading of an investigative story. As British investigative journalist Jonathan Calvert observed: 'Some stories you make five calls on, some twenty. When you are making a hundred, that's investigative journalism' (Calvert 1999, cited in De Burgh 2000, p. 25).

The types of sources used in investigative stories matter too. Ettema and Glasser argued that beat reporting is characterised by the auto-legitimisation of certain sources of information, particularly 'official' sources that tend to be institutional, like the courts and Parliament. Official sources provide a steady stream of news that is tacitly assumed to be credible. With investigative reporting, by contrast, the reporter will often have to determine whether or not certain information is legitimate, rather than assuming it is (Ettema and Glasser 1984).

Ettema and Glasser's research (1984, p. 17) found that investigative journalists use a hierarchy of evidence, with weightings given to different information sources. Video evidence is seen as most convincing, followed by paperwork, then accounts from participants, and then non-participating witnesses. Below these are journalistic 'hunches', and on the last rung of evidence are anonymous phone calls.

Investigative reporters typically present both sides of a story, as daily reporters do, but also *weigh* both sides, asking of themselves: On what side of the story does the greater weight of evidence sit? What type of evidence (in the hierarchy of evidence) rests on each side? The investigation is then abandoned or pursued depending on whether 'the scales tip decisively toward the exculpatory evidence or if, after much effort, the scale cannot be made to tip' (Ettema and Glasser 1989, p. 19).

Assembling the story can be seen like a jigsaw puzzle, in which chronology and relationships are seen as central to determining what 'fits' where. The more the pieces fit cleanly together, the more confidence in the 'truth' of the story. Yet, an important distinction is drawn between 'justification' and 'verification'. Sometimes the reporter, rather than proclaiming the absolute truth of a story, may determine if they are 'comfortable in presenting the facts which justify reporting the story', according to Ettema and Glasser (1989, p. 24). They described a four-step process of investigative reporting. First, a tip is examined to see whether it can justify an investigation. Second, evidence is collected not to verify, but to be tested to see whether airing the story can be justified. Third, it is determined whether pieces of evidence can be assembled in a coherent manner that seems to support the story narrative. Fourth, attempts are made to find a plausible alternative narrative to the story. Ettema and Glasser argue: 'A fully justified story is, then, one in which the pieces fit so well that the reporter has become morally certain that he cannot disconfirm it' (1989, p. 23).

James Aucoin, like Calvert, highlighted the strenuous efforts required to verify information in investigative journalism, relative to daily reporting: 'Journalistic investigation must involve the search of numerous public records and interviews with dozens, if not hundreds, of people', he observed (2006, p. 102).

For Brant Houston (2016, interview with the author, 23 September), quality, evidence-based investigative reporting provides an avenue to rebuild the public's trust in journalism. In a news environment that includes 'clickbait' and fake news, he observed that too much quality control has been lost in journalism: 'If you're going to do journalism, what's going to make you distinct from everybody else is verification, which leads to credibility, which leads to trust', Houston said. McClymont agreed. She argued that the post-truth era is in fact a golden time for investigative journalism.

> The Trump effect has meant that people are willing to read and believe credible sources and . . . it's really important for the major news organisations, or particular journalists, who do have credibility in readers' eyes, take up that mantle and be the public's eyes and ears.

It is a form of public service, presenting the facts and trying to present them in an unemotional way.

(McClymont 2017, interview with the author, 16 March)

Exposing Hidden Information or Suppressed Facts

Linked to verification is truth-telling, or unearthing hidden information. While this revised 'truth' might not always be possible to fully verify, as discussed, attempts to do so are central to the investigative journalist's methodology and quest.

ICIJ Director Gerard Ryle (2016) said of all the outcomes resulting from the Panama Papers, the investigation's single greatest impact was to breach the law firm Mossack Fonseca's method of secrecy behind the offshore tax havens. 'The offshore world only has one product and that is secrecy. Once you take that away then they're going to be nervous forever', he said.

More often than not, investigative reporting is about the detail behind information that may already be in the public sphere but is lacking context (Tiffen 1999, p. 46). Most investigative reporting is the result of 'the media's attempts to penetrate the mystery behind events which are already publicly known', Tiffen stated. Therefore, the issue being investigated need not be 'exclusive', but if the story adds previously hidden information, then it can be called investigative. Tiffen (1999, p. 33) identified three categories of investigative reporting involving exposing hidden information: investigations of neglected issues; revision of major events, such as an unsolved crime; and gathering new information by disclosing a secret wrongdoing. All expose hidden information of some sort to convey a new public understanding of the 'truth'. For example, the reinvestigation of cold case crimes or the discovery of the mystery behind an historical event such as a shipwreck or plane crash is investigative reporting that can reveal new details or context. Contemporary examples include a spate of cold case crime investigations, such as the 2014 global hit podcast *Serial* by *This American Life* producers with Chicago Public Media, about the murder of Baltimore high school student Hae Min Lee; and Australia's Walkley winning podcast 'The Teacher's Pet' by the *Australian*'s Hedley Thomas, which led to charges against school teacher Chris Dawson for the murder of his wife Lynette, 36 years after her disappearance.

Morality

Investigative journalists have tended to be romanticised in the public imagination and in literature and cinema. The popular image of the lone wolf reporter operating *outside* the established order was typified in Al Pacino's portrayal of *60 Minutes* producer Lowell Bergman in *The Insider*

(1999). Yet as de Burgh noted, real investigative reporters tend to work *within* societal norms, and stories exposing wrongdoing tend to appeal to widespread moral standards or values (2000, p. 22). De Burgh argued that investigative journalists police the boundaries between order and deviance, and thus appeal to a general public sense of existing standards of morality (De Burgh 2000, p. 15). Consider the investigation by journalist Glenn Greenwald and documentary maker Laura Poitras into the claims of National Security Agency whistleblower Edward Snowden about the US government spying on its citizens. Their press reports, book, and documentary *Citizenfour* condemned covert government wiretapping practices and information sharing with other nations' intelligence agencies. The journalists in this situation made an implied judgement that the moral imperative of protecting individual citizens from being spied on by their own government outweighed the moral argument of the government—that such surveillance was necessary for the national security of US citizens generally. In this example, the investigative journalists were tapping into a moral orthodoxy at odds with the standard set by the nation state, but in common with perceived public sentiment and widely expressed international opinion of the time.

De Burgh argues that investigative journalists are also motivated by their own sense of morality and desire for change: 'The fact that much investigative journalism ends with legislation or regulation being promised or designed is not therefore an accident' (2000, p. 22). Ettema and Glasser favour the pursuit of public morality over objectivity in storytelling because all information selected for inclusion in a story contains some form of value judgements. They say the tools of the investigative journalist should be used to serve as an exercise in public consciousness:

> The work of these reporters calls us, as a society, to decide what is, and what is not, an outrage to our sense of moral order and to consider our expectations for our officials, our institutions and ultimately ourselves. In this way investigative journalists are custodians of public conscience.
>
> (Ettema and Glasser 1998, p. 3)

They point to the role of journalists in re-establishing the moral order, through the fact that they must show 'that transgressions are, in fact, transgressions'; journalists 'locate, select, and interpret the standards that can be used by the public to make such judgements' (Ettema and Glasser 1989, pp. 2–3). However, Leen (2016, interview with author, 30 August) makes a distinction between the personal morality of some journalists and their work:

> The morality of it is a complicated question because some of the best investigative reporters I know have no politics and they're almost completely immoral in their outlook. But they are scientists for the

truth. I think that what gives investigative reporting its power and its strength is that investigative reporting in the public good makes it easier for me to do my job and to put up with the slings and arrows and the difficulties because you feel like there's a larger purpose.

Victims and Villains

Hugo De Burgh, like Robin Fields in the quote at the start of this chapter, observes that investigative reporting often involves stories about villains and victims—and the power differentials that define their respective roles. Powerful villains targeted by investigative reporting can be individuals, or they may be collectives like governments, bureaucracies, statutory authorities, or companies. Ettema and Glasser documented interviews with investigative reporters who felt it was their primary role to give a voice to the voiceless and, in some cases, to conduct their work as a form of activism (Ettema and Glasser 1989, p. 7). Fields, however, does not equate investigative journalism with advocacy:

> If you look at our stories you will see a thread running through them of moral outrage and I don't think that it crosses the line into advocacy because we don't give you a three-point plan about what you are supposed to do to fix things, although often the story will point to the way toward things that have worked or potential solutions because on some level we do want our journalism to make a difference and to lead the way to some form of change.
>
> (Fields 2016, interview with the author, 6 September)

The Public Interest

The IRE and others have referred to the importance of the public interest in investigative reporting. But what is the public interest? And how do reporters decide whether it is in the public interest to pursue and tell a story? *The Australian*'s investigative journalist Hedley Thomas acknowledges that not all investigative journalism is in the public interest: 'There will be investigative journalism that has outcomes that will probably not be in the public interest' (Thomas 2012, interview with the author, 18 July). A notorious example of this was Britain's now defunct *News of the World*, which relied on covert phone hacking to expose the private lives of celebrities and victims of crime, including murdered schoolgirl Milly Dowler. Emily Bell described this as 'a fishing exercise' to find stories that would attract readers' interest rather than be in their interest:

> They didn't have a specific story in mind. They just wanted to hear what celebrities and footballers and things like that were saying. They didn't target politicians around particular stories.
>
> (Bell 2017, interview with the author, 14 March)

Former editor of *The Guardian* Alan Rusbridger uses the ideal of the public interest to differentiate between what is exposure journalism and reporting in the public's interest. He said that it was clear that not all revelations or 'truths' are worth pursuing, and particularly not in the name of the 'public interest'. He suggested that it was the 'quality' of the target, and its relationship to the public interest, that elevated a story to the genre of quality investigative reporting, rather than mere smear or exposure journalism:

> What's the public interest in a cricketer having a love romp in a hotel room. . . . But if elected representatives are arguing a case in Parliament but not revealing that they are being paid to do so, then that strikes at the heart of democracy. That's public interest.
>   (Rusbridger 1999, cited in De Burgh 2000, p. 22)

What this tells us is that context is important in determining what is in the public interest. Author of *Understanding Journalism*, Lynette Sheridan Burns (2012) lists other social concerns that might need to be weighed up alongside investigative reporting. These might include an individual's right to privacy, legal considerations, and the potential for other harms such as national security risks.

The concept of the 'public interest' cuts across many professions and is an 'ideal' often examined alongside similar concepts such as the 'common good', 'common interest', and 'public good'. Some have argued that because it depends on context, scope, and field of practice it should not be defined. For example, the Australian Law Reform Commission (2019) expressly noted, 'Public interest should not be defined'. The UK Joint Committee on Privacy and Injunctions (2012, p. 19) also concluded that there should not be a statutory definition of the public interest, as 'the decision of where the public interest lies in a particular case is a matter of judgment'.

In considering the difficulty of pinning down this concept in the context of journalism, media scholar Jay Blumer (1998, pp. 54–5) made three useful points. First, the public interest, like its application in government is about authority and power: In government, 'the justification for their freedoms, their wide-ranging roles in society, politics and culture and their place in regulatory orders depends ultimately on the public interests presumed to be served thereby'. He argued that media power should also be used in a legitimate way to responsibly serve the interests of the public. It ought to consider the needs of those beyond the immediate term and in this way has a 'certain transcendent quality' that is superior to any one particular interest, rather it requires a wider perspective, even one that may extend to the interests of future generations. Second, others like *The Guardian*'s Andrew Sparrow (Elliot 2012) remind us that what is in the public interest can change over time in accordance with social mores and therefore this concept should be reviewed periodically: '50 years ago it was assumed that there was a public interest in knowing that an MP was gay, but little or no public interest in whether he drove home drunk. Now, obviously, it's the other way round'. Third, Blumer acknowledges that the public interest operates in an imperfect world and thus its application can bring about contestation and compromise. On this point, Denis Muller and Bill Birnbauer (2018) argued that watchdog reporting by its nature does do harm, to those that it exposes, and inadvertently in its dealings with vulnerable or traumatised people (Muller and Birnbauer 2018, p. 87). The public interest test for journalists is therefore not to do 'no harm', but rather to minimise harm to achieve outcomes for the greater good. The Australian Press Council (2011) applies a general description about what the 'greater good' is in relation to the public interest, which involves 'a matter capable of affecting the people at large so they might be legitimately interested in, or concerned about, what is going on, or what may happen to them or to others'. Although a broad description, it covers all matters that may be important to citizens such as public safety, social, political, economic or other forms of public well-being.

Some media scholars consider the public interest less in terms of specific reportage but in terms of how media systems are structured to serve society. For example, through the liberal democratic lens, the public interest role of news media is seen as providing citizens with diverse and plural voices, which are generally regarded as enriching public discourse. Denis McQuail (2001, p. 144) devised nine criteria of 'public interest' requirements of the mass media. These involved offering plurality of ownership, freedom to publish, diversity of views and opinion, quality of information and audience reach, capacity to support democracy, and respect for law and human rights.

Another dimension to the public interest outlined at the start of the chapter involves the techniques used by journalists to get their information. While a story's outcomes may be in the public interest, the means used to unearth the information may not automatically justify the ends. Since Nellie Bly's feigned mental illness to expose mistreatment in a women's asylum in the 19th century, investigative reporters have grappled with the ethics of using deception to expose wrongdoing. To this day, reporters and their employers commonly rely on a 'means justifies the end' argument. Even in the earliest days, however, the use of subterfuge by reporters did not escape criticism. Some critics saw it as cheap exposure journalism, and editors were accused of exploiting women reporters, like Bly, on investigative projects to avoid the suspicion of their targets (Thyer 2016, p. 9).

The argument that subterfuge can be a legitimate technique for verifying the facts of a story (provided publication of the story is in itself in the public interest) continues to be relied upon in modern investigative reporting. For example, Britain's Channel 4 News investigative team went undercover to tell the story of the misuse of data in major election campaigns in 2018. Its journalists used hidden cameras to expose Cambridge Analytica executives who misused Facebook data in attempts to manipulate elections, including the 2016 US presidential election.

The 'means to an end' argument for undertaking investigative reporting, while problematic and hypocritical when deception is used to expose wrongdoing, does highlight the ethical issues involved and the media's wider role as a social and political reformer when it exposes wrongdoing in society. A focus on public outcomes of stories is often used to defend and define investigative journalism. Stapenhurst (2000) identified that public outcomes can be direct or indirect. Tangible effects could include judicial inquiries, legislative reform, criminal charges, or political and bureaucratic sackings flowing directly from the reporting. Intangible effects might include impacts on public opinion generally, raising the public's awareness of certain topics and prioritising these issues on the political agenda. This in turn can raise the threshold of the public accountability asked of political figures, and it might deter them from unlawful or unethical acts through the fear of exposure (Schudson 2008). Protess and colleagues referred to this emphasis on the effects of reporting, rather than its methods, in *The Journalism of Outrage*:

> Investigative journalists are reformers not revolutionaries. They seek to improve the American system by pointing out its shortcomings rather than advocating its overthrow. By spotlighting specific abuses of particular policies or programs, the investigative reporter provides policy makers with the opportunity to take corrective actions without changing the distribution of power.
>
> (Protess et al. 1991, p. 11)

Thus, the public interest is a multifaceted concept. It encompasses a range of concerns for journalists and their editors to consider on a case-by-case basis when weighing up disclosing information against the potential for causing other harms. It is inextricably linked to the role of journalists to watch over institutions and public figures with power in which the public have invested trust (Muller 2014, p. 65).

Exposing Breaches of Public Trust

Exposing breaches of public trust, like exposing hidden information, is a staple of the investigative journalist. James T. Hamilton in *Democracy's Detectives* identifies five areas that reporters focus on when investigating if individuals within institutions have failed in their responsibilities. The five areas in which breaches of trust tend to occur involve effort (a waste or lack thereof), money, perks, power, and information (2016, p. 31). Breaches of trust can have multilayered impacts. A breach of trust between a principal and agent within an organisation—for example, the committing of a fraud within a bureaucracy or a company—can also impact on the public's trust in that organisation or someone in public life. In the political realm, an effective democratic government relies to some degree on public trust. Exposure of a breakdown of the lines of delegation and trust between decision makers and implementers can chip away at public trust. An example is the Panama and Paradise Papers exposure of elites' use of tax havens to hide their true wealth and reduce their tax.

Gerard Ryle (2016, interview with author, 29 August) explains how individuals using tax havens failed to live up to their responsibilities, which impacted on social trust. In the case of Icelandic Prime Minister Sigmundur Davíð Gunnlaugsson, he lost his job:

> Having an offshore company by itself is not illegal. But when, for instance, you are a politician and you don't declare it then it becomes an issue for you, or if you don't actually declare your tax and you get found out by your tax office, then it's a problem.
> (Ryle 2016, interview with author, 29 August 2016)

Exposure of hypocrisy or double standards in public life is less straightforward for the investigative reporter. As Muller explained (2014, p. 64), the double standards of a public figure need to bear in some way on their public duties or utterances. Any intrusion into a public figure's private life—a concept repeatedly raised during the British 2011–12 Leveson inquiry into the culture, practices, and ethics of the British press—must be justifiable and proportional to the degree of intrusion. The establishment of the British Independent Press Standards Organisation (IPSO) as a result of the inquiry, expects editors to comply with an Editor's Code of Practice. In doing so, they must fully justify intrusions to an individual's privacy without their consent. According to the code, the use of subterfuge to expose breaches of public trust must be demonstrably in the public interest, and the information must not be obtainable by other means.

Exclusive and Sets the Agenda

Investigative journalism is further distinguishable from daily news reporting by its unique contribution to the public sphere. Most daily journalism is reactive, gathered from attendance at press conferences, or replicating details from media releases and other supplied information. It does not require the effort and active investigation of watchdog reporting.

De Burgh argues that investigative journalism 'selects its own information and prioritises it in a different way' (2000, p. 14). It sets the news agenda rather than responding to it. It operates outside of the cycle of leaked information and 'news drops' and, in doing so, plays an active role researching and revealing new information.

Some apply a broader definition than De Burgh. Leen, speaking about the Snowden leaks, and McClymont, referring to *WikiLeaks*, both argue that leaked information or information drops (where information is supplied selectively to one media outlet, or to a small number) can constitute investigative reporting; the information still must be put into context and verified. 'I think leaks is a way to get material into the public realm that's being hidden. So, it fits that part of the definition'. Reflecting on the NSA leaks on which *The Washington Post* reported, Leen observed that:

> Getting the leak was only a piece of it, there was a lot of effort put in to trying to put the leak in context, to understand the leak, to make selections about what's the most important journalistically and in terms of public knowledge.
>
> (Leen 2016, interview with the author, 30 August)

Ettema and Glasser observed that 'hard news' in daily reporting tends to be either *unscheduled* (e.g. an unexpected event such as a natural disaster) or *prescheduled* (e.g. something planned such as a press conference); soft news also tends to be *non-scheduled* (e.g. it is less reliant on a timed event such as a profile of a remarkable person). The authors argue that 'the only time a non-scheduled event qualifies as hard news is in the case of "investigative reporting"' (1984, pp. 5–6).

Active Reporting: Investigative Skills and Personal Attributes

Alan Kohler, the founder of Australia's *Business Spectator* and a former editor of *The Age* and the *Australian Financial Review*, says some of what is called 'quality' journalism is not. Kohler (2010, interview with the author, 5 October) cites the example of reporters who accept leaks from vested interests and report on them uncritically in the expectation that they will continue to be supplied with 'exclusive' stories. This is not quality investigative journalism because it fails to challenge the veracity of the information and therefore does a disservice to the reader, he argues.

Michael Isikoff (2016, interview with the author, 30 August) argues that while there is little difference in the tools and the skills required for everyday and investigative reporting, there are particular personal qualities required to be an investigative journalist, starting with inquisitiveness and doggedness to get to the bottom of a story and to penetrate public relations' lines. McClymont agreed that investigative reporters must have persistence and patience. 'You can make a hundred calls and three of them are worthwhile, but you've got to make them', she says (McClymont 2017, interview with the author, 16 March). The other necessary quality is to be open to the facts, particularly when they go against the imagined narrative of the story. She adds:

> You can have an idea of what you're looking for, but as we know, sometimes it just doesn't pan out. Your original source gave you a bum steer and you have to be big enough to not try and squeeze facts into proving something that just isn't there.

Leen adds that investigative reporters need precision and courage.

> I always say that (with) investigative reporting you have to have the mind of an accountant, because you have to be able to get a thousand details exactly correct, but you also need to have the soul of a gambler because you have to be willing to take risks that other people won't.
> (Leen 2016, interview with the author, 30 August)

Having the right psychological disposition to deal with loneliness, high expectations and the ability to sort through lots of facts, and then to find energy for the next story are other necessary qualities of investigative reporters, according to *New York Times* investigative reporter, David Barstow. He said:

> With these stories you're just carrying a kind of a giant weight because you're carrying so many more facts on your shoulders and trying to assess constantly what does it add up to, what does it mean, what does it reveal. So, you need the ability to carry that weight and to be patient and to handle the rising expectations. Every one of these stories takes its pound of flesh up, they're mentally exhausting, they physically wipe you out.
> (Barstow 2016, interview with the author, 5 May)

Veteran Australian investigator Chris Masters, who exposed systemic police corruption in Queensland in the 1980s resulting in a royal commission and jailing of corrupt police, also speaks to the personal toll:

> You wear these stories, you carry them around with you. You can't put them down, you think about them all the time, even when you do your job well and you want to say goodbye to them, you can't because you will spend the next 10 or 20 years in court for the really important ones. It is really easy to feel like a martyr and it is easy to get really angry with how lonely you feel when you are in a big fight that goes on forever, and it seems that so often you have to wear most of it on your own.
> (Masters 2011, interview with the author, 15 February)

Operative Definition

From the interviews with journalists and other experts and review of the existing literature, I have identified five essential features and four secondary features that distinguish 'quality' investigative reporting from straight news storytelling for the purposes of the research within this book (see Table 2.1).

These key features are framed as questions, or criteria, in order to form an operative definition of investigative journalism, which is necessary to identify and measure it, using content analysis. Each criterion, when present, attracts 1 point out of a total of 9. If there is more than one story as part of the investigation, the questions are asked of the overall body of work relating to the investigation, not just of the single story. For details on sampling methods used to find the stories in order to evaluate them, see Chapters 4 and 5.

Mandatory Fields of the Operative Definition

It is clear that some investigative stories will not contain every distinguishing element of investigative reporting, as detailed in Table 2.1, while others will. The important consideration when deciding whether to classify a story as investigative is that must contain the essential elements of the genre. For this reason, based on the preceding discussion, I have designated five mandatory elements for a story to be considered investigative, and these are marked with asterisks in Table 2.1.

The four non-essential criteria are salient features of investigative journalism in their own right, and help to further distinguish between stories that meet the minimum standard (5 points), and those with more of

Table 2.1 Criteria for Identifying Investigative Journalism in Content Analysis

1. *Does the article set the public agenda/or is it exclusive to that publication?
2. *Does the story provide evidence of skills, and techniques of active reporting?
3. *Is there evidence of time, research, and effort in the story, or series of stories?
4. *Does the story investigate (and verify 'facts'), rather than rely on a compilation of opposing viewpoints?
5. *Does the revelatory information belong in the public rather than private sphere (e.g. is it in the public interest)?
6. Does it identify victims or villains?
7. Does it investigative a breach of public trust?
8. Does it expose hidden information or pursue a suppressed truth, and is it in the public interest to do so?
9. Is a moral standard implied?

Source: Author.

*denotes mandatory elements.

the hallmarks of investigative journalism (maximum of 9 points) in this constructed measuring scheme. The full rules used to evaluate whether stories were investigative journalism or not are displayed in a detailed matrix in the Appendix.

Applying a Sliding Scale to Investigative Journalism

For simplicity, and to get a snapshot of investigative stories over time, a traffic light sliding scale was applied to the scoring system. For example, stories with the *most* features of investigative reporting scored 8 or 9 points, and were placed in the green zone (the green zone is represented in a grayscale here in sections 8 and 9 of Figure 2.1). Investigative stories that met the *minimum* requirements, scoring either 5 to 7 points, were placed in the amber zone. Stories that *failed* to meet the five core fields were not considered investigative journalism and fell into the red zone (see Figure 2.1). Thus, stories might score higher than 5, but were not considered investigative reporting because they did not possess the five mandatory elements; see Figure 2.1.

Conclusion

It is argued here that investigative journalism is different to other types of reporting both because of its function—what it aims to do—and its methods. This chapter has examined investigative journalism over time, the scholarly literature and, combined with expert interviews, highlighted nine features of investigative journalism that collectively enable us to identify examples of the genre. Not every investigative story will have all nine elements, but each must have at least five essential elements to be considered investigative for research purposes here. Of the mandatory fields, the literature review and expert interviews suggest that the story must be exclusive or revelatory in a way that sets the news agenda rather than follows it; the revelation belongs in the public domain and it is in the public's interest to know about it; and the story (or story series) contains evidence of serious efforts to verify information rather than simply compile competing perspectives. Investigative stories also show evidence of active reporting and are not the result of a press release or passive observation such as a court report. Lastly, through the examination of the investigative series or story, it is apparent that it took time and effort by the journalist to produce.

In arriving at the working definition, this chapter has highlighted four waves of investigative reporting—from the Antebellum period through

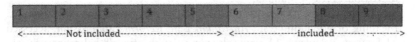

Figure 2.1 The Traffic Light Scale Used to Define Investigative Journalism

to the digital age—which are generally considered to be important moments in the evolution of its practice and public impact. In tracking these epochs, we discover that the objectives of investigative reporting have remained largely constant: to expose wrongdoing on behalf of the public for the common good. What has changed temporally are the methods and scale of investigations, which in the digital age have come to transcend national borders. This is made possible through journalists' unprecedented access to data, highly skilled data journalism, and cross-national collaborations. It is also important to remember, however, that over time investigative journalism has always remained the outlier in the field of reporting. As stated by Leen:

> Maybe only one per cent of journalism is true investigative journalism. And that's journalism that's done by well-funded mainstream outlets just because it's so expensive and so difficult and takes so much time.
>
> (Leen 2016, interview with the author, 30 August)

Leen's observation also emphasises the historical role of traditional established media in producing quality investigative journalism, particularly newspapers. While this chapter has addressed the question of what is investigative journalism and why journalists do it, Leen's observation leads us to the important questions examined in the chapters ahead about the viability of watchdog reporting in the digital age, and which outlets are likely to undertake it in the future. We begin this task in the next chapter by examining a theoretical framework to explain why watchdog reporting endures in the digital age. Chapters 4 and 5 provide empirical evidence to show that both established and digital-only media outlets are producing quality examples of investigative reporting, offering some confidence about its future.

Note

1. Aucoin, J. 2006 notes that reform journalism, muckraking, and investigative reporting were used interchangeably, citing Carey Williams, editor of *The Nation*, and Jessica Mitford, a freelance reporter who exposed the unethical practices of the funeral industry in America in *The American Way of Death* in 1963.

References

Aucoin, J 2006, *The Evolution of American Investigative Journalism*, University of Missouri Press, Columbia.
Australian Law Reform Commission 2019, 'Balancing privacy with other interests: Meaning of public interest', *Australian Law Reform Commission*, accessed 31 January 2019 from 11, www.alrc.gov.au/publications/8-balancing-privacy-other-interests/meaning-public-interest.

The Australian Press Council 2011, *General Statement of Principles*, accessed 2 February 2019, from www.presscouncil.org.au/uploads/52321/ufiles/APC_General_Statement_of_Principles.pdf.

Birnbauer, B 2012, 'The power of investigative journalism and why it is needed more than ever', in M Ricketson (ed), *Australian Journalism Today*, Palgrave Macmillan, Melbourne.

Blumer, JG 1998, 'Wrestling with public interest in organized communications', in K Brants, J Hermes & L van Zoonen (eds), *The Media in Question*, Sage, London.

Canada, M 2011, *Literature and Journalism in Antebellum America: Thoreau, Stowe and Their Contemporaries Respond to the Rise of the Commercial Press*, Palgrave Macmillan, London.

Carson, A 2014, 'The political economy of the print media and the decline of corporate investigative journalism in Australia', *Australian Journal of Political Science*, 49(4), 726–42.

De Burgh, H 2000, *Investigative Journalism: Context and Practice*, Routledge, New York.

Elliot, C 2012, 'The readers' edition on . . . how should we define "in the public interest"', 21 May, accessed 30 January 2019, from www.theguardian.com/commentisfree/2012/may/20/open-door-definition-public-interest.

Ettema, J & Glasser, T 1989, 'Investigative journalism and the moral order', *Critical Studies in Mass Communication*, 6(1), 1–20.

Ettema, J & Glasser, T 1998, *Custodians of conscience*, Columbia University Press, New York.

Ettema, J & Glasser, T 1984, 'On the epistemology of investigative journalism', in *Annual Meeting of the Association for Education in Journalism and Mass Communication*, Gainesville, FL, August 4–8.

Evans, H 2010, *My Paper Chase: True Stories of Vanished Times*, Abacus, London.

Feldstein, M 2006, 'A muckraking model', *Harvard International Journal of Press/Politics*, 11(2), 105–20.

Hamilton, J 2016, *Democracy's Detectives: The Economics of Investigative Journalism*, Harvard University Press, Cambridge, MA.

Hills, B 2010, *Breaking News: The Golden Age of Graham Perkin*, Scribe, Melbourne.

Joint Committee on Privacy and Injunctions 2012, 'Privacy and injunctions', *Joint Committee on Privacy and Injunctions*, accessed 31 January 2019, from www.parliament.uk/business/committees/committees-a-z/former-committees/joint-select/privacy-and-superinjunctions/.

Lewis, C 2014, *935 Lies*, Public Affairs, New York.

Lloyd, C 2002, 'The historical roots', in S Tanner (ed), *Journalism: Investigation & Research*, Longman, Frenchs Forest, NSW.

McKnight, D 1999, 'The investigative tradition in Australian journalism 1945–1965', in A Curthoys (ed), *Journalism: Print, Politics and Popular Culture*, University of Queensland Press, St Lucia.

McQuail, D 2001, *McQuail's Mass Communication Theory*, (4th edn), Sage, London.

Mitford, J 1979, *The Making of a Muckraker*, Michael Joseph, London.

Muller, D 2014, *Journalism Ethics for the Digital Age*, Scribe Publications, Melbourne.

Muller, D & Birnbauer B, 2018, 'The ethics of reporting national security matter', in J Lidberg & D Muller (eds), *In the Name of Security: Secrecy, Surveillance and Journalism*, Anthem Press, London.

Nerone, J 1987, 'The mythology of the penny press', *Critical Studies in Mass Communication*, 4(4), 376–404.

The New York Times 1886, 'The Tweed Ring', accessed 2 December 2018, from https://timesmachine.nytimes.com/timesmachine/1886/08/08/103969247.pdf.

Oxford Dictionary 2018, *Definition of Muckrake in English by Oxford Dictionaries*, accessed 11 November, from https://en.oxforddictionaries.com/definition/muckrake.

Protess, D, Cook, F, Doppelt, J, Ettema, J, Gordon, M, Leff, D & Miller, P 1991, *The Journalism of Outrage: Investigative Reporting and Agenda Building in America*, Guilford, New York, NY.

Schiffrin, A 2011, *Bad News: How America's Business Press Missed the Story of the Century*, New Press, New York.

Schudson, M 2008, *Why Democracies Need an Unlovable Press*, Polity Press, Cambridge, UK.

Schultz, J 1998, *Reviving the Fourth Estate: Democracy, Accountability and the Media*, Cambridge University Press, Melbourne.

Smith's Weekly 1923, 'Were forceps left inside her? Woman's sensational allegations', 3 February, p. 1.

Stapenhurst, R 2000, *The Media's Role in Curbing Corruption*, World Bank Institute, Washington DC.

Stiglitz, J 2011, 'The media and the crisis: An information theoretical approach', in A Schiffrin (ed), *Bad News: How America's Business Press Missed the Story of the Century*, New York Press, New York.

Strausbaugh, J 2016, *City of Sedition: The History of New York City during the Civil War*, Twelve, New York.

Thyer, D 2016, 'Reporting the "unvarnished" truth: The Origins and Transformation of Undercover Investigative Journalism in Nineteenth Century New York', unpublished PhD thesis, University of Sydney, Sydney.

Tiffen, R 1999, *Scandals, Media, Politics & Corruption in Contemporary Australia*. UNSW Press, Sydney.

Tiffen, R 2010, 'The press', in S Cunningham & G Turner (eds), *The Media and Communications in Australia*, Allen & Unwin, Crow's Nest.

Ullman, J & Honeyman, S 1983, *The Reporter's Handbook: An Investigator's Guide to Documents and Techniques, Under the Sponsorship of Investigative Reporters & Editors*, Inc. (IRE), St. Martin's Press, New York.

3 Why Watchdog Reporting Endures

Theories About the Public Sphere, Media Power, and Democracy

> I think that *The Washington Post* still believes that investigative reporting is part of its brand. Top editors like Marty Baron fully support it and I believe one testament to how they feel about it here is that they maintained a separate investigative unit for over 30 years. That's a big commitment in terms of resources and it shows you that they're willing to spend . . . put their money where their mouth is in terms of the most difficult, risky journalism that you can do in the public service.
>
> (Leen 2016, interview with the author, August 30)

Introduction

This chapter challenges the popular view that as traditional media outlets have been weakened financially, investigative journalism has also declined. It addresses the theoretical question of *why* watchdog reporting can endure in the digital age when the profitability of commercial media outlets is greatly diminished compared to the 20th century.

The theoretical framework builds on the media power theories of 'chaos' and 'control', as advanced by scholars such as Brian McNair, James Curran, Virginia Berridge, Denis McQuail, James McChesney, Edward Herman, Noam Chomsky, and others. Together these media theories speak to the civic and market functions of news media in democratic society. The pluralist (chaos) and dominance (control) theories of the media underpin the conceptual framework used here to explain what motivates media outlets to produce investigative journalism, even in difficult economic times. This framework is developed to explain *why* investigative reporting has survived the transition from the analogue to the digital age.

The chaos paradigm, a pluralist theory of the news media, belongs to the liberal democratic tradition. This tradition proffers the notion of a central role for the news media in democratic society, which is to facilitate the participation of diverse and multiple voices in political discourse. It also embraces the view of the news media fulfilling a 'fourth estate' function in a democracy (Schultz 1998, p. 3). Investigative journalism stands apart from everyday reporting for its particular capacity to fulfil this 'fourth estate' role by challenging the exercise of authoritative power on the public's behalf. In this way, the news media is considered an important agent of public accountability, an essential check on power and abuses thereof in a well-functioning democracy. Pluralist media theories therefore generally provide a positive view of the news media's role in society. As Chapter 2 showed, this positive framing of the role of watchdog reporting as an essential component of a democratic society is widely embraced by journalists and their editors.

The chaos paradigm is typically contrasted with theories that fall within the 'control' or 'dominance' orthodoxy of media theories. These include political economy explanations of the news media, such as Herman and Chomsky's propaganda theory (Herman and Chomsky 2002). Control theories focus on the market imperatives of the commercial media and media companies' positioning within their political environment to maximise profits and political power for their owners. The control orthodoxy posits that the news the audience receives is filtered to the advantage of capital and elites, and thus it plays little role in serving as a check on power on the public's behalf, unless this also serves proprietorial interests.

Clearly, the two theoretical strands of chaos and control are somewhat at odds. Yet, it is proposed here that the civic functions (chaos) and market imperatives (control) of the media need not be mutually exclusive, but that they can coexist on a conceptual continuum where there is potential for overlap. This is a departure from earlier thinking that has largely viewed these theories as oppositional (see Curran 2005). Specifically, with respect to investigative reporting, the foundational theories of the mass media can produce a common outcome—watchdog reporting—notwithstanding different objectives or motivations driving their news agendas. This overlap helps explains why investigative reporting remains viable in the digital age, albeit with some compromises described elsewhere in this book. Empirical evidence for watchdog reporting's durability from the 20th to the 21st century (and its limitations) is detailed in Chapters 4 and 5. The explanatory basis for these empirical findings begins here.

The introductory chapter included a discussion of the public sphere, its origins, its importance to democracy, and its relevance to investigative journalism. The public sphere as conceptualised by German critical theorist Jürgen Habermas (1992) in his book, *The Structural Transformation of the Public Sphere*, is a well-worn path for scholars. I reference it because liberal democratic theory of the media was rejuvenated by Habermas' early work, which provides a normative model of the media (Curran 2005, p. 233). His pessimistic conclusions about the modern state of the public sphere, which he attributed to the hyper-commercialisation of the media, also provide a convenient segue to control theories of the media. We consider how these theories relate to democracy, and specifically investigative journalism, to address two related questions:

1. Does investigative journalism matter in the digital age?
2. Why do media outlets continue producing costly and time-consuming watchdog journalism in an era of extreme financial austerity in newsrooms?

Normative Functions of the Press in a Democracy

In its most ideal imagining, the public sphere provides a communal public space facilitated by the media to allow citizens informed choice, participation, and the ability to monitor the deeds of public officials. This watchdog role undertaken by the media ensures those with power follow the rules and laws of society (constitutionality), thus helping to sustain a healthy democracy (McNair 2003, p. 18).

The media fulfil these preconditions of liberal democracy through different types of news reporting. Schudson (2012) lists seven ways in which media reporting enhances democracy: providing information, investigation, analysis, social empathy (the human interest story), mobilising opinion, providing a forum for debate, and publicising representative democracy. This last function, he says, requires journalists to cover 'more carefully some institutions and relationships that today they take for granted' (Schudson 2012, p. 24). It is one thing for the government to be accountable to the people through elections (vertical accountability), but another for the various branches of government to hold one another accountable through formalised processes and procedures (horizontal democracy). Schudson calls for the media to provide greater publicity to parliamentary workings so that horizontal accountability is better realised.

The Role of the Investigative Journalist

At various times, an investigative journalist might contribute stories that serve each of the aforementioned functions of the media in democracies. But the watchdog role is perhaps most commonly aligned with investigations and scrutiny of political institutions to keep them accountable to the citizens they represent. *Washington Post* reporters Carl Bernstein and Bob Woodward famously demonstrated this role with their groundbreaking reporting of the Watergate scandal, which resulted in Richard Nixon resigning the US presidency in 1974. The media's monitorial role provides an important linkage between democracy and representation by seeking to ensure openness, transparency, and accountability, which are all necessary for meaningful representation.

The News Audience Compared to the Citizen

There is an important distinction between the media serving its audience and serving the wider citizenry. A criticism of the Habermasian public sphere model is that it assumes that citizens *actively* reflect on issues in the public domain, engage in rational-critical discourse about policy matters, and form opinions about issues, which in turn informs their votes.

However, a list of political scientists from John Stuart Mill and Hanna Pitkin to Joseph Schumpeter and Walter Lippmann have decried the level of ignorance that underlies public opinion, the absence of voter rationality, and a general lack of political knowledge. Lippmann (1993, p. 29) stated: 'The individual man does not have opinions on all public affairs. . . . He does not know what is happening, why it is happening, what ought to happen'.

Sally Young (2011) and others have identified a number of practical problems with the idealised conception of the media's role in democracies. First, citizens are not always 'active' in their consumption of news and may engage with media content for many non-political reasons like relaxation and pleasure. Second, this thinking may not only purport to demand too much of citizens, but also of the news media and its role in facilitating an 'idealised' public sphere which, as McNair (2000, p. 12) notes, 'may never exist outside the intellectual imagination'. Third, as Michael Schudson (1998, p. 258) has argued, citizens might be better viewed as monitorial rather than 'active' and ready to react if triggered, much like a watchful parent beside a child in a swimming pool: 'They look inactive, but they are poised for action if action is required'.

Schudson underscores how watchdog reporting need not have a large or knowledgeable audience to be effective in safeguarding democracy for all citizens.

> Journalism performs its institutional role as a watchdog even if nobody in the provinces is following the news. All that matters is that people in government believe that some people somewhere are following the news. This is sufficient to produce in leaders a fear of public embarrassment or public discrediting, public controversy, legal prosecution, or fear of losing an election.
>
> (Schudson 2012, p. 14)

Of course, watchdog journalism extends beyond scrutiny of government to other public and private organisations as well as to individuals who wield power in society. Lucy Bernholz and colleagues remind us that a functioning democracy consists of a tripartite classification of government, market, and civil society. While the exact boundaries of these three domains are not fixed, norms and rules about legitimacy, accountability, transparency, participation, financing, beneficiaries, and governance exist for public, private, and independent institutions (Bernholz et al. 2013, p. 6). If these are violated in some way, the overall system of democratic governance can suffer. Thus, the watchdog reporter investigates transgressions across public and private institutions, and one can spill over to the other. For example, *The Boston Globe*'s Spotlight team's 2003 investigation into child sex abuse within the Catholic Church was not an expose of government but of a religious institution. That investigation had a global ripple effect and eventually led to investigative journalists around the world prodding governments to launch inquiries into institutional responses to child sex abuse in their jurisdictions, such as the 2012 Australian Royal Commission. It referred more than 2,500 suspected abuse cases to authorities following watchdog reporting by the *Newcastle Herald* and the public broadcaster Australian Broadcasting Corporation that triggered the inquiry (Royal Commission into Institutional Responses to Child Sex Abuse 2019). A major global consequence of reporters' investigations into alleged crimes by members of the Catholic Church was the Australian conviction and sentencing in February 2019 of the Vatican's third most senior clergyman, Dr George Pell, for historic cases of child sexual abuse (Davey 2019).

Schudson (2012, p. 14) argues that investigative journalism, particularly by newspapers, engages attentive elites and triggers public debate about issues of democratic accountability. He describes newspaper journalists as assembling the frontline of this type of news and says the print investigative journalist's role is essential to democracy: 'The investigative reporter is the star of a watchdog press . . . democracies need an unlovable press' (Schudson 2012, p. 8).

Various types of societal outcomes occur because of watchdog reporting. David Protess and colleagues (1991, p. 23) identify three broad categories: individualistic (e.g. the sacking of a dodgy doctor); deliberative (e.g. initiating public debate and triggering further investigation or policy change); and substantive, such as the *Boston Globe* investigation that led to substantive changes around institutional processes, jailing of pedophile priests and compensation for victims of sex abuse in many countries. In accordance with the discussions in the last chapter, we might also distinguish between single-issue investigations (individualistic) and systemic-issue investigations (deliberative and substantive) with intangible (heightened debate) and tangible outcomes (establish a royal commission).

A final point here is that investigative reporting is not the only means of exposing transgressions—parliamentary hearings (horizontal accountability), police, and whistleblowers do this too—but the media's monitorial role is the central interest of this study. This is an important point because it differentiates the pluralist media theorists' position from constructivists. From the perspective of a pluralist such as political scientist Pippa Norris, the media are just one instrument contributing to the functioning of a political system. From a constructivist's viewpoint, the media are everything; they are akin to its grand architect (see Street's *Mass Media, Politics and Democracy* 2011, pp. 289–302 for a full account).

Critiquing the Liberal Media System

I have focused on the liberal model, rather than other democratic models, because it best fits the country case studies of Britain, Australia, and the United States analysed in Chapters 4 and 5.

Central tenets of the liberal model of media are weak state intervention, predominantly self-regulation (with the exceptions of provisions to protect against defamation, hate speech, and national security), and an emphasis on free market media ownership (see Hallin and Mancini 2004). As Curran (2005) details in *Media and Power*, this model is premised on elevating the watchdog role of the media as its principal democratic function: to act as a check on the state on behalf of the citizenry. It is argued, and vehemently prosecuted in the United States, that critical distance between the media and the government is best achieved through private media ownership in order to watch over the state. History shows this is not always true. Curran (2005, p. 221) observes that market forces influencing commercial media can produce 'corporate mercenaries which adjust their critical scrutiny to suit their private purpose'.

In recognition of the media's novel role in society and the dangers of leaving media ownership entirely to market forces, countries such as the United Kingdom, Canada, Ireland, and Australia use taxpayers' money to subsidise or fund sections of their media through public broadcasting. However, in each of these countries public broadcasters are the subject of frequent controversy, with accusations of political bias from politicians and the imposition of budget cuts and staff redundancies (Carson 2014). They have also been accused of competing unfairly with commercial media organisations, which as this book highlights have had increasing difficulty maintaining the profitability necessary to fund their journalism.

The Chaos Paradigm

The chaos model described by Brian McNair falls under the broad banner of a liberal democratic theory of the media. While acknowledging the economic difficulties for traditional mass media, such as falling print circulations and closures of mastheads in liberal democracies, he takes a generally optimistic view about the mass media's contribution to the public sphere in the internet era. McNair borrowed the 1944 term 'cultural chaos' from critical theorists Theodor Adorno and Max Horkheimer and playfully turned it sideways to describe the current state of the global media, which can be marked by anarchy and disruption but also allows for 'dissent, openness and diversity rather than closure, exclusivity and ideological homogeneity' (2006, p. vii). Although the word 'chaos' often has negative connotations, McNair applies it in a positive way to rethink contemporary media in its various guises: the commercial broadcast and print media, social media, public broadcasters, web-based citizen journalists, bloggers, and others. Power in society is not simply exercised from the top down but may also come from the ground up or sideways. This is a useful conception for understanding the viability of investigative journalism this century.

However, since writing *Cultural Chaos*, McNair and others have acknowledged the public sphere's quantitative expansion, digitisation, and globalisation, which have simultaneously enhanced and frustrated public discourse (McNair et al. 2016). On one hand, the internet has provided new opportunities for public participation and engagement in political affairs. On the other hand, the volume of information available at any time, alongside the rise of fake news, can complicate, overwhelm and distort political communications and deepen public mistrust of the news media (and of political elites) in democracies. The ease with which false information spreads has heightened the need for citizens to identify what is trustworthy journalism and to understand why it can be trusted. This has serious implications in the electoral cycle, when democracy is predicated on the ideal, discussed earlier, of an informed citizenry capable of making rational choices to select their elected representatives.

In recent decades public trust in the media has fallen, as recorded by various studies of public opinion including Pew, Oxford's Reuters Institute, and Edelman's Trust Barometer. In the wake of Donald Trump's presidential election victory, when the term 'fake news' became part of the public lexicon, the Center for Public Integrity (Sutton 2016, n.p.) argued we need 'independent, serious investigative journalism unraveling for people what's really going and what's really changing, in the nation's capital and around the world'. The public seemed to agree. Sales of quality newspapers and donations to investigative outlets in the United States hit new highs after the 2016 presidential election, in a phenomenon dubbed the 'Trump bump'. *ProPublica*, a specialist investigative reporting bureau, experienced a major influx, with philanthropic income tripling from US$14.3 million in 2016 to US$43.5 million in 2017 (Nisbet et al. 2018). In this way, investigative reporting as evidence-based news offers a counter to fake news (see Chapter 5). Thus, while the chaos model is conducive to the production and valuing of investigative journalism by welcoming openness and diversity of news, paradoxically it also opens the door to the viral spread of fake news that exacerbates public distrust of media.

Political Economy Theories of the Media

A key reason that the political economy orthodoxy is typically viewed as oppositional to a liberal democratic paradigm is that power tends to be imposed from the top down. It highlights the limitations of the journalist trying to critique the powerful due to the overwhelming strength of political and economic forces that are set upon reinforcing and protecting the dominant paradigm. This may involve political interference, market corruption that can lead to suppression of investigative journalism, or market failure resulting in concentrated media ownership and the absence of real market choice. In each instance, we see the potential for a compromised news media with journalism that cannot live up to its idealised role in democratic society.

This theoretical perspective reiterates the use of the mass media to recast society not as it is, but as it is perceived to be to uphold the status quo, or as stated by Walter Lippmann, to 'manufacture consent' of the public. In other words, it is used to control or reinforce the economic, social, and political agendas of the powerful through their own construction of what is news.

Public Opinion and Manufactured Consent

Lippmann (1922) first articulated how the mass media could alter the nature of public political discourse with its capacity to mediate reality. Having witnessed propaganda in World War I, Lippmann was on alert for the misuse of media power for political purposes. His argument in *Public Opinion* was that political leaders understood that there were more facts than any of us could know, and that opinion was thus often unreliable. In his assessment, 'every leader is in some degree a propagandist' because 'the official finds himself deciding more and more consciously what facts, in what setting, in what guise he shall permit the public to know' (Lippmann 1922, p. 158). Here, Lippman brings to attention the dependence of the audience on the primary sources of information: the elites. His worldview is *not* that the media is 'a mirror to reality' as it has been conceived at various times and reflected in countless newspaper titles, but an organ of selected stories with particular perspectives decided by others (Vos 2011).

State influence over the news media is exerted in other ways beyond propaganda, such as broadcast licensing controls, surveillance, censorship, intimidation, and violence towards journalists, as the annual Freedom House reports reveal (see Chapter 6). Recent reports paint an alarming picture of how press freedom has declined globally in recent years, as the media is constrained by both illiberal and liberal governments (Freedom House 2017).

Media Power and the State

Deregulation of rules designed to protect diversity of media voices and owners, such as the relaxation of cross-media ownership laws, can distort the public sphere by allowing 'the power of a very few men to influence the outlook and opinion of large numbers of people' (Norris 1981, pp. 217–18). For example, the left-of-centre Australian Labor government made changes to ownership laws in the 1980s that led to a spate of take-overs and acquisitions, and reduction in the number of owners and mast-heads (see Chapter 1). Paul Chadwick (1989) wrote that in the lead-up to these events there was an organised tactical alliance between media proprietors and the government of the day, which was duly rewarded with favourable media coverage at the 1987 election. Further media ownership consolidation was made possible in 2018 when the conservative Liberal National Coalition additionally relaxed cross-media ownership laws, enabling a A$4 billion merger between a major television network (Nine) and the second-largest newspaper group (Fairfax Media) following persistent lobbying efforts by the major media owners. These changes reduced the number of major news players from five to four (ACCC 2018). Such ownership concentration arguably serves the media proprietors and their shareholders at the expense of the public by potentially limiting diverse viewpoints within the established media landscape.

In Britain in 2012, former Prime Minister David Cameron admitted the news media and his government had become too close in the years leading up to the *News International* phone hacking scandal. As a witness called before the Leveson Inquiry into the culture, practices, and ethics of the British press, he conceded: 'I think in the last 20 years the relationship has not been right, I think it has been too close' (Halliday and Baird 2012). In the circumstances, it appeared that the relationship was distorted, or arguably corrupted, by both the media and government putting their own interests and agendas ahead of the public interest.

Australian and British prime ministers have long been sensitive to and wary of media power and have gone out of their way to meet with media moguls, particularly Rupert Murdoch, over recent decades. However, Rodney Tiffen reminds us that the influence of media owners can be overestimated. Murdoch has on multiple occasions backed losers in both British and Australian elections, despite overtly partisan coverage in his newspapers. Tiffen (2014, p. 120) concludes that it is 'impossible to quantify the impact of Murdoch's editorial positions on public opinion, let alone on election results'.

Yet in the three countries studied in detail in this book—Australia, the United States, and the United Kingdom—Murdoch has accumulated enormous economic power through his media interests. His News Corp Australia network dominates the Australian media market; its listings include metropolitan and regional newspapers, magazines, and the only cable television network, Foxtel. In the United States, Murdoch's media assets include the US$11.7 billion Fox television network, which broadcasts into 90 million homes, and significant magazine, book, and newspaper holdings including *The Wall Street Journal, New York Post,* and Dow

Jones Newswire. News UK's media assets include radio and newspaper listings such as the popular downmarket tabloid *The Sun* and elite masthead *The Times*.

Edward Herman and Noam Chomsky (2002) systematically addressed the economic and political power of 20th-century mass media in *Manufacturing Consent: The Political Economy of the Mass Media*. Their concerns align with Habermas' (1992) pessimistic conclusions about the media using its power to uphold the interests of elites and capital. Their propaganda model of the media takes Lippmann's famous phrase to build a significant account of how the media reinforce the economic, social, and political agendas of the powerful in society through their construction of what is news. They outline five news filters that commercial media organisations in the West activate to reinforce commercial and political interests when deciding what news is 'fit to print' (see Box 3.1).

21st-Century Media Power

Herman and Chomsky's thesis has received renewed attention this century because, notwithstanding democratising effects of the internet and new media digital entrants, the owners of existing large media companies have continued to acquire media assets and thereby increase the concentration of media ownership. In the 19th century, newspapers typically began as family-owned enterprises. Then, as newspaper businesses started changing hands, society witnessed the rise of the media baron.

Box 3.1   The Essential Elements Informing Herman and Chomsky's Propaganda Model

The essential elements informing Herman and Chomsky's propaganda model are:

1. The size of the media outlet, its ownership structures and wealth
2. The influence of advertising as the primary media income source for the mass media
3. Reliance on information provided by government and business 'experts' who reinforce the dominant paradigms
4. Reliance on information provided by perceived purveyors of propaganda, such as public relations specialists and government lobbyists
5. Anti-communism—the negative reaction to any news that seemed to support communist ideology. In the 21st century, this last point could be reasonably perceived as another 'other' that challenges Western ideology, such as Islamism.

During the 20th century, large numbers of newspaper publishers were sold to corporate conglomerates. In the 21st century, conglomerate media businesses have continued to expand through mergers and acquisitions, in some cases on a global scale. The largest media deal in history came in 2017–18 when Rupert Murdoch's 21st Century Fox was sold to Disney Corporation for US$71.3 billion, further consolidating the number of global owners that produce the world's cultural media products (Jacobs 2018).

Herman and Chomsky concluded that the net effect of transnational consolidation was particularly bad news for investigative reporting:

> The increase in corporate power and global reach, the mergers and further centralization of the media, and the decline of public broadcasting, have made bottom-line considerations more influential both in the United States and abroad. The competition for advertising has become more intense and the boundaries between editorial and advertising departments have weakened further. Newsrooms have been more thoroughly incorporated into transnational corporate empires, with budget cuts and a further diminution of management enthusiasm for investigative journalism that would challenge the structures of power.
>
> (Herman and Chomsky 2002, p. xvii)

The late Ben Bagdikian found that from 1983 to 2004, corporate media ownership in the United States had consolidated from 50 major media enterprises to just five, including Time Warner, the Walt Disney Company and Rupert Murdoch's News Corporation. And in 2018, two of those were merging. The remaining hegemons have commercial interests across different aspects of the supply chain ('vertical integration') and distribute their media products across multiple media platforms and markets. Bagdikian's conclusions were stark:

> They are American and foreign entrepreneurs whose corporate empires control every means by which the population learns of its society. And like any close-knit hierarchy, they find ways to cooperate so that all five can work together to expand their power, a power that has become a major force in shaping contemporary American life.
>
> (Bagdikian 2004, p. 3)

Other media scholars in the first decade of the 21st century echo Herman and Chomsky's concern that investigative journalism is under threat because of these consolidating market forces and hyper-commercialism (Franklin 2008; Dahlgren 2009; Curran 2005). These conditions preference advertising over news, or at least favour news stories that attract advertising such as easy-to-digest 'clickbait' stories. These stories are typically about celebrities, often blurring the lines between private and public realms with a view to maximising the story's appeal and reach across social media and other networks.

Dumbing Down the News? Tabloidisation and the Rise of the 'Broadloid'

British academic Bob Franklin (2008, p. 3) argued in the early 2000s that investigative journalism was under serious threat in print because of this downmarket approach to news selection (see introductory chapter). Colin Sparks, John Street, and Peter Dahlgren have also asserted that increasing tabloidisation of content can impede the workings of democracy through self-serving populism, with an emphasis on the private over public interest stories. Dahlgren's (2009, p. 47) general view was that tabloids and tabloidisation of 'serious' papers were a threat to communicating important matters in the public sphere because news content that was 'offering more fun and placing less demands on the audience leads to expectations of, well, more fun and less demands'. Sparks identified a 'moral panic' about tabloids, which he argued existed because changes in education levels, feminisation of the general workforce, and social mobility were redefining readerships and throwing the news market into chaos. This, in turn, engendered the 'broadloid' (a broadsheet, tabloid hybrid) and other tabloidisation trends in the writing style and physical layout of papers to appeal to more readers.

James Curran (2005, p. 225) also feared that market pressures would lead to the 'downgrading of investigative journalism in favour of entertainment'. Street maintains that any discussion of the fate of investigative journalism was inevitably linked to 'churnalism' (the practice of journalists recycling second-hand information, such as from press releases, rather than doing original research) and the 'dumbing down' of news. Yet, Street (2011, pp. 194–5) suspected that if investigative journalism had declined, undoubtedly part of the reason was its high cost and the commercial interests of proprietors. But other factors had to be considered too, such as how media and digital technologies shape the character of coverage, the role of professional journalistic norms and practices, and the overall regulatory environment for news. Media academic Alan Doig argued at the end of last century that any revival of investigative journalism . . . must work within a very different environment than that which promoted investigative journalism in earlier decades (1997, p. 206). Referencing Doig, Street argued it must address the commercial pressures that make 'ratings and profits' of greater importance than 'performance and the public interest' (Street 2011, p. 207). Street also acknowledged this revival might lie in new technologies, such as sites like *WikiLeaks*.

Applying the chaos-and-control framework, I argue that commercial imperatives as well as the public interest are motivating factors for newsrooms influencing investigative journalism's future. Watchdog reporting survives, even thrives, in the digital age because traditional news outlets identify economic value in branding themselves as trustworthy and accurate, as they have in the past. This distinction is more pressing in a fake news era, when public trust of media is generally falling in democracies (Edelman 2018; Mitchell et al. 2016).

Some media outlets like *The New York Times* and *The Washington Post* engage in investigative reporting because it is central to their values, as the *Post*'s chief investigative journalist Jeff Leen explained in the opening quote of this chapter.

New technologies are a key *means* for aiding investigative journalism's brighter future, in that they play an increasing role in the gathering, analysing, and distribution processes of investigative stories. The effects of, and reactions to, economic and political globalisation provide the *mechanism* that offers a different environment for the promotion of investigative journalism. This occurs in remarkable circumstances whereby news can travel across the globe in seconds, and the local story can also belong to a global narrative. This local/global nexus is exemplified by stories about global concerns like climate change and stories about its local impacts such as bushfires, or the broader narrative of economic unfairness and the downfall of a local politician caught using secret offshore tax havens.

Comparing Chaos and Control Theories

Table 3.1 shows a somewhat binary division whereby media power is seen as either dispersed (pluralist view) or concentrated (dominance view) (Corner and Robinson 2006). In the table, I build on these 20th-century oppositional models (the shaded columns) which categorise the two media paradigms by the following: type of outlets, mass media's general effects, audience reactivity, pervasive ideology, and modes of production in order to show their difference.

Table 3.1 represents the broad-brush differences between the dominance and pluralist features of the liberal media system by adapting the mass media theory of the late Denis McQuail. The features that Brian McNair identifies that can shift the control paradigm towards chaos in the digital age are highlighted (in bold). I then insert a new column (in italics) between the two existing media power paradigms to indicate areas where I consider overlap is possible in the digital age, where the two models share key features. The central argument of this chapter is that while differences might still exist between the two models (see Table 3.1), some features are now common, or available, to both. Significantly, this overlap can be advantageous for the production of investigative journalism

Table 3.1 Comparison of Chaos and Control Media Models With Reference to Investigative Journalism

FACTORS	CHAOS THEORY (pluralism)	POTENTIAL OVERLAP (shared features)	CONTROL THEORY (dominance)
Sources (primary)	Competing political, social, cultural interests of groups	*Combination of chaos and control outcomes, depending on circumstances*	Dominant elites, those with capitalist power
Media type	Many and independent of each other, **networked, open**	*Extending reach through social media promotion*	Concentrated ownership, hierarchical and **centralised**, dominance
Production	Creative, free, and original	*Collaborative between media and non-media organisations; agnostic about the media platform; data driven, greater journalistic agency*	Standardised, routinised, **controlled**, exclusive
Worldview (ideology) represented in content	**Diverse** and competing views, responsive to audience demand, transparent, **heterogeneity**	*Gatekeepers circumvented or replaced with 'sense makers'*	Selective and coherent, decided from above; **opaque**; homogeneity
Audience	Fragmented, selective and active and reactive	*Participatory and/ or monitorial rather than passive*	Dependent, passive, **limited access to information**
Effects of reportage	Numerous without consistency or predictability of direction, including 'no effect'	*Combination of outcomes- transnational, potential to have global impact*	Strong and confirmative of established social order

Sources: Author adapted from McNair, B (2006) *Cultural Chaos*, and McQuail, D. (1987), *Mass Communication Theory*.

by both traditional and non-traditional media, and commercial and non-commercial outlets.

Rethinking the Control and Chaos Paradigms

McNair (2006, p. 88) has suggested that commercial viability and political radicalism can coexist in contemporary capitalist societies. Curran

(2005) observed that the literature on the dominance model tends to simplistically dismiss countervailing influences on commercial media, such as the need to remain profitable and to be regarded as legitimate news organs to keep their audiences on side. In Curran's words:

> Privately owned media need to maintain audience interest in order to be profitable; they have to sustain public legitimacy in order to avoid societal retribution; and they can be influenced by the professional concerns of their staff.
>
> (Curran 2005, p. 223)

Curran's point is that distinctions between one paradigmatic model and another are less neat in practice. Certainly, established media have suffered under market forces in the digital age, as evidenced in Chapter 1, but their responses to these changed circumstances have varied. Some outlets have retreated to churnalism and clickbait to save costs and attract mass online advertisers, while others have decided that to compete in a globalised media sphere, they must not only remain relevant and trustworthy to their readers, but they must be *seen* to be doing so. To this end, many media groups laud their investigative reporting in ways that clearly imply a higher status for it than for their other work. *The Washington Post*'s motto, 'Democracy Dies in Darkness', is an example of how commercial outlets signal the value of investigative reporting. Likewise, Australia's second-largest newspaper company, Fairfax Media, now Nine, has in recent years profiled its award-winning investigative journalism in its annual report to shareholders, stating: 'We celebrate and promote this position as our point of difference and competitive advantage in news media' (Fairfax Media 2018). News Corp, owner of mainly tabloid brands but also elite titles such as *The Times* in London, *The Wall Street Journal*, and *The Australian*, uses its annual report to publish improving digital reader subscription figures, reasoning that 'this success vindicates our commitment to quality journalism' (News Corp 2016).

It is perhaps unsurprising that in both the Fairfax and News annual reports to shareholders, the emphasis in their language is on the commercial value of investigative journalism rather than its possible contribution to democratic accountability or other altruistic goals. James T. Hamilton agrees with the view that investigative journalism can still make money in the digital age: 'Some outlets do profit from developing a brand name for exposés' (Hamilton 2016, p. 33). Of course, for the many other media outlets that rely principally on online advertising and clickbait stories to attract audience share, a traditional political economy approach best explains their business practice.

Some media organisations profess a commitment to investigative journalism for its civic functions rather than as a branding strategy designed for market success. *ProPublica* in the United States is one example. As a non-profit organisation, its mission is not to impress the market but to enlighten its readers about misuses of power. Its mission statement is unambiguous:

> To expose abuses of power and betrayals of the public trust by government, business, and other institutions, using the moral force of investigative journalism to spur reform through the sustained spotlighting of wrongdoing.
>
> (*ProPublica* 2019)

American media academic Philip Meyer (2009, p. 214) argued that quality print newspapers could remain viable, albeit with a smaller audience share, if they retained local community trust. A way to do this was to provide readers with evidence-based journalism that regained public trust and empowered the media to continue to demand political accountability. He stated that at the core of evidence-based journalism was investigative journalism. But in order to meet the costs associated with this type of reporting, newspapers needed to aim for 'quality' readers who sought the truth as a defence against political and advertising spin (Meyer 2008).

Meyer recommended that newspapers reassign resources used to gather frivolous, non-consequential news, which in the current information-rich environment, he argued, failed to add value to mastheads' brands. Anderson and colleagues (2015, p. 87) also argued that newsrooms of the future would be smaller, with more diverse revenue streams, and that to survive they would need to collaborate and engage in subject specialisation. They also argued (2015, p. 107) that quality reportage was key: 'So many sources of news are now available that any publication with a reputation for accuracy, probity or rigor has an advantage over the run-of-the-mill competition'. *The Washington Post* is an example of Meyer's model. Out of 47 Pulitzer Prizes won during its long history, six came during the global financial crisis. Hence, rather than retreating from quality reporting in difficult times, it doubled down.

A compelling explanation for why both *The Washington Post* and the downmarket *Daily Mail* in Britain would persevere with investigative journalism in times of financial hardship is offered by Hamilton's *Democracy's Detectives*. Hamilton lists five motivations for why outlets would produce investigative journalism this century, each of which aligns approximately with at least one of the different contemporary funding models for media. In doing so, Hamilton also demonstrates the limitations of viewing media power solely through the binary lens of control and chaos.

Box 3.2 adapts Hamilton's five reasons for outlets to pursue investigative reporting, and I have added a sixth, based on Meyer's emphasis on trust.

Box 3.2   Six Reasons Why Media Outlets Would Pursue Investigative Reporting

1. The traditional commercial model that use revelations to sell a readers' attention to others (advertising-based)
2. The user-pays model that engages in investigative reporting to offer unique information to sell to the reader (subscription model)
3. The partisan model that seeks to influence readers' vote through political exposés (this is more likely in places known for politically partisan media)
4. The worldview model that undertakes investigations to reset the issue agenda by 'changing what you think about' to change the world (an ideological motivation)
5. The shareability model for 'sharing my ideas with you' by investigating an area of interest, as might be the case with self-funded passion projects

Models 4 and 5 could be funded through non-profit models, sponsorship, or a hybrid funding model (see Chapter 7 for details). To this list, I add:

6. The trust model. This motivation aligns with goals of both the commercial and non-profit media sector. It provides evidence-based investigations to rebuild public trust in the media, which in turn builds audience and the means to pay for further investigations. Media trust is vital if news outlets are to stay relevant to their audiences.

Hamilton provides a mix of motivations for why investigative reporting continues to happen. Hamilton (2016, p. 26) also offers several additional reasons why individuals pursue watchdog reporting, such as reporter prestige, career advancement, or personal satisfaction in the sense of 'making a difference' to the world. Together, institutional and personal motivations give us an understanding of *why* investigative journalism continues this century. However, the question of *how* it continues, beyond its obvious requirements for funding and staff (see Chapter 7), brings us back to the question of the *means* for producing investigative journalism. This involves age-old necessities such as a journalist's skills and time, combined with new-age tools such as digital technologies, big data, computational journalism, and information networks that allow information to spread far and wide (see Chapter 6). In this way, the internet has had a revolutionary impact akin to the invention of the printing press centuries earlier, which paved the way for the communal public sphere. Today the internet makes possible a global digital public sphere.

The Digital Public Sphere

In the second decade of the new millennium, information transcends state and global borders, quickly and seamlessly, and digital media is central to the process (Castells 2009). The emergence of Facebook in 2004, YouTube in 2005, and Twitter in 2006, among other forms of social media and information sharing platforms, has enabled citizens to participate, comment, and engage with ideas in varied and new ways. Manuel Castells, McNair, and others consider this digitised network information space as forming an emergent globalised digital public sphere (McNair et al. 2016, p. ix; Volkmer 2014). It includes both the traditional media of television, radio, and the press, as well as other forms of digital communications that bypass mainstream media and government controls.

Castells proffered the view that the digital public sphere was where citizens could come together to express their autonomous views to influence the political institutions of society. Thus civil society was the 'organised expression of these views' (2009, p. 78). He contended that the digital communication tools and information networks available to us in the 21st century would pave the way for the formation of global civil society, enabling 'ad hoc forms of global governance' to address problems that transcend the nation state. Put simply, media networks would exercise significant political power in a globalised world.

Habermas (2006, p. 426), revisiting his own theory and commenting on the globalising effects of the internet on the public sphere, wrote in 2006: 'The internet has certainly reactivated the grassroots of an egalitarian public of writers and readers'. However, he argued that although it can undermine the censorship of authoritarian regimes that try to control and repress public opinion,[1] it has weaknesses in liberal regimes:

> In the context of liberal regimes, the rise of millions of fragmented chat rooms across the world tend instead to lead to the fragmentation of large but politically focused mass audiences into a huge number of isolated issue publics. Within established national public spheres, the online debates of web users only promote political communication, when news groups crystallise around the focal points of the quality press.
>
> (Habermas 2006, p. 423)

In other words, established 'quality' media still play a necessary role in making sense of the vast 'issue publics' online in liberal societies. According to Castells' network theory of communication, the internet has played a democratising role, enabling citizens to come together to overcome traditional 'flows of power'. Previously, those with power used the mainstream media to spread or control information to their advantage (Castells 2013). Castells argues that the internet has reversed this paradigm, creating 'power of flows', which enables journalists and citizens to work together, beyond state boundaries, to report crimes against the previously silenced. Therefore, digital communication technologies have enabled the classical definition of the public sphere to be extended sideways to allow for more inclusive space(s), beyond the bourgeoisie who were central to the Habermasian model.

The digital tools and networks of the global public sphere have enabled investigative reporters to critique global power in ways not previously possible. The ICIJ collaborations, like the medical Implant Files, enabled individual journalists from various media organisations to work together to show how patients around the world had become unwitting test subjects for new medical technology that did them harm. The journalists were able to tell this global story, while also communicating local aspects of it. The Global Investigative Journalism Network (GIJN) has estimated that more than 100 investigative outlets in almost 50 nations are driving this new form of large-scale collaborative journalism, mostly funded through philanthropy (Kaplan 2013).

Peter Berglez and Amanda Gearing (2018) apply Castells' network society view to emerging forms of global collaborative investigative journalism, arguing the ICIJ could be viewed as a global fourth estate that holds power accountable across countries and continents. What is most pertinent about their theory of global network journalism here is that it includes mostly reporters at traditional media outlets who unite to use the digital tools and international networks to challenge various forms of global inequality such as tax evasion. Accordingly, Berglez and Gearing argue:

> The global fourth estate expands the domestic space of politics. In this new domestic-global political terrain, those who could be held accountable for unjust actions might represent global or transnational institutions but also domestic ones.
>
> (Berglez and Gearing 2018, p. 4585)

This heralds a seismic shift in reporting practice from the 'old model' of single newsroom investigations marked by cutthroat rivalry to a 'new model' of multiple newsrooms and countries cooperating and sharing information to expose systemic wrongdoing. This emergent form of collaborative watchdog reporting represents another reason for understanding the chaos and control traditions along a continuum rather than in opposition to one another in the digital age. It shows that the 'old' binary model does not adequately explain the new environment for investigative journalism.

Investigative journalist and academic Brant Houston (2010) argued three phenomena were playing a prominent role in this new landscape for investigative journalism: the rise of non-profit media, machines (computers and their software), and journalism networks. He wrote: 'These factors mean more focus to the investigative journalism itself, more citizen involvement in shaping stories, and more collaboration rather than competition'. Houston argued somewhat prophetically in 2009 that growth in the number of non-profit newsrooms, and groups of journalists working with computer scientists and citizens making use of data analysis and software, would 'create networks of newsrooms to share information, to improve the quality of their investigations, and to create cost efficiencies'. Further, Houston (2010, p. 51) observed: 'The advent of the non-profits has led newspapers to embrace collaboration, especially with non-profits, as one way to counter the decline of staff and resources'.

Comparing the chaos and control approaches to media allows us to view through a multifocal lens how the changing reporting environment impacts upon investigative journalism and the organisations and people undertaking it. The chaos-and-control framework, previously seen as comprising distinct spheres, is reconsidered here as a conceptual space where overlap is possible in the global digital age, as in a Venn diagram (see Figure 3.1). At this juncture investigative journalism has economic, political, and cultural viability because of the varying motivations (and

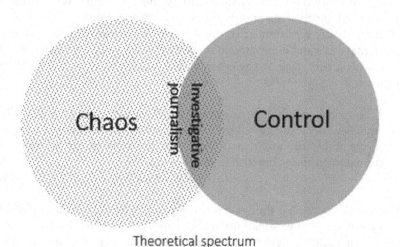

Theoretical spectrum

Figure 3.1 A Venn Representation of Conceptual Common Space Between the Chaos and Control Models, Where Investigative Journalism Is Likely to Endure in the Digital Age

Source: Author.

their combinations,) driving it—be they political, ideological, commercial, personal, or otherwise.

The former investigative editor at Fairfax Media, Mark Baker, stated that the primary motivation for preserving Fairfax's investigative reporting tradition was commercial. However, its reporting outcomes—such as exposing sex abuse of children in institutional care that led to a royal commission and national apology—strengthened Fairfax's reputation for providing democratic accountability, thus highlighting the overlap between the two models. Baker explained:

> What is going to sell in the future is the product of investigative journalism. So, we need to do more of it and not less, and it is by developing that high end content that nobody else has, that is what will continue to persuade people to buy you . . . news is a universal commodity now, everybody has it and everybody gets it for nothing, it is highly competitive . . . but where we want to make money is on the strength and credibility of our investigative journalism.
>
> (M. Baker 2012, interview with the author, 11 January)

Conclusion

While newsrooms have suffered significant setbacks in the 21st century with the collapse of their main revenue source (analogue advertising), the assumption that investigative journalism is therefore also in decline is a less straightforward proposition. In answer to the earlier questions posed in this chapter, investigative journalism still matters in the digital age because it supports different media outlets' varied motivations for undertaking watchdog reporting.

Ideological, economic, and civic values of news organisations are among various drivers of the continued pursuit of investigative journalism in the 21st century. In this context, there has emerged a synthesis between the control and chaos paradigms that can be seen to have *enabled* investigative journalism's endurance. Amid the substantial newsroom cutbacks that impacted on other forms of reporting and editorial spending, watchdog reporting has been afforded considerable protections.

The chaos-and-control framework accommodates these varied motivations for undertaking investigative journalism. The *mechanism* that enables a reappraisal of how investigative journalism fits within the framework relates to economic and political globalisation. While these forces have placed financial pressures on established media outlets, they have also opened up new audiences and opportunities for collaboration within the digital public sphere. The *means* for this reappraisal is the technological developments providing journalists with new tools, digital platforms, and access to 'big data' to connect reporters to citizens and other collaborating partners, resulting in unprecedented information flows within, and between, nations. Indeed, as Doig had foreseen, investigative journalism exists and endures in a different environment (as it must) 'than that which promoted it in the past' (1997, p. 206).

Sustainable funding remains a perennial challenge for watchdog reporting. Its future is also made vulnerable by governments enacting laws that limit media freedom and diversity. To assist our understanding of how watchdog reporting can survive into the future, the next chapter explores its past, and in particular how it has changed and developed since the mid-20th century.

Note

1. The internet's egalitarian power was mobilised through social networking sites such as Twitter during the 2009 Iranian elections. The voices of many allowed greater international scrutiny of the corrupt conduct of those elections.

References

ACCC 2018, *ACCC Will Not Oppose Nine-Fairfax Merger*, accessed 5 January 2019, from www.accc.gov.au/media-release/accc-will-not-oppose-nine-fairfax-merger.

Anderson, C, Bell, E & Shirky, C 2015, 'Post-industrial journalism: Adapting to the Present', *Geopolitics, History & International Relations*, 7(2), 32–123.

Bagdikian, B 2004, *The New Media Monopoly*, Beacon, Boston.

Berglez, P & Gearing, A 2018, 'The Panama and Paradise Papers: The Rise of a Global Fourth Estate', *International Journal of Communication*, 12.

Bernholz, L, Cordelli, C & Reich, R 2013, *The Emergence of Digital Civil Society*, Stanford PACS, Stanford, CA.

Carson, A 2014, 'ABC cuts a tale of two Australias: Sydney-Melbourne and also-rans', *The Conversation*, 23 November, accessed 1 January 2018, from https://theconversation.com/abc-cuts-a-tale-of-two-australias-sydney-melbourne-and-also-rans-34424.

Castells, M 2009, *Communication Power*, Oxford University Press, Oxford.

Castells, M 2013, *Networks of Outrage and Hope*, Polity Press, Cambridge.

Chadwick, P 1989, *Media Mates: Carving Up Australia's Media*, Sun Books, South Melbourne.

Corner, J & Robinson, P 2006, 'Politics and mass media: A response to John Street', *Political Studies Review*, 4(1), 48–54.

Curran, J 2005, *Media and Power*, Routledge, London.

Dahlgren, P 2009, *Media and Political Engagement: Citizens, Communication and Democracy*, Cambridge University Press, New York.

Davey, M 2019, 'George Pell: Cardinal found guilty of child sexual assault', *The Guardian* 26 February, accessed 26 February 2019, from www.theguardian.com/australia-news/2019/feb/26/cardinal-george-pell-vatican-treasurer-found-guilty-of-child-sexual-assault.

Doig, A 1997, 'The decline of investigative journalism', in M Bromley & T O'Malley (eds), *A Journalism Reader*, pp. 189–213, Routledge, London.

Edelman, R 2018, *Trust Barometer: Global Report*, Edelman, accessed 5 January 2019, from www.edelman.com/sites/g/files/aatuss191/files/2018-10/2018_Edelman_Trust_Barometer_Global_Report_FEB.pdf.

Fairfax Media 2018, *Fairfax Media Annual Report 2018 'Going for Growth'*, Fairfax Media, accessed 1 December 2018, from www.fairfaxmedia.com.au/ArticleDocuments/193/2018%20FXJ%20Annual%20Report_FINAL_14AUG2018.pdf.aspx?Embed=Y.

Franklin, B 2008, *Pulling Newspapers Apart: Analysing Print Journalism*, Routledge, Abingdon.

Freedom House 2017, *Freedom of the Press*, accessed 1 December 2018, from https://freedomhouse.org/report/freedom-press/freedom-press—2017.

Habermas, J (trans T Burger) 1992, *The Structural Transformation of the Public Sphere*, Polity Press, Cambridge.

Habermas, J 2006, 'Political communication in media society: Does democracy still enjoy an epistemic dimension? The impact of normative theory on empirical research', *Communication Theory*, 16(4), 411–26.

Halliday, J & Baird, D 2012, 'David Cameron at the Leveson inquiry: As it happened', *The Guardian*, accessed 4 May 2017, from www.theguardian.com/media/2012/jun/14/david-cameron-leveson-inquiry-live.

Hallin, D & Mancini, P 2004, *Comparing Media Systems: Three Models of Media and Politics*, Cambridge University Press, Cambridge.

Hamilton, J T 2016, *Democracy's Detectives: The Economics of Investigative Journalism*, Harvard University Press, Cambridge.

Herman, E & Chomsky, N 2002, *Manufacturing Consent: The Political Economy of the Mass Media*, Pantheon, New York.

Houston, B 2010, 'The future of investigative journalism', *Daedalus*, 139(2), 45–56.

Jacobs, D 2018, 'Rupert Murdoch's children are in line for $2 billion: Each: From 21st Century fox sale', *Business Insider*, 17 October, accessed 17 October, from www.businessinsider.com.au.

Kaplan, D 2013, *Global Investigative Journalism: Strategies for Support*, Center for International Media Assistance, Washington.

Lippmann, W 1922, *Public Opinion*, Harcourt, USA.

Lippmann, W 1993, *The Phantom Public*, Transaction Publishers, London.

McNair, B 2000, *Journalism and Democracy: An Evaluation of the Political Public Sphere*, Routledge, London.

McNair, B 2003, *An Introduction to Political Communication*, (3rd edn), Routledge, London.

McNair, B 2006, Cultural Chaos: Journalism, News and Power in a Globalised World, Routledge, London.

McNair, B, Flew, T, Harrington, S & A Swift 2016, *Politics, Media and Democracy in Australia: Public and Producer Perceptions of the Political Public Sphere*, Routledge, New York.

McQuail, D 1987, *Mass Communication Theory*, Sage, Thousand Oaks.

Meyer, P 2008, 'The elite newspaper of the future', *American Journalism Review*, 30(5).

Meyer, P 2009, *The Vanishing Newspaper: Saving Journalism in the Information Age*, University of Missouri Press, Columbia.

Mitchell, A, Holcomb, J & Barthel, M, 2016, 'Many Americans believe fake news is sowing confusion'. *Pew Research Centre*, 15 December, accessed 1 March 2017, from https://www.journalism.org/2016/12/15/many-americans-believe-fake-news-is-sowing-confusion/.

News Corp 2016, *News Corp Annual Report*, News Corp.

Nisbet, M, Wihbey, J, Kristiansen, S & Bajak, A 2018, 'Funding the news: Foundations and nonprofit media', *Shorenstein Center*, accessed 1 December 2018, from https://shorensteincenter.org/funding-the-news-foundations-and-nonprofit-media/.

Norris, J 1981, *Report of the Inquiry into the Ownership and Control of Newspapers in Victoria*, Department of the Premier, Victoria.

ProPublica 2019, *About Us: ProPublica*, accessed 5 January 2019, from www.propublica.org/about/.

Protess, D, Cook, F, Doppelt, J, Ettema, J, Gordon, M, Leff, D & Miller, P 1991, *The Journalism of Outrage: Investigative Reporting and Agenda-Building in America*, Guilford Press, New York.

Royal Commission into Institutional Responses to Child Sexual Abuse 2019, accessed 5 March 2019, from www.childabuseroyalcommission.gov.au/.

Schudson, M 1998, *The Good Citizen*, Martin Kessler Books, New York.

Schudson, M 2012, *Why Democracies Need an Unlovable Press*, Polity, Cambridge.

Schultz, J 1998, *Reviving the Fourth Estate: Democracy, Accountability and the Media*, Cambridge University Press, Melbourne.

Street, J 2011, *Mass Media, Politics and Democracy*, Palgrave Macmillan, London.

Sutton, K 2016, 'Nonprofit newsrooms fundraise off Trump win', *Politico*, 11 November, accessed 5 January 2019, from https://www.politico.com/blogs/on-media/2016/11/non-profit-newsrooms-fundraise-off-trump-win-231246.

Tiffen, R 2014, *Rupert Murdoch: A Reassessment*, UNSW Press, Sydney.

Volkmer, I 2014, *The Global Public Sphere: Public Communication in the Age of Reflective Interdependence*, Polity, Cambridge.

Vos, T 2011, '"A mirror of the times" A history of the mirror metaphor in journalism', *Journalism Studies*, 12(5), 575–89.

Young, S 2011, *How Australia Decides: Election Reporting and the Media*, Cambridge University Press, Cambridge.

4   Six Decades of Investigative Journalism
The 1950s to the 2000s

> The thing about journalism, what is going on is that the traditional cartels, owned by wealthy people, are being broken up. If it were not for the fact that journalism also has a role in the public interest, in the stability of the democracy, we would not care. If it were a bunch of confectionery companies, we would be celebrating it.
>
> (Kohler 2010, interview with the author, 5 October)

Introduction

How has investigative reporting developed and changed since the mid-20th century? And how has it fared since the arrival of the digital revolution? Earlier chapters have shown that the traditional print media are at an economic crossroads. Their business model has been fractured chiefly by the digital revolution and the resulting loss of lucrative print advertising revenue streams that previously underpinned journalism, particularly in newspapers. The industry's financial crisis has added to the historical tension between maximising profits and providing quality newspapers, described as the 'profit controversy' by US media academic Philip Meyer. 'Investors and their advisors tend to focus on short-term financial results, and this puts pressure on newspaper managers to cut back on resources in order to maintain steady earnings growth year to year', wrote Meyer and Koang-Hyub (2003, p. 1). This raises an important question: Have the unprecedented newsroom cutbacks of recent years affected the quantity and quality of investigative journalism?

This chapter employs empirical methods to identify and track the development of investigative journalism over six decades, using Australia as its case study. The analysis begins in the 1950s when the first Australian national journalism awards began. It spans the heyday for newspaper print circulations in the 1970s and 1980s, through to the economic hard times for mastheads brought on by the digital age.

To show how investigative journalism has developed and changed, a content analysis of investigative journalism in key Australian broadsheet-style mastheads, introduced in Chapter 1, is undertaken. A second analysis of six decades of award-winning investigative journalism of Australia's only national peer-reviewed journalism awards, the Walkley Awards (which includes awards for some television, online and radio investigative reporting) is also performed. These analyses are complemented by interviews with 22 Australian media professionals to illuminate the data findings. They enable a survey of investigative journalism in all media forms, not just newspapers. The findings provide valuable insights about the quantity and quality of investigative journalism in Australia over time. Given the many similarities between the media landscape in Australia and other developed nations, the findings may resonate in other mature economies.

This study is important because of widely held concerns that established newsrooms are producing fewer investigative stories in response to falling print circulations and advertising revenues (Franklin 2008, p. 15; Street 2011, pp. 191–5). By tracking investigative reporting over decades, I identify various patterns and trends—such as the increase in one-off investigative specials. As outlined in Chapter 3, this enables us to explore not only if investigative journalism has endured in tougher times, but if so, for what purposes? Is it primarily to provide democratic accountability? Or is it a branding strategy for mastheads to demonstrate to the market their 'quality' and unique worth? Or, as proposed in the previous chapter, is it both?

Data presented in this chapter debunks the myth that investigative journalism has been in decline in Australia (Schultz 1998; Bruns, Wilson and Saunders 2008; Whitton 2012, interview with the author, 8 February; Masters 2011, interview with the author, 15 February). Contrary to widely held perceptions, it demonstrates that by the end of the first decade of the 21st century—as the effects on publishers of the digital age were intensifying—the quantity and quality of investigative journalism was in reasonable shape. It also confirms that Australia's broadsheet-style mastheads have produced more investigative journalism than tabloids over time, and the press is the major source of it.

The Quantity of Investigative Journalism

The longitudinal broadsheet study examined more than 21,100 news pages of selected broadsheet mastheads. Every news story for an entire month (April) was examined, and this was repeated at ten-year intervals from 1971 to 2011[1] (for the operative definition of investigative journalism, see Chapter 2).

Through this process, it was found that each sampled month of each year yielded an increase in the quantity of investigative journalism stories compared to the previous decade. It should be emphasised in this context that investigative journalism that meets the definition of this study is, as expected, not commonplace in the daily media landscape. This is reflected in the low numbers of examples detected and concurs with the experiences of interviewees.

The Australian Walkley Awards are analysed in the second content analysis and present an exceptional opportunity to understand Australian investigative journalism over time because they represent the only peer-reviewed national pool of journalism, including investigative journalism, since the awards' inception in 1956. The awards are useful for triangulation of methods in this chapter because they showcase examples of journalism and investigative journalism in every year since 1956 (unlike the broadsheet study which uses ten-year periods), and thus provide a year-by-year sample of investigative journalism. As some of the award categories have changed in number, name, and criterion over time, the categories analysed were those that remained largely unchanged and where it was reasonable to expect to find an example of investigative journalism. Thus an award category such as 'best headline' was excluded from analysis. In all, nine categories of awards were analysed,[2] which yielded a population of 187 stories to be examined. The same content analysis recording sheet as the broadsheet study was used to record details for each of the 187 Walkley-winning stories in the sample. The societal outcomes of winning investigative stories were cross-referenced with digital newspaper archives and newspaper databases LexisNexis and Factiva, through interviews, and when necessary, through correspondence with the authoring journalists to gain further details. Of the 187 stories analysed, 101 passed the operative definition described in Chapter 2 for investigative journalism.

While datasets for the broadsheet newspapers and the Walkley Awards are separate, both show a growing number of examples of investigative reporting over the years up to and including the first decade of the new millennium. *The National Times* began in 1971 and ceased publication 16 years later due to the financial crisis of that period, yet the volume of investigative stories, even with one fewer masthead in the dataset, continued to rise. The quantum peak came *after* newsrooms across the country had engaged in a spate of cost-cutting in 2001, with 16 investigative stories recorded in one month across the studied mastheads. The number of investigative stories, for the month, eased slightly to 13 by 2011 (see Figure 4.1). This trajectory suggests a delayed impact on investigative reporting as a consequence of cost-cutting exacerbated by the financial downturn of the GFC in Australia, consistent with the observations in Chapter 1. However, more data points are needed after this time to be certain.

It is also found that the number of investigative journalism print stories (both tabloid and broadsheet) that pass the operative definition increased over time.[3] The Walkley Awards are not a completely reliable indicator of quantity because the number of entries has increased in each year. However, the Walkleys data suggests more stories, judged by their peers to be exceptional, were investigative stories.

As more entries were competing for awards,[4] more categories were added and more winning stories were available for analysis. To adjust for this, the number of winning investigative stories was expressed as a

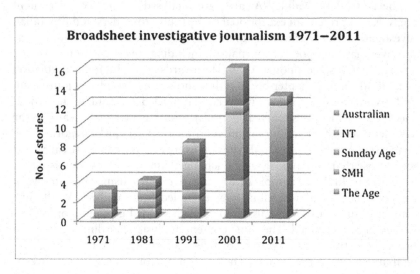

Figure 4.1a Amount of Australian Broadsheet Investigative Journalism, 1971–2011

Source: Author

Note: N = 45

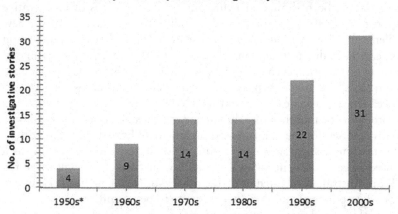

Figure 4.1b Amount of Australian Newspaper Investigative Journalism Winning Walkley Awards, 1950s–2000s

Source: Author

*incomplete decade, as Walkley awards began in 1956

Note: n = 101

percentage of the total number of entries for that decade. This allowed for the number of stories that passed the test for investigative journalism to be compared across time. It revealed two peaks for the quantum of investigative journalism over time (see Figure 4.2).

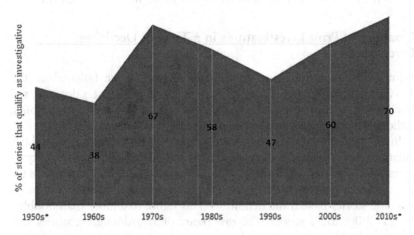

Figure 4.2 'Golden Eras' for Australian Print Award-Winning Investigative
    Journalism, 1956–2011

Source: Author

*incomplete decades (Walkley awards began in 1956 and 2010s yet to conclude)

Notes: n = 101; N = 187

Golden Times for Investigative Journalism

Using the Walkley data, the decades 1970–79 and 2000–09 were peak
times for investigative journalism. In the 1970s, 67 per cent of award-
winning stories qualified (using the operative definition) as investigative
journalism. In the 2000s, 60 per cent of winning stories were investigative
journalism, and all of the awarded print stories met the investigative journalism definition.[5] A specific 'investigative journalism' Walkley category
was not established until 1991, and it was not available to *all* forms of
media as an 'all media' category until 1997. Nonetheless, in the 21 years
that this category was available to all platforms, print won it 15 times
(71 per cent). All except two winning stories originated from broadsheets,
highlighting the role of that particular medium in producing award-
winning investigative journalism.

Contrary to popular perception, the 1980s was not a 'golden era' for
print investigative journalism in Australia in terms of the *quantity* of peer-
reviewed award-winning print stories (see Chapter 2) (Amos 2005, p. 1).
However, this perception about watchdog reporting in the 1980s might
arise from a series of high-profile and consequential television and radio
investigations. One example was Chris Masters and Bruce Belsham's
1985 Gold Walkley for their ABC TV *Four Corners* investigation into the
fatal explosion on the Greenpeace ship, the *Rainbow Warrior*, in New

Zealand's Auckland Harbour (Masters 2011). Another example was Dr Norman Swan's 1988 Gold Walkley for his exposé on ABC radio of the fraudulent medical claims of Dr William McBride erroneously linking antidepressants to birth defects, which led to his medical deregistration.

Quantity of Print Investigations in a Time of Declining Circulations

Print paid circulations and advertising revenues have fallen since the 1990s in Australia (see Chapter 1). The peak for print sales was the late 1980s for most broadsheets, and a decade earlier for most tabloids, although these peaks varied from masthead to masthead.

In an apparent paradox, and contrary to popular perception, as paid circulations and revenues of most mastheads started declining, the quantity of investigative stories was increasing decade upon decade. For example, if we only consider the stories that passed the investigative test, in the 1980s, 14 winning stories passed the definition. This figure had more than doubled by the 2000s to 31 stories. The raw figure of award-winning stories was of course higher, but not all of these passed the investigative test as applied here. Between 1980 and 2009 inclusive, 67 stories passed the investigative test. The overwhelming majority of award-winning investigative reporting was published in broadsheets: 48 investigations compared to 7 in tabloids, with the remainder in magazines. The figure for broadsheet-style publications climbs higher (another ten award-winning stories) if we include the compact *Australian Financial Review*. The data shows that since the awards began in 1956 until 2011, Fairfax's broadsheet newspapers produced the most investigative story winners. This is also the conclusion of Souter (1991, p. 146). With their respective Sunday papers included, Fairfax's *The Age* (17) ranks slightly ahead of its *Sydney Morning Herald* (16) with News Corp's *The Australian* equal third with the Fairfax financial compact, *The Australian Financial Review* (10).

An important finding is that there is no positive correlation between print's circulation decline and their capacity to produce quality investigative journalism. Rather, contrary to concerns about the state of investigative reporting (see introductory chapter), the opposite is realised here—an inverse relationship between falling newspaper circulations and the amount of Walkley-winning investigative reporting until the end of the first decade of the 2000s (see Figure 4.3).

This finding is contrary to many popular and academic concerns and predictions about newspaper investigative journalism in developed democracies (Harrison 2006; Jones 2009; Kelley 2009; Sampson 1996). Bob Franklin has argued that in order to sustain newspapers' profitability as paid circulations and revenues shrank, newsrooms would abandon expensive investigative reporting. Relating to the press in the United Kingdom, he said: 'newspapers seem less concerned to report news,

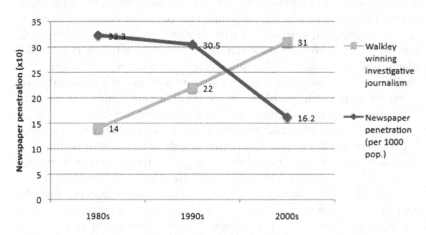

Figure 4.3 Australian Paid Print Circulation (per 1,000 Population) Compared to Amount of Investigative Journalism (Number of Broadsheet Stories per Month)

Source: Author compiling Australian Audit Bureau of Circulation and Walkley award data

especially . . . investigative stories' (Franklin 2008, p. 15). Such concerns were also prevalent in Australia, but do not bear out in the Australian findings (Beecher 2007). A contributing factor to this pessimism is the decline in the relative audience reach of print media since the 1980s as media consumption has become more fragmented and fewer Australians are reading print newspapers.

Qualitative Features of Investigative Journalism

Quality investigative reporting is not easily defined. By its nature, quality can be subjective and may relate to different aspects of journalism. Penny O'Donnell and colleagues highlight how the term has different meanings for different stakeholders (O'Donnell et al. 2012). For example, newspaper managers, driven both by commercial and public interest considerations, seek a 'sweet spot' between commercial success and informing readers. By contrast, media industry regulator the Australian Communications and Media Authority (ACMA) places less emphasis on the commercial aspects, saying quality journalism enables access to fair, ethical, and accurate information—which, by extension, is fundamental to constructive participation in Australian democracy (O'Donnell et al. 2012, p. 7). Journalists, on the other hand, tend to use the term 'quality' as 'shorthand for news content that readers will pay for because it is distinctive (value adds) and meets their particular information needs and interests' (O'Donnell et al. 2012, p. 7).

For the purposes of this book, quality is measured with reference to several distinctive qualitative features of investigative journalism. These include the extent to which a story fulfils the operative definition of investigative journalism; whether the story is about a single issue or systemic issue in society, and whether it is a one-off or story series. It is acknowledged here that while single-issue stories might be impactful, generally speaking systemic-issue stories require greater investigation to bring attention to systemic problems in society that cause injury or injustice and require reform (see Ettema and Glasser in Chapter 2). I also look at how mastheads display and promote their stories in their print versions. Together, these measurements provide insight into the thoroughness of reporting, its depth and its visibility that speaks to its capacity to impact on the audience and, perhaps ultimately, effect societal change.

To decide which stories are counted as investigative reporting, the operational definition codified aspects of investigative journalism out of 9 points (see Chapter 2). A high score suggests more qualitative features of investigative journalism were identified. It is important to note that the Walkley Awards were already judged for 'quality' using 11 Walkley Awards criteria. These were ethics, newsworthiness, public benefit, originality, research, impact, writing, creative flair, inclusiveness, innovation, and production (O'Donnell et al. 2012, p. 38).

For a story to be rated as a 9, it must pass the mandatory fields that required exclusivity, evidence of active journalism, time and research, the verifying of facts (where possible), and reveal a transgression of sorts that is in the public interest (see Chapter 2). The highest-ranking stories (green zone stories) also passed the test of the four discretionary fields that included 'standing up for the powerless by identifying victims or villains', 'pursuing a supressed truth', 'uncovering a breach of public trust', and operating 'within a normative moral framework'.

The Walkley data revealed that stories classified by their authors as investigative have tended to score highly and be located in the green zone (see Figure 4.4). An exception to this was in the 1950s, when investigative reporting was less common and more investigative stories belonged within the amber zone. This reflects an early period of watchdog reporting in Australia, before it was popular in newsrooms and specialist reporting units had been created. The 1980s had the highest proportion of green stories compared to amber (93 per cent).

The study's analysis of broadsheet mastheads—these stories were not necessarily award-winning and thus represent a wider sample of investigative stories—also showed both the 1980s and the 1990s had the highest proportions of green zone stories.

While the longitudinal broadsheet study was independent of the Walkley analysis, both produced similar trend lines (see Figure 4.4). From the

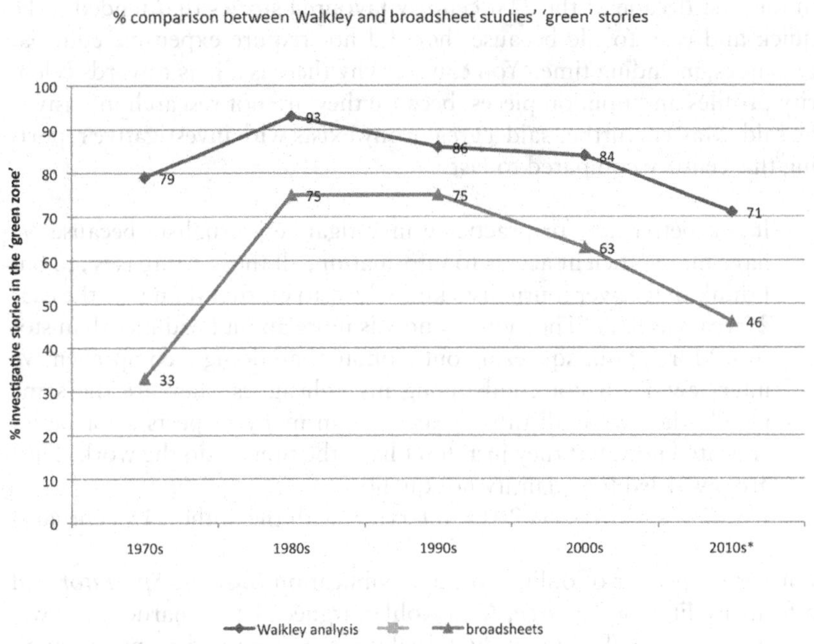

% comparison between Walkley and broadsheet studies' 'green' stories

Figure 4.4 Percentage Comparison of Australian Walkley and Broadsheet Investigative Stories Defined as 'Green Zone' Stories, 1970–2011

Source: Author using Walkley award data and content analysis from Australian Broadsheet study.

* = not a full Walkley Award decade

Note: n = 146 investigative stories

1960s until the 1980s, investigative stories had more qualitative features of investigative journalism than each prior decade.

But after the 1990s, certain qualitative features were less frequently observed. Thus the 1980s stands out as a peak time for *quality* watchdog reporting and again might explain the lingering perception that it was a 'golden era' of investigative journalism in Australia.

After the 1980s, only a minority of stories were able to satisfy the test that the journalism had 'uncovered a breach of public trust'. This is a discretionary field of the content analyses but a noteworthy one, given that trust in the media itself and other public institutions has fallen over time (Edelman 2018).

A subtle pattern emerges after 1981. Each decade has slightly fewer qualitative attributes than the preceding one. This pattern coincides with falling revenues and circulations of print mastheads over time, which began to affect newspaper operations from 1991, with increasing effects over the following two decades (see Chapter 1). Yet over the same period the *quantity* of investigative stories increased.

Investigative journalist Chris Masters has argued that news journalism in the first decade of the 21st century favoured stories that tended to be quick and easy to file because they did not require expensive editorial resources, including time. 'You can see why there is a bias towards celebrity profiles and opinion pieces, because they are not research intensive', he said. Masters further said a great irony exists with investigative reporting this century compared to last:

> It is a better age for practicing investigative journalism because we have more efficient access to information, all those databases . . . but I think that fewer journalists know how to do that than was the case 25 years ago. . . . The industry now is more about headlines than stories. More about squeezing out a quote than doing a comprehensive interview. I am not condemning my colleagues, they are the same people they were all those years ago, in many respects a lot better educated now, but they just don't have the time to do the work. They are rewarded for quantity not quality.
>
> (Masters 2011, interview with the author, 15 February)

Former proprietor of online business publication *Business Spectator* and a former editor of *The Age*, Alan Kohler argued that as hardcopy newspaper revenues fell prior to digital editions, editors had to make tough choices about how to use their editorial resources within a defined budget. If they constantly pursued expensive stories with no gain, their job or promotion could be at risk:

> The editor gets to decide how those resources are allocated but there is really no measurement [offline] of any individual article or section or type of journalism. Nobody really knows what is successful and what is not, nobody knows what anybody is reading. Everyone assumes that they know, but they do not. So, what is going on then, is that the whole package is being created by an editor, and if that does not work, they sack the editor and start again or give someone else a go and he will kind of adjust it slightly and see if that works. If it works, everyone is happy and the editor has a long and happy life but, as for whether the investigative stories are important over the sports stories or opinion pages or the page three picture story, nobody knows.
>
> (Kohler 2010, interview with the author, 5 October)

By comparison, Kohler points out that in the digital era, a story's online audience can be precisely measured: 'We do watch how our stories rate and although we are sort of a subset of journalism on business, we can see that stories that are what I might call sensationalist or populist do rate quite well', he said about his experience editing *Business Spectator*, which he sold in 2012 to News Corp (Kohler 2010, interview with the author, 5 October).

He said the challenge for editors in the digital age has been to find a balance, or 'sweet spot', between 'maximizing the clicks on the story, with the idea also of creating a brand that has a certain set of values' (Kohler 2010, interview with the author, 5 October). This idea of balance between the budget and the reporting might, in part, explain why 1980s investigative journalism ranked highly for its qualitative measures—cost (and time) were not such barriers in that era. The values that resonated in the 1980s investigative stories reinforced the normative moral framework, and the journalists had the time, resources, and as Masters suggests, the training to produce stories that defended the powerless, pursued suppressed truths, or uncovered breaches of public trust, more so than in later years.

In the new millennium, investigative reporting still operates within a moral framework, and journalists are still pursuing suppressed truths. But the broadsheet data shows that investigations have less often been specifically about defending the powerless or unearthing breaches of public trust compared to newspaper investigations in the 1980s and the 1990s. Still, the *quantum* of investigative journalism has increased each decade. These findings might be best understood by considering that notwithstanding the high cost of investigative journalism (compared to other stories), editors persisted with it. As will be shown, they adapted practices to save costs where they could because it remained important for the maintenance of a 'quality' brand, and (for some) to challenge wrongdoing to provide democratic accountability. This compromise fits with the framework identified in the previous chapter, whereby editors and proprietors persist with investigative journalism for a variety of reasons notwithstanding difficult economic times for commercial news media.

Former ABC managing director and Fairfax editor-in-chief Mark Scott says Australian investigative journalism has always been financially subsidised by proprietors. Media outlets had made this sacrifice because of watchdog reporting's 'value' to their media brands:

> It is very rare for an investigative story to drive a spike that is going to drive the big circulations and increase ad revenues. Investigative journalism is all part of the brand of who you are. It can be subsidised by public broadcasting. It can be subsidised by philanthropy. It can be subsidised by other parts of your media organisation, but you will do it because it is an important part of the integrity of your brand to have content of consequence. Fundamentally, that is what it boils down to. If you have compelling stuff that people want to read and they think it is important and their life is less without it, and so I would argue, in

an ABC context, you will still certainly have investigative journalism, that is a lot of what ABC's *Four Corners* is all about.

(Scott 2010, interview with the author, 19 August)

Scott argued that the commercial broadcast sector was affected by the 'profit controversy' more now than when media moguls such as Australian billionaire Kerry Packer owned Fairfax and a free-to-air television station, Nine:

> I think the difficulty with the commercial television model now, and commercial radio, is that they do not think in terms of brand building over time. They think in terms of profit maximization now. Once, Kerry Packer would think, in terms of [investigator] Ross Coulthart on *Sunday*. He would think: 'I am not going to make money out of that, but that is going to make me the news leader and I will make money off the back of that'. Now the commercial sector says, 'How do I maximise profit: Cartoons, or *Weekend Today* or *Two and a Half Men*?'
>
> (Scott 2010, interview with the author, 19 August)

Scott argues investigative journalism will need to be subsidised into the future to survive: 'I still think there will be arguments for newspapers to be subsidised because of the brand' (Scott 2010, interview with the author, 19 August). He identified that the ABC's collaborations with Fairfax journalists to pursue investigative stories in the public interest as a new form of subsidisation. But there are many ways that investigative journalism could be funded:

> There might well be a model where an independent philanthropic kind of organisation is funded, so that is doing the digging and making the stuff generically available, the way an AAP [news wire] works. But you have got to try a whole lot of these things. I still think though, that for certain kinds of organisations, investigative journalism will need to be cross-subsidised as it has always been cross-subsidised.
>
> (Scott 2010, interview with the author, 19 August)

Since Scott's comments, the public broadcaster's number of investigative collaborations with Fairfax's investigative units have sharply risen to bring a larger audience and greater impact to its stories (see Chapter 5). It reflects the experience of US newspapers also. Michael Schudson and Leonard Downie Jrn, writing about US newspapers in 2009, predicted:

> The remaining economically viable newspapers—with much smaller staffs, revenues, and profits—will try to do many things at once: publish in print and digitally, seek new ways to attract audiences and

advertisers, invent new products and revenue streams, and find new partners to help them produce high-quality news at lower cost.

(Downie and Schudson 2009, p. 25)

Mark Scott also predicted that philanthropy would increasingly be relied upon to sponsor investigative journalism. Online tycoon Graeme Wood was the first Australian to follow the example of US philanthropists funding public interest news outlets like *ProPublica*. Wood funded the *Global Mail* in 2012. While that venture did not last, Wood then committed funds to the online start-up Australian edition of Britain's *The Guardian*. Both beneficiaries of Wood's financial support produced investigative journalism.

Despite an uninspiring economic outlook for commercial media organisations, the emergence of media collaborations, cross-subsidisation within a media organisation, and philanthropic support collectively suggest a willingness within the media community to experiment to provide public interest investigative journalism. Emerging business models and trends for funding and producing investigative journalism in the future are addressed further in Chapter 7.

Australian Investigative Journalism Over the Decades

To delve further into the data and gain a much deeper understanding of the character and style of investigative journalism over time each decade is analysed separately for both the quantity and quality of Australian watchdog reporting.

The 1950s

In the 1950s, Melbourne's evening broadsheet newspaper, *The Herald*—which closed after 150 years of publishing in 1990—was the standout provider of award-winning investigative journalism.[6] Its stories had a human interest focus and tended to report on individuals more than systemic, societal issues. As discussed in Chapter 2, McKnight found single-issue reporting was commonly associated with 'muckraking' or exposure journalism and focused on individual transgressions, whereas systemic investigative journalism focused on widespread wrongdoing such as corruption within a system. The Walkley data shows that systemic-issue investigative reporting was more common in Australia from the 1960s onwards (McKnight 1999, p. 155).

What is instructive here is that the news cycle was much slower than the digital age and newspaper readership measured as a proportion of the total population was much greater. Thus, prolonged accounts of a story, such as Hogg's four-part series, were common. These factors assisted investigative stories to reach a very large audience and to stay perhaps in the public consciousness for longer.

Box 4.1   The 1950s Investigative Reporting: The Melbourne *Herald*

The Herald's award-winning investigative story of 1957 is a prime example of the human interest focus of investigative reporting of the era. The story did what the police were unable to do at the time: it tracked down a missing Ukrainian stewardess who had deserted her ship while docked in Melbourne for the 1956 Olympic Games. In Lionel Hogg's four-part series, the stewardess, Nina Paranyuk, gives a first-person account of how tough life was in the Baltic state during the Cold War. Hogg details how he used his extensive contacts to find Paranyuk, who was accommodated in three different safe houses in Melbourne during her two months on the run from authorities. The series began with Paranyuk telling Hogg:

> Ever since Stalin ordered the demolition of our tiny stone church, I have prayed for somebody or something to take me away from the USSR. That was 24 years ago. I was only 10. I had to wait a long time before my prayers were answered.
>
> (Hogg 1957)

The 1960s

A unique feature of Australian journalism in the 1960s is the tabloid dominance of the Walkley Awards. McKnight argued the transition from single-issue muckraking and exposure journalism to systemic investigative reporting was delayed by a period of reporting complacency during the Cold War years. Broadly speaking, the mass media in Australia, as in Europe and the United States, was largely complicit with anti-Communist government positions and agendas during the Cold War (McKnight 2008, pp. 5–17). *The Herald*'s award-winning 1957 story portraying the Ukrainian stewardess as a victim of Stalinism fits with this profile. The collaborative relationship between the press and the political establishment eventually started to fall apart as social and political movements, such as the feminist movement and Vietnam War protests, gained strength. Until then, Evan Whitton recalls: 'Organs of the media did not tell the customer what was really going on' (Whitton 2012, interview with the author, 8 February).

But there were exceptions to this rule—notably, Australia's irreverent tabloids. Newspapers like the weekly *Truth*—which at its peak had a circulation exceeding 400,000—broke significant 'big target' stories in the 1960s that prefigured the rise of systemic-issue investigative journalism. In this period, some tabloid journalists experimented with 'new journalism' storytelling. Long, descriptive passages were traded in for snappier reportage using more dialogue and favouring the present tense. Newspaper feature writers started to play around with 'new journalism' inspired by American writers like Tom Wolfe. (Whitton, 2012, interview with the author, 8 February). Here is a reconstruction that Whitton wrote about one of his meetings with anti-corruption and pro-choice campaigner Dr Bertram Wainer in the 'new journalism' style:[7]

> Judith got me a vodka, which seemed to be the tipple I'd fallen into in that place, and improved on the Scotch she and Wainer were drinking. Wyatt [former policeman, turned backyard abortionist] absentmindedly sipped away at the London Dry. The atmosphere, at this stage, was quite matey, despite the fact that, during the Winter Offensive, Wainer and Mrs Berman [whistleblower] had done their damndest to have Wyatt put away, and despite the fact I had written a piece called 'Harry, the Backyard Aborter', which was a thinly disguised account of Wyatt's career to that point. It posed the question to Inspector Jack Ford: 'Well, here's old Charlie scraping away in the backyard and the very dogs are barking the fact, so why haven't the cops been able to find him?'
>
> (Whitton n.d.)

Whitton recalled how his editor at *Truth*, Sol Chandler, saw value in seemingly insignificant details, and so he combined these with Wolfe's literary techniques to write vivid non-fiction news (Whitton 2012, interview with the author, 8 February). Whitton's award-winning 1969 investigation into police corruption and illegal abortion was an early Australian example of a systemic-issue investigation with significant public interest outcomes using the techniques of 'new journalism'.

Truth, along with some of the Sunday papers led the way in publishing investigative journalism in the '60s, with their longer deadlines enabling them to deviate from the daily news agenda and devote more resources to investigations. Sydney's *Sunday Telegraph* was the most prolific winner of awards for investigative stories in the industry. For the last four years of the 1950s, the data sample shows an even split between single-issue and systemic investigative reporting. But in the 1960s, we see the emergence of the trend for more systemic investigative reporting than single-issue reporting. The majority of award-winning stories were about international issues, followed by stories about indigenous affairs. The international stories included series about apartheid in South Africa, the future of the two New Guineas, and the effects of the Vietnam War on the North Vietnamese.

The 1970s

Investigative journalism was in vogue in the 1970s for several reasons, including the success and glamourisation of *The Washington Post*'s

Watergate investigation (Henningham 1990, p. 138). According to former *Age* and *Herald Sun* editor Bruce Guthrie, another factor was the maverick editorship of Graham Perkin (Guthrie 2010, interview with the author, 11 February). Perkin, who edited *The Age* from 1966 to 1975, imported the idea of the specialist print investigative unit after visiting London's *Sunday Times* (Hills 2010, p. 294). This period also marked the start of a shift in the culture of Australian journalism, from its historical status as a craft or trade in which school leavers learned on the job to a profession increasingly populated with university graduates, many with journalism degrees. Walkley-winning investigative journalist Paul Robinson, one of the first university graduates entering Australian journalism, explains:

> I was part of a changing world that rebelled against the Vietnam War, was suspicious of authority and contemptuous of the strict morality of past generations. Journalism was the job of a lifetime. It presented the opportunity to challenge authority, to be close to the decision-making process and a chance to play a critical part in political life.
>
> (Robinson 2012, interview with the author, 20 January)

In the 1970s, the greatest number of investigative journalism pieces were published in two papers that had both changed size: *The West Australian* (four awards), a broadsheet that converted to tabloid following a newsprint shortage in 1947, and *The National Times*, a now defunct weekly national tabloid that turned into a broadsheet. *The National Times* also won four consecutive awards for 'Best Newspaper Feature' from 1975 to 1978.

Box 4.2   The 1970s Investigative Reporting: *The National Times* and *The West Australian*

The National Times was unusual compared to other newspapers of the era, in part for its particular focus on commentary and long features. Often its stories extended beyond 100 column inches, or 3,500 words. Other newspapers at the time tended to report news 'straight', invoking the inverse triangle formula (reporting information in descending order of importance and/or interest), and answering the questions of 'who', 'what', 'where', and 'when' before finishing the story with quotes and background facts. *The National Times*, by contrast, experimented with feature writing in news telling and some stories filled several pages, extending beyond 10,000 words.

The National Times' winning stories in the 1970s were a three-part series about Vietnam (by Evan Whitton); a profile on Bob Hawke, a future prime minister (by Craig McGregor); the collapse of an old Australian commodities trading company the Gollin

---

group (by Robert Gottliebsen); and an inside account on a prison riot where guards attacked prisoners at Sydney's Long Bay jail (Anne Summers) (Whitton 1974; Summers 1976; McGregor 1977; Gottliebsen 1978). All but the Hawke profile passed the definition of investigative journalism.

The West Australian's reputation for investigative journalism in the 1970s was due almost entirely to the work of one young journalist, Catherine Martin. She investigated the use of the Tronado microwave machine, a since discredited invention used to treat cancer (Martin 1975, p. 1). She won the 1975 Walkley for 'Best Piece of Reporting for the Year'. Two years earlier, Martin won a Walkley for her feature series involving a two-week expedition to remote Australia to report on the health conditions of indigenous Australians (Hurst 1988, p. 135). But her most celebrated investigative series (1978) exposed the deadly effects of blue asbestos on mining workers' health. Her stories forced CSR, the owner of Western Australia's blue asbestos mine, to establish the Wittenoom Trust for victims (Martin 1978, p. 1). For this series, Martin won the inaugural Gold Walkley ('Gold Award—Best Piece of Journalism, Newspaper, Television or Radio') and again the Walkley for 'Best Piece of Reporting for the Year'.

Box 4.3   The 1980s Investigative Reporting: *The Age*

Freelancer Jan Mayman won two of *The Age*'s three awards in this decade, taking out the 1984 Gold Walkley for exposing the cover-up of the death of an indigenous youth in police custody (Mayman 1983). Michael Gawenda, a future *Age* editor, won *The Age*'s other 1980s investigative reporting Walkley Award for a highly controversial 1982 series about life in Melbourne's high-rise social housing blocks. He did so from an insiders' view, posing as an occupant and enraging some ethicists at the time for not disclosing his identity to his interview subjects (Gawenda 1982). This style of undercover reporting reflected the reporting techniques of America's Gilded Age, and was similar to Whitton's award-winning story 'Life on the Pension', which won the 1967 Walkley for the tabloid muckraking *Truth* newspaper.

The 1980s

As *The Age*'s circulation was peaking in the 1980s—with average sales of about 250,000 copies a day—its 'Insight' investigative unit, along with its Fairfax stablemates, was dominating the Walkley Awards (Hills

2010, p. 505). *The Age* won three Walkleys for investigative reporting during the decade, while *The Sydney Morning Herald* and *The National Times* won two each. Other award winners were New Limited's *The Courier Mail* (two awards)[8] and the weekly magazine *Time Australia* (two awards).

The 1990s

While most investigative reporting in the modern era has focused on systemic wrongdoing, a small increase in single-issue reporting occurred in the 1990s. Although the change was subtle, it may have significance in the context of what was happening more broadly in media at the time. With the arrival of the digital age—and with it a faster, more frenetic news cycle—many journalists faced unprecedented pressure to produce volumes of news copy quickly. In such an environment, single-issue investigations might have become more attractive and feasible than long and detailed investigations of systemic wrongdoing.

A breakdown of the Walkley data reveals that profiles of criminals and corporate figures—which in many cases could be classified as single-issue investigations—dominated investigative reporting in the 1990s and beyond. This might partly explain the slight rise observed in single-issue reporting generally during this decade. It may also reflect a global trend described in the United States by Michael Schudson, who identified the increasing prominence and frequency of crime stories as a feature of tabloidisation (Schudson 2003, p. 90).

Corporate investigative stories of this era also tended to focus on individuals rather than systemic wrongdoing. Australian academics and journalists have harshly critiqued the business press during this decade, and also found an absence of critical reporting of the corporate sector in the lead-up to the 1987 global stock market crash (Toohey 1994; Sykes 1994; Turner 1994). Kitchener argued that finance journalists had acquiesced to the narrative of capitalism:

> By nature, business reporting has always been 'pro-business', preferring to oil the wheels of capitalism rather than offer critical insights into the economic system and act as a counter-balance to abuses of power. And for as long as the commercial media have existed there has been a tension between advertising and marketing goals and editorial objective.
>
> (Kitchener 1999, p. 243)

Following the collapse of the Australian stock market in 1987 and associated high-profile failures of businesses such as Victoria's Pyramid Building Society, there was renewed interest in investigative business reporting at

The Australian Financial Review (see Figure 4.7), but less so in general news mastheads. Overall, broadsheets dominated award-winning investigative reporting in the 1990s, with *The Courier Mail* and *The Sunday Age* winning the most awards. Figure 4.7 shows how closely the winning investigative stories were divided among the mastheads, just as they were in the 1980s.

Since *The Adelaide Advertiser* became a tabloid in 1997, like its sister paper, *The Courier Mail* in 2006, it has not produced Walkley-winning investigative journalism in the studied time frame. Similarly, since 1998, when the Fairfax-owned *Newcastle Herald* converted to tabloid, it experienced two decades without winning Walkley Awards for investigative journalism. As a broadsheet, it had produced many award-winning investigative stories and had won the coveted Gold Walkley.[9] This is consistent with Franklin's argument about the tabloidisation of news—that tabloid journalism tends to 'retreat from investigative reporting to the preferred territory of "lighter stories"' (Franklin 2008, p. 3).

The 2000s

Following the trend of the previous two decades, Fairfax produced the most Walkley Award–winning investigative journalism in the 2000s. But this time it did so for the first time with large contributions from its financial tabloid, *The Australian Financial Review* (AFR), which won seven Walkleys, of which five met the operative definition of investigative reporting. *The AFR*'s investigative story topics were evenly divided between individual and corporate corruption.

Box 4.4   The 2000s Corporate Investigative Reporting:
The Australian Financial Review

The 2000s included a profile by *The AFR* team on high-flying stockbroker Rene Rivkin and his undisclosed Swiss bank accounts (Chenoweth et al. 2003, p. 1). The story won both the 2004 Gold Walkley and 'Business Journalism Award'. The following year, the late Morgan Mellish wrote a 3,500-word profile on Liberal Party donor and multimillionaire businessman Robert Gerard, who was investigated by the Australian Tax Office for avoiding tax using an elaborate and fraudulent offshore insurance scheme (Mellish 2005, p. 58). The corporate stories focused on shareholders who lost millions following the collapses of financial companies Opes Prime and Storm (Chenoweth et al. 2008, p. 1; Hughes 2009).

The Rise in Syndication of News Stories

Two other significant trends for investigative journalism became apparent in the digital age. The first was the increase in syndicating stories across mastheads within the same group. Fairfax began this in the late 1980s, and by the 2010s its syndicated award-winning efforts had more than quadrupled. The rise in story sharing coincided with falls in advertising revenue and circulations. Sharing the costs of producing stories through a more centralised editorial approach allowed individual mastheads to maintain high levels of investigative journalism despite their reduced resources.

In an extension of the trend of sharing resources within a media group, collaborations between discrete media organisations also developed. One example of this was the use of *WikiLeaks* material as a starting point for investigative stories in Fairfax publications in late 2010. *The Age* and the ABC have also collaborated on multiple stories, resulting in a wider audience reach for individual investigations around the same time.

The most notable of these collaborations was the 2011 Walkley-winning story 'The Money Makers' by *Age* journalists Richard Baker and Nick McKenzie, which uncovered Australia's biggest bribery scandal involving the Reserve Bank of Australia's subsidiary currency firms, Note Printing Australia and Securency. The story resulted in Australia's foreign bribery laws being invoked for the first time, with corruption charges levelled against the firms involved and local and international senior managers (McKenzie and Baker 2012, p. 2).

Former investigative bureau chief Mark Baker explained *The Age*'s decision to share story resources with the ABC:

> I saw it as a good opportunity to raise the profile of the story because we had been plugging away at it for over a year or so, at that stage, and we had had significant impact: the police investigation was under way and all the rest of it. But the story was hard to get traction outside of Victoria and I felt that, and the outcome has vindicated it, that by doing this with the ABC we broadened its profile. After *Four Corners* the story got a new lease of life and got a better national profile and we were then able to drive it to new heights, and then of course we saw charges being laid and the story continues to evolve, so it was a good deal.
>
> (M. Baker 2012, interview with author, 11 January)

In 326 newspaper pages analysed for 2011, nine stories involved collaborations with an outside media organisation; one of these was an investigation between *WikiLeaks* and Fairfax about David Hicks, an Australian overseas combatant controversially detained by the United States in Guantanamo Bay from 2002 to 2007 on terrorism charges: 'Hicks had leadership qualities US feared' (Dorling 2011, p. 1). Another investigative story involved a collaboration between Fairfax mastheads: 'Murdered by death squad' (Lester and Young 2011, p. 1). The trend for collaboration coincides with the declining relative influence of the press, and appears to be an attempt to regain and extend audience reach at a time of fragmentation in media consumption (Tiffen 2010, pp. 81–2).

Other Features of Investigative Journalism: 'Depth' of a Story

Beyond the operative definition, a variety of contextual factors were used to gauge the editor's intended reception on the audience of the investigative reporting, which speaks to the depth of editorial treatment of the story. This involved assessing the priority that a masthead gives to investigative journalism through its page placement, story follow-ups, use of promotional tags such as 'exclusive', and accountability to the public through acts such as naming sources in the story, and following up on its outcomes.

The Decline of the Follow-Up Story

When considering the intended impact on the audience, it is worth examining if investigative stories were more or less likely to be part of a series of articles. This speaks to the probable audience impact because a series is more likely than a one-off story to keep an issue burning on the public agenda. *Age* investigative journalist Richard Baker argues that inter-media effects are also important for a story's longevity and that 'often the magnitude or significance of a story is defined by other media' (R. Baker 2011, interview with the author, 21 March). Thus it is a desirable outcome when competitors follow up on an investigative story. When they do, it suggests the story was of such significance that it was too difficult to ignore.

The Walkley analysis over time revealed most winning stories (84 per cent) were published in a series. This is expected given that 'impact' is one of the criteria that Walkley judges use to determine the winner. One way to have audience impact is to persist with publishing stories about a particular issue over time. For example, in 1957 *The Sydney Morning Herald*'s Selwyn Speight spent months travelling around rural Australian towns to gauge how migrant workers adapted to life in a new country and how the locals reacted to them. His five-part series, printed over two months, recorded conversations between migrants and locals. It entwined the narrative with census data and facts. The 'Report on Migration' series won the 1957 'Best Feature' Walkley Award (Speight 1957).

The broadsheet study, which includes some stories that did not win awards, provides a different picture to the Walkley study. It showed that, over time, fewer investigative stories were part of a series (see Figure 4.5). The broadsheet study trend line showed that in 1971 all investigative stories were part of a series, but by 1991 the number of print investigations published in a series hovered around 50 per cent.

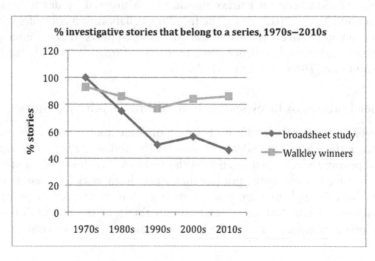

Figure 4.5 Percentage of Australian Print Investigations That Are Part of an Investigative Series, 1970–2011

Source: Author

Note: n = 146

One of the reasons why broadsheets do less follow-up on their own stories than they did in the past is that the news cycle has become faster and editorial resources scarcer. Journalists feel pressure to continue to come up with fresh news stories rather than invest time on the same issue, especially if the follow-up stories are considered less newsworthy. British academic Stephen Cushion, writing on this subject, found that the influence of rolling 24-hour television news coverage had 'moved print journalism away from supplying news and information towards the promotion of ideas and opinions' (Cushion 2011, p. 62). Former *Age* investigative journalist and 774 ABC *Drive* presenter Rafael Epstein found that when he broke a significant defence story at *The Age* he decided not to follow it up beyond two stories:

> It disappeared without a trace. The ideal thing would be to follow it for another month and chase all the loose ends that I didn't develop. But I just let it go because I didn't know for sure that I was going to get anything by the end of the month . . . the reality of the paper is that everyone has to produce, I don't think we have as much pressure as the other reporters, but you have to produce at some stage.
>
> (Epstein 2011, interview with the author, 21 March)

The faster news cycle can create competition between stories for attention and can make the public space for information crowded and noisy. Media proprietor and former editor Alan Kohler argued that due to the pace of the digital news cycle, newspapers might be disinclined to pursue investigative journalism because they no longer get a strong return benefit from the efforts and resources put into their investigations:

> When you have an investigative team what you're trying to get is a scoop right? When I was writing in *The Age*, we set up an Insight team. In those days, before the internet, your scoop was yours for 24 hours, till the next day. Now, as soon as you publish it [online], it is gone. So, scoops last a minute. There is nothing to do about that. It is really out of everyone's control. Scoops are only for bragging rights, you get to say that this was your scoop, but I do not think [the audience] really care that much
>
> (Kohler 2010, interview with the author, 5 October)

For this reason, Kohler said that when considering what content would go into the digital-only *Business Spectator*, the editorial team decided not to invest in investigative journalism:

> We took the view that news, that is to say the new information about what is happening in the world, is a commodity everyone knows that, it is everywhere, it is on the internet, it is on the news, on the TV and radio, there is absolutely no need for us to have news reporters because we can buy it from AAP and Reuters, so we do that. What we have is commentary to tell people what it means and the commentators get paid a lot of money and they are expected to be fairly expert in that, and to be good writers and so on. We do not have any investigative reporting at all because that just is not part of our model now.
>
> (Kohler 2010, interview with the author, 5 October)

In the preceding example, investigative journalism did not figure in the media outlet's business model; in other cases, adaptations are made to continue to produce costly investigations rather than abandon them because they are considered important for the overall branding of the outlet. The presentation of investigative reporting in leaner time for media can take various forms. Some publications, instead of running a series of stories about one issue over a number of days, will dedicate many pages to a single 'special report' or to an online multimedia feature in one hit. One reason for this, at least in the Australian context, is the lack of follow-up by other media in an era of highly concentrated print media ownership. News Corp and Fairfax Media together own approximately 90 per cent of Australia's metropolitan daily newspapers (see Chapter 1) (Tiffen 2010, p. 3). Fairfax's joint ABC collaboration, 'The Money Makers', received little acknowledgment or follow-up from other media, including News Corp publications. Richard Baker explained it this way:

> Because Australia's media landscape is so small you have got News Limited and Fairfax in the press as rivals, both companies are reluctant to follow each other's stories and that is probably not a good thing for readers, for the public. I think we have to get over that.
>
> (R. Baker 2011, interview with the author, 21 March)

Complicating matters was that 'The Money Makers' was a dense story to understand. It lacked high-profile villains. So it was easy for the Murdoch press to ignore it. However, that said, Masters argues that the media's failure to follow up public interest stories in rival publications was a grave disservice to the public: 'One of the reasons that these stories aren't going further, is because sometimes the competition is so poisonous that a story won't have carriage because competitors refuse to acknowledge that it existed' (Masters 2011, interview with the author, 15 February). In the past, different media organisations worked together on important stories to serve the public interest, Masters recalled:

> When I think about my story the 'Moonlight State' in Queensland, I was really angry at that time that *The Courier Mail* kind of pinched the story from me because I had been working on it for a long time, and I didn't feel they had done their dues at all, but because they were aware of what I was doing they sort of jumped on the bandwagon at the last minute and made a bit of a splash about it. But fortunately, the splash was the same splash. It was the same splash I made. But even though we were uncomfortable allies, we were effective allies at the end of the day. . . . When I look at the reporting of similar scandals in Victoria sometime later, every little corner of the media taking its own position and determinedly fighting each other really, and not taking the side of the public. We are really not collectively representing the interests of the public; I think that is quite telling when you consider the outcomes.
>
> (Masters 2011, interview with the author, 15 February)

This failure to follow up rival outlets' stories epitomises a time when collaboration outside of the news organisation's stable mastheads was rare and investigative stories were more locally or nationally focused rather than transnational. As the next chapter will show, collaboration has become more commonplace in the second decade of the 21st century, and through collaboration investigative journalism is able to transcend national borders, leaving behind this 'old model' of rivalrous newsrooms.

Self-Promotion of Investigative Journalism

In the last few decades of the 20th century, newspapers, and in later years their online versions, began more actively marketing stories and their authors—a trend confirmed by the broadsheet analysis. For example, in 1971 stories rarely carried the author's name (a byline) unless it was a column or opinion/commentary piece. By 1981, most major stories carried bylines, and by 2011, almost all stories, regardless of their weight or profile, carried bylines. By 2019 it was also common for newspapers to publish journalists' photos and Twitter addresses. McNair argued that because there is now so much information and noise in the public sphere, the power to influence can be returned to the traditional media gatekeepers to fill the role of 'sense makers' (McNair 2006, p. 154). Newspapers are using picture bylines and other tools to try to build the profile and reputation of journalists, and by extension their own masthead's authority and trust in the role of 'sense-maker'.

In some cases, a journalist's byline has arguably become more influential than the masthead itself, whereas once it was the reverse. While most print journalists tend to still rely on their employer for their profile, there are examples of journalists who do not rely on their primary employer for their high profile and influence. It is an example of the rise of individualism on which modern culture thrives. It is also one consequence of changes to media labour markets, particularly in Australia. With fewer staff journalists and a greater reliance on freelancers and casuals, developing an individual profile is important for a reporter's longevity in the industry, and it returns agency back to reporters. As hardcopy mastheads lose circulation, revenues, and ultimately influence, some individual journalists benefit from these power shifts and have gained personal public authority from them.

Significantly, the broadsheet analysis in its final years highlights a form of promotion that was not possible in the past. As Kohler noted, newspapers can track online readers' engagement with a story, and readers can promote stories for the masthead by sharing them on social media (Kohler 2010, interview with the author, 5 October). This is a powerful endorsement if a reader has many followers. It also provides the story with a bigger audience. Social media shareability of news stories and active engagement with the audience became even more important in the second decade of the millennium (see Chapter 7). Epstein argues these forms of online measurement through Twitter, Facebook, or any number of 'below-the-line' comments following a story have become the key performance indicators for news managers. The danger in this, he argues, is that these online numbers often reflect a particular audience that is reactive to certain types of stories: 'We have all become consumers, and in a news environment like that, no one cares about serious stories, just the big impact stories' (Epstein 2011, interview with the author, 21

March). He argued that the 'The Money Makers' was an important story about corporate corruption, yet it did not become a popular online story for *The Age* until it involved prostitutes, and only then did its online readership surge (Epstein 2011, interview with the author, 21 March). The ABC's former managing director Mark Scott found this online reach could be very powerful.

> Twitter is the best mechanism for disseminating fast breaking news that we have ever discovered. There are some algorithms you can run. I sent out a message I think when News 24 was going live [in 2010], and it was retweeted 150 times in 30 minutes, and if you look at all those figures it got up to 300,000 people in a quarter of an hour. That's just amazing kind of multiplying.
>
> (Scott 2010, interview with the author, 19 August)

Third-party promotion through social media and strategic promotion within a newspaper can give an investigative story a bigger readership over a shorter time than in the past. But the downside is that this promotion occurs within a modern news cycle that delivers many more stories in a shorter time frame than in the past, which means stories can disappear from the public's attention very quickly.

This century, print newspapers are much more likely than in the past to promote their stories using tags such as 'exclusive', 'special report', and 'investigative report'. Sometimes the labels are applied to articles that arguably do not meet conventional definitions of exclusive, special, or investigative. For example, in April 2011 *The Australian* newspaper marked 20 front-page stories as exclusives. The same month, *The Age* marked 19 stories as exclusive. A decade earlier, none of *The Australian*'s front-page stories in April were labelled exclusive, while *The Age* had three. At the same time, the number of stories appearing on the front pages of the broadsheet newspapers were fewer than the past, as advertisements and pictures grew bigger. Overall, the papers averaged 3.5 stories on their front pages, down from 8.9 in 1971. The point here is that if news organisations overuse promotional tags, it creates the risk that readers will become desensitised to these labels and possibly more indifferent to genuine investigative or 'special' reporting when it is produced. This in turn might help explain the pervasive (and false) perception that there is less investigative reporting now than in the past.

Placement of Stories

In 1971 and 1981, investigative stories were typically placed inside the newspaper on a dedicated page for longer news stories, rather than on page one. This was not the case in 1991, when most investigative stories featured on the front page. Since 1991, investigative stories have increasingly been promoted on page one, with the full story displayed as the main feature of a particular section such as sport, business, or a weekend magazine. Investigative stories generally need space to be told, and sections can provide this. As mentioned, front pages, on the other hand, have become increasingly unable to accommodate long stories due to a number of trends in newspaper design, including increased picture sizes, the introduction of display advertising to front pages, and what Franklin (2005) has described as the 'McDonaldisation' of the print medium with short, bite-sized stories.

Naming of Sources

The broadsheet analysis shows that most investigative journalism has included named sources. Essentially this practice has endured over time, although the use of unnamed sources has increased slightly in recent times. In 1971, *all* sources in investigative stories analysed for this study were named. In the 2011 analysis, four out of five watchdog stories named their sources (see Figure 4.6). McKnight's research found that unnamed sources could be a key indicator that the media are serving others' propaganda campaigns (McKnight 2008, p. 10). While this is concerning, most investigative stories still name sources. Naming sources is also an important element of Australian journalists' own MEAA Code of Ethics (MEAA 2013).

In sum, this section has identified some effects of a faster-paced news cycle over time on the qualitative features of investigative reporting. While the number of investigative stories has increased, and investigative

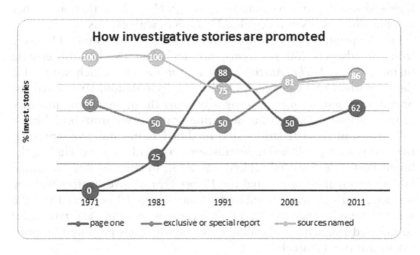

Figure 4.6 Promotion of Investigative Stories (Australian Broadsheets) Over Time, 1971–2011

Source: Author

Note: n = 45 broadsheet investigative stories

journalism is prioritised on front pages, its capacity for impact might suffer in the modern news environment. Adaptations have been made to overcome this. For example, there is evidence of increased self-marketing of investigative stories using promotional tags such as 'special investigation'. Investigative journalism has moved to the front page—even if it is as a pointer to the main story inside the paper. Yet, accountability, assessed through the follow-up of stories and the naming of sources within a story, has deteriorated. This suggests that at the end of the 20th century, while editors and proprietors still identified a need to produce investigative reporting, they were perhaps more demure about their commitment to providing democratic accountability. This commitment is further explored by comparing different proprietors' investigative stories.

Size, Owners, and Platforms: What Matters for Investigative Reporting?

Size: Tabloid Versus Broadsheet

It is not surprising that Australian broadsheets have produced more award-winning investigative journalism than tabloids. According to Franklin, Sparks, Dahlgren, and others, tabloids are more interested in content that is enjoyable and entertaining (see Chapter 3). As Sparks argues, tabloids have 'a greater stress on the personal and private at the expense of the public and structural' (Sparks 2000, p. 36). The Walkley Award analysis showed Australian broadsheets contributed more peer-reviewed investigative journalism to the public sphere than any other news medium over seven decades. This comes with caveats.

Of 187 print Walkley Award–winning stories in the study, 113 were from broadsheets (60 per cent), not including the broadsheet-style financial tabloid *The Australian Financial Review*, which would lift the proportion to 71 per cent. Of the story population, 101 passed the operational definition of investigative journalism; again, the majority of investigations that met the definition criteria were from broadsheets (67). Thus, of the 101 stories that qualified as investigative reporting, two thirds were published in broadsheet mastheads, again excluding the broadsheet-style financial tabloid *The AFR*. In comparison, Australian tabloid newspapers accounted for 19 per cent of investigative Walkley winners, and the financial tabloid accounted for 10 per cent from the selected sample since the Walkley's inception in 1956. The remainder constituted magazine and online-only investigations produced by print mastheads (see Figure 4.7).

In 2013 Fairfax sold its broadsheet printing presses and converted its major broadsheets, *The Age* and *SMH*, to tabloid-sized papers. A short time later, Fairfax's *The Canberra Times* also downsized to tabloid, leaving one remaining broadsheet in Australia, News Corp's *The Australian*.

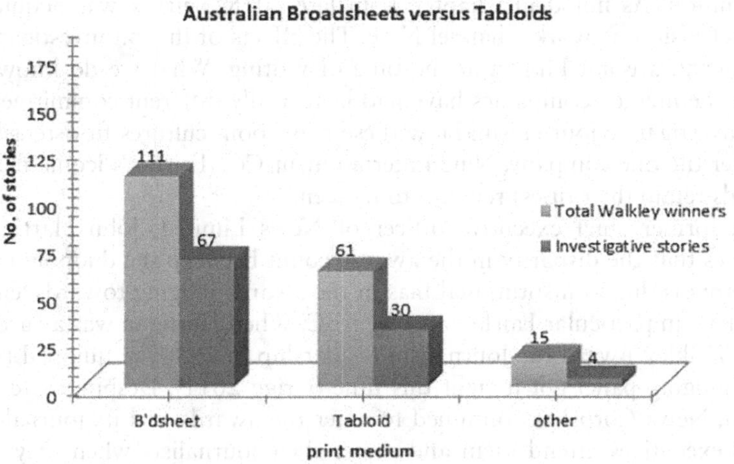

Australian Broadsheets versus Tabloids

Figure 4.7 Press Walkley Awards: Amount of Australian Broadsheets Versus Tabloid Investigative Stories, 1956–2011

Source: Author, N = 187

This chapter has established that in the 20th century broadsheet-style mastheads produced more award-winning investigative journalism. How the size change might affect Fairfax's future investigative content is difficult to predict, especially as there are other variables that might affect its investigative outputs such as the deterioration of the financial operating environment for press. However, extending the Walkley analysis to 2014–16 (the award period after which Fairfax mastheads had converted to tabloid), only 3 of the 27 awards (in the same categories as the earlier analysis) for investigative reporting that met the definition in this period were won by Fairfax's converted tabloids, excluding its cross-media collaborations. Significantly, six investigative reporting awards went to cross-media collaborations (22 per cent), which mainly included former broadsheets, now compacts (*The Age* and *Sydney Morning Herald*) working with television. Moreover, in the digital age, the preliminary data suggests that collaboration is key for producing quality investigative journalism.

Owners: Fairfax Media Versus News Corp

Fairfax has won more Walkleys than any other Australian print media organisation since the awards began in the analysed categories. Fairfax collected 96 Walkleys, compared to News Corp's 64.[10] The remaining 27 selected awards over this period were divided among smaller media organisations. Exactly half of News Corp's (then News Limited) awards pass the operative definition for investigative journalism. Fairfax is similar, with 53 per cent of its award-winning stories passing the investigative definition. As noted in Chapter 1, in late 2018, Fairfax was acquired by television network Channel Nine. The effects of this on investigative reporting are not known at the time of writing. What we do know is that the merged companies have had historically different commitments to investigative journalism. How these newsroom cultures fit ostensibly under the one company, Nine Entertainment Co. (Fairfax's iconic mastheads retain their titles) remains to be seen.

A former chief executive officer of News Limited, John Hartigan, argues that the disparity in the awards count between the duopoly proprietors is due to institutional bias in the awards judging towards 'elite' media—in particular Fairfax and the ABC. When Hartigan was awarded the Walkley Award for Journalism Leadership in 2008, he quipped that the judging panel got it right this time (Grigg 2011). Despite the criticism, News Corp has continued to enter the awards and its journalists and executives attend them and praise their journalists when they are successful.

Platform: How Print Compares to Other Media

There is a perception among media professionals that print media does more investigative journalism than other media forms. Most of the 22 Australian media practitioners and professionals interviewed for this study agreed that print was most likely to produce more investigative journalism than other media platforms. It was noted in this context that this might be partly due to newspapers collectively employing more journalists than other types of media outlets. Some argued newspapers have fewer logistical hurdles to producing investigative stories than platforms like television, which require moving images and words. Yet investigative journalists with experience across multiple platforms such as Linton Besser, Chris Masters, and Jonathan Holmes perceived that while the print media might produce more stories, television had greater public impact. Former ABC *Media Watch* host, investigative journalist, and executive producer of *Four Corners* Jonathan Holmes stated:

> On the face of it, it is a lot easier to do [investigative journalism] with newspapers. Because the unnamed sources are a lot more useful to a newspaper journalist. . . . It is ok to say a source close to the subject and people will accept it, but they won't really accept it on television, it is much rarer. So, in that sense it's easier to do in newspapers. Newspapers should find it easier and should do more of it than television. Plus, apart from anything else it is cheaper because you only have one or two people doing it.
>
> (Holmes 2011, interview with the author, 19 December)

Holmes identified two distinct advantages that television had over print for producing investigative journalism:

> Its lead times are long anyway, the sheer mechanics of shooting and editing, mean that to do a long program like *Four Corners* takes you weeks, and even short form programs like 7.30 takes several days to a week. Within that time is the opportunity to do a lot of research even if you have not been given an extended deadline. The second advantage is the sheer impact of the story. If you do get it, it is vastly greater on television. Even stories that aren't that visual, when they are on television, they just seem to have more impact.
>
> (Holmes 2011, interview with the author, 19 December)

Holmes' assessment is pertinent to the enduring notion that the 1980s was a peak period for investigative journalism, as there were several high-profile television investigative reports during this era. Some had significant audience impact with important public outcomes, such as Queensland's Fitzgerald inquiry following Chris Masters' *Four Corners* police corruption investigation, 'Moonlight State'. It coincided with Phil Dickie's newspaper reporting about the same issues for *The Courier Mail* and resulted in four government ministers and police commissioner Terry Lewis being jailed and the establishment of Queensland's first anti-corruption body.

Masters agreed with Holmes that no medium beats television for impact:

> I have certainly found that for a piece to work television does a much better job, even though it is much harder to make the piece for television. The fact is obviously you are reaching a much bigger audience, and newspaper audiences are shrinking. I see fantastic stories being printed on the front page of *The Age*, or whatever, and going nowhere, absolutely nowhere, you know they are dead the next day and you really have to wonder why that is. And so, I think that television does a better job of introducing the subject to the public and maybe it is because you can get to know the characters a bit better and maybe you care a bit more about it. But the record of television investigative journalism, even though it fights with both hands tied behind its back, to me has done a hell of a lot better than newspapers in the last 20 years or so.
>
> (Masters 2011, interview with the author, 15 February)

Yet Masters also believed that newspapers were a more natural home for investigative journalism:

> Newspapers are better suited to investigative journalists because you don't have a whole range of problems when it comes to

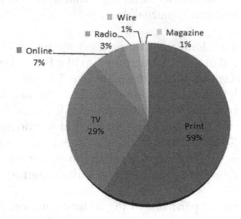

Figure 4.8 The Medium That Produced the Most Australian Walkley Award-
       Winning Investigative Journalism

Source: Author, N=187

> identifying sources, even forming the narrative and the speed at
> what you can do the work. If I come upon a good story and I want
> to get it out there as quickly as I can, I am much better off working
> for a newspaper.
>
> > (Masters 2011, interview with the author, 15 February)

When different media have competed in the same investigative journalism
categories of the Walkley Awards (since the advent of 'all media' categories in 1978), print has dominated with 59 per cent of awards (see Figure 4.8). Television had the second-highest contribution with 29 per cent;
online was third with 7 per cent; radio won 3 per cent, and wire services
and magazines rarely won investigative journalism awards (1 per cent).

However, digital-only media was eligible only since 1997 to receive
Walkley Awards for its journalism. The next chapter will provide more
detailed insights into differences between the media platforms in the production of investigative reporting.

Conclusion

This chapter addresses the question of whether newsroom cutbacks in
the digital age have affected the quantity and quality of investigative
journalism using Australia as the case study. In terms of quantity of investigative stories over time, falling newspaper revenue and the amount of
print investigative reporting are not synchronous. In fact, the number of
investigative stories has generally increased each decade since the 1950s.

Yet, some types of watchdog reporting appeared to have stagnated or
declined in the early stages of the 21st century. The decline in business

investigative reporting by general newspapers in the lead-up to the global financial crisis (GFC) of 2007–09 is particularly notable. The next chapter shows that the fallout of the GFC witnessed a renewed interest in watchdog journalism of the corporate sector in general news mastheads.

Fairfax broadsheets contributed more award-winning investigative journalism than any other media outlets in 55 years. This is a key finding for Australian investigative reporting for two reasons. The first is Fairfax's perilous financial position in 2018 and subsequent merger with the Nine television network, which has a limited contemporary record of producing quality investigative journalism. Any prediction on the future of investigative journalism in Australia will depend on how this merger of different newsroom cultures works in practice.

The second reason is that Australian broadsheet-style mastheads have produced more award-winning investigative stories than tabloids. But the study finds that generally, when broadsheets have converted to a tabloid format, their award-winning investigative reporting, in the absence of collaboration, had declined. This also has implications for Fairfax's investigative tradition. It downsized its metropolitan mastheads to tabloids from 2013. There are too few data points available to judge its effects on its investigative reporting, but preliminary analysis since conversion suggests a negative one. Past examples of conversions to tabloid after the 1970s by *The Newcastle Herald* and *The Courier Mail* also revealed a shift away from watchdog reporting.

More broadly, the analysis shows systemic-issue investigations are more prevalent than single-issue (or muckraking) reporting, consistent with the scholarship, although a slight increase in single-issue reporting since the 1990s has been identified. However, overall 127 stories out of 187 were about systemic issues. The incremental rise in single-issue reporting in recent decades could be attributed to the popularity of criminal and corporate stories, which are well suited to individual investigations, the tight editorial budgets of the digital era, and tabloid editorial sensibilities.

Investigative reporting of the 1980s stands apart from other periods on the 'quality' measures applied here. This period can be seen as the 'sweet spot' for investigate journalism in Australia, when newspaper circulations and revenues had yet to begin falling and the 'profit controversy'—the tension between journalism quality and business success—was low. Since then, print media ownership has become more concentrated in Australia. Evening papers no longer exist, and with fewer journalists employed in newsrooms, investigative reporters have less capacity to follow up their own stories, or even their competitor's investigations. Newspapers' front-page formats have changed to display more advertising at the expense of news stories. Yet, investigations are more likely to be placed or promoted on front pages, suggesting investigative journalism is considered by editors to be important for newspapers' brand and status.

Another way of understanding the modern phenomena of fewer investigative series, less mainstream media follow-up, and more intense short-term promotions is that investigative stories can achieve a bright initial flare of interest, but the flame does not last as long as it once did—such as the time when a newspaper would write a series to keep the issue on the public agenda for months, or even years, as was the case in the 1950s. This difference might create the (false) perception that there are fewer investigative stories—or, perhaps more arguably, that investigations are of lesser quality.

The second question relating to the quality of investigative journalism over time is more complicated. As circulations and revenues fell from the late 1980s, investigative journalism experienced qualitative changes. Fewer investigative stories defended the powerless or uncovered a breach of public trust. But to argue the 'quality' of investigative journalism is less now than in the past would be to overlook critical changes that have enabled investigative journalism to survive to continue producing public interest investigations. The finding that watchdog reporting endures suggests, as argued in the previous chapter, its continuation is important both as a branding strategy for mastheads to demonstrate their unique worth to shareholders and also as a means for monitoring power in democracies.

Significantly, the emergence of collaborative investigative reporting denotes a seismic shift in reporting practice from the 'old model' of single newsroom investigations marked by cutthroat rivalry to a 'new model' of multiple newsrooms cooperating and sharing information to expose systemic wrongdoing. As the next chapter will show, these collaborations extend to transnational investigations on a scale not previously thought possible. While this chapter has shown Australian newspapers have lost some cultural power and investigative journalism has had to adapt to tougher economic conditions at the end of the 20th century, the opportunities born from these changes pave a future for investigative reporting in the 21st century.

Notes

1. The start date of 1971 was selected because it represents the start of the 'second wave' of investigative journalism in Australia, and captures *The Australian* and *National Times*, which did not exist a decade earlier. This content analysis ends at the beginning of the second decade. Further analysis is undertaken after this date later in the chapter. April was selected because it is outside the summer festive season, when newsrooms tend to be less intense with staff on holidays. April is also sufficiently distant from the end of the financial year of June 30, when newspapers (and news pages) can be limited if the masthead experiences a budget shortfall.
2. The nine Walkley categories selected for story analysis between 1956 and 2011 inclusive were: 'Best News Report' (1956), 'Newspaper Feature Writing' (1956), 'Best Online Journalism' (1997), 'Best Use of the Medium'

(2003), 'Business Journalism' (1993), 'Investigative Journalism' (1991), 'Sport Reporting' (1997), 'Gold Walkley' (1978), and 'shared Winners' (1956). The date in parentheses is the year the award was first introduced. All except 'Best News Report' and 'Newspaper Feature Writing' were open to all media forms at the time of analysis.

3. The Walkley data for 2010 and 2011 is excluded because it was not a complete decade and therefore made comparisons with the other decades less useful.
4. Five inaugural categories in 1956 swelled to 34 categories by 2011.
5. Winning stories were blindly tested for 'investigative journalism' without the author identifying beforehand the particular Walkley category to which they belonged. This ensured that stories that won the 'investigative' Walkley category were not favoured inadvertently when tested to see whether or not the story possessed the hallmarks of investigative journalism.
6. The longitudinal study did not examine the *Herald*'s contribution in the 1950s, because this content analysis began at 1971.
7. The original series of stories was in the Melbourne *Truth*. This extract was reprinted a few years later for *Man* magazine, and was also recognised with a Walkley award.
8. The *Courier Mail* was a broadsheet at this time (until 2006).
9. In 1981, journalist John Lewis won the Gold Walkley and 'Best Piece of News Reporting' for his story 'Battle for Control of Newcastle-Based Television Company NBN', *Newcastle Herald*, 4 May 1981, no page number recorded in archive.
10. In 1966, Fairfax acquired a minority stake in the paper owned by David Syme and Co., and in 1972 Fairfax bought a controlling interest. It bought out the remaining shares in 1983. For the purposes here, *The Age* is considered a Fairfax masthead. In late 2018, Fairfax merged with Channel Nine.

References

Amos, J 2005, *The National Times: Bastard of a Paper*, University of Wollongong Thesis Collection, unpublished MA.

Beecher, E 2007, 'War of words: The future of journalism as public trust', *The Monthly*, accessed 5 May 2018, from www.themonthly.com.au/issue/2007/june/1283826117/eric-beecher/war-words.

Bruns, A, Wilson, J & Saunders, B 2008, *Club Bloggery: Once Were Baron*, ABC, Sydney, accessed 10 November 2010, from www.abc.net.au/news/2008-02-28/club-bloggery-once-were-barons/1057802.

Chenoweth, N, Drummond, M, Nicholas, K & White, A 2008, 'Inside job: Who killed Opes Prime', *Australian Financial Review*, 12 June, p. 1.

Chenoweth, N, Elam, S & Ryan C et al. 2003, 'Rivkin's swiss bank scandal', *Australian Financial Review*, 30 October, p. 1.

Cushion, S 2011, *Television Journalism*, Sage Publications, London.

Dorling, P 2011, 'Hicks had leadership qualities US feared', *Sydney Morning Herald*, 26 April, p. 1.

Downie, L & Schudson, M 2009, 'The reconstruction of American journalism', *Columbia Journalism Review*, 19.

Edelman, R 2018, *Trust Barometer: Global Report*, Edelman, accessed 5 November 2018, from www.edelman.com/sites/g/files/aatuss191/files/2018-10/2018_Edelman_Trust_Barometer_Global_Report_FEB.pdf.

Franklin, B 2005, 'The local press and the McDonaldization thesis', in S Allan (ed), *Journalism: Critical Issues*, Open University Press, Maidenhead.

Franklin, B 2008, *Pulling Newspapers Apart: Analysing Print Journalism*, Routledge, Abingdon.

Gawenda, M 1982, 'Ghettos in the sky', *The Age*, 29 May.

Gottliebsen, R 1978, 'Gollin' the $120 million crash', *National Times*, 3 October.

Grigg, A 2011, 'The news agent', *Australian Financial Review Magazine*, 10 November.

Harrison, S 2006, 'Local government public relations and the local press', in B Franklin (ed), *Local Journalism and Local Media: Making the Local News*, pp. 157–88, Routledge, London.

Henningham, J 1990, *Issues in Australian Journalism*, Longman Cheshire, Melbourne.

Hills, B 2010, *Breaking News: The Golden Age of Graham Perkin*, Scribe, Melbourne.

Hogg, L 1957, 'Nina tells: Why I fled', *Herald*, 9 February, page not recorded in archive.

Hughes, D 2009, 'ASIC knew about Storm for months', *Australian Financial Review*, 2 April, p. 1.

Hurst, J 1988, *The Walkley Awards: Australia's Best Journalists in Action*, John Kerr Pty Ltd, Melbourne.

Jones, A 2009, *Losing the News: The Future of the News That Feeds Democracy*, Oxford University Press, Oxford.

Kelley, S 2009, 'Investigative reporting, democracy, and the crisis in journalism', in *Centre Blog*, 21 May. The Canadian Centre for Investigative Reporting, Ottawa.

Kitchener, J 2019, 'Business journalism in the 1980s', in A Curthoys & J Schultz (eds), *Journalism: Print, Politics and Popular Culture*, University of Queensland Press, St Lucia.

Lester, T & Young, T 2011, 'Murdered by death squad', *The Age*, 4 June, p. 1.

Martin, C 1975, 'Tronado cancer device blasted', *West Australian*, 16 April, p. 1.

Martin, C 1978, 'Blue asbestos: The latent killer', *West Australian*, 20 February, p. 1.

Masters, C 2011, 'Four Corners stories', *Australian Broadcasting Corporation*, accessed 30 July 2012, from www.abc.net.au/4corners/stories/2011/08/08/3288488.htm?site=50y.

Mayman, J 1983, 'A town with two names and two laws', *The Age*, 14 October.

McGregor, C 1977, 'Inside Bob Hawke', *National Times*, 9 May.

McKenzie, N & Baker, R 2012, 'Reserve chief admits bank knew of corruption', *The Age*, 25 February, p. 2.

McKnight, D 1999, 'The investigative tradition in Australian journalism 1945–1965', in A Curthoys & J Schultz (eds), *Journalism: Print, Politics and Popular Culture*, University of Queensland Press, St Lucia.

McKnight, D 2008, '"Not attributable to official sources": Counter-propaganda and the mass media', *Media International Australia*, 128, 5–17.

McNair, B 2006, *Cultural Chaos: Journalism, News and Power in a Globalised World*, Routledge, London.

MEAA 2013, 'Media alliance code of ethics', accessed 4 February 2013, from www.alliance.org.au/code-of-ethics.html.

Mellish, M 2005, 'The rise and fall of a liberal bankroller', *Australian Financial Review*, 29 November, p. 58.

Meyer, P & Koang-Hyub, K 2003, *Quantifying Newspaper Quality: "I Know It When I See It"*, Newspaper Division for Education in Journalism and Mass Communication, Kansas City.

O'Donnell, P, McKnight, D & Este, J 2012, *Journalism at the Speed of Bytes*, The University of New South Wales, Sydney.

Sampson, A 1996, 'The crisis at the heart of our media', *British Journalism Review*, 7(3), 42–56.

Schudson, M 2003, *The Sociology of News*, W.W. Norton & Company, San Diego.

Schultz, J 1998, *Reviving the Fourth Estate: Democracy, Accountability and the Media*, Cambridge University Press, Melbourne.

Souter, G 1991, *Heralds and Angels: The House of Fairfax 1841–1992*, Melbourne University Press, Melbourne.

Sparks, C 2000, in C Sparks & J Tulloch (eds), *Tabloid Tales: Global Debates Over Media Standards*, Rowman & Littlefield Publishers Inc, Lanham.

Speight, S 1957, 'Report on migration: What the first million mean', *Sydney Morning Herald*, 23 April.

Street, J 2011, *Mass Media, Politics and Democracy*, Palgrave Macmillan, London.

Summers, A 1976, 'The day the screws were turned loose', *National Times*, 19 April.

Sykes, T 1994, *The Bold Riders*, Allen & Unwin, Sydney.

Tiffen, R 2010, 'The Press', in S Cunningham & G Turner (eds), *The Media and Communications in Australia*, Allen & Unwin, Sydney.

Toohey, B 1994, *Tumbling Dice*, William Heinemann, Melbourne.

Turner, G 1994, *Making it National: Nationalism and Australian Popular Culture*, Allen & Unwin, Sydney.

Whitton, E 1974, 'The truth About Vietnam', *National Times*, 28 April.

5 The Rise of Collaborative Investigative Journalism[1]

> Journalism is based on geography. It's all based on the city and who the readers are. And yet most of the increasing issues that confront human-kind are not in a city, they're global, they're regional, they're beyond countries, even, in a lot of cases, and who's covering that?
>
> (Charles Lewis, founder Center for Public Integrity, interview with the author, 31 August 2016)

Introduction

Investigative journalism's important role exposing abuses of public trust in society has not only endured but taken on a new global focus, notwith-standing the challenging contemporary financial environment for it. This was no more evident than in 2016. 'Spotlight'—a *Boston Globe* investiga-tion into Catholic Church sex abuse—inspired an Oscar-winning film. In the same year, more than 300 members of the International Consortium for Investigative Journalism (ICIJ) broke the global story of tax evasion with the Panama Papers. It was journalism's largest data leak at the time.

These were exemplar moments for watchdog journalism in an age increasingly said to be characterised by fake news and labelled as a 'post-truth' era. These great examples of the power of investigative journalism also serve to illustrate a significant change in its practice—from an 'old model' of a highly competitive single newsroom environment—like the *Boston Globe*'s initial 'Spotlight' investigation in 2003—to a 'new model' of multiple newsrooms (and countries) unprecedentedly sharing informa-tion to expose wrongdoing on a global scale, as seen with the Panama Papers stories.

This chapter explores these important shifts in investigative journal-ism through expert interviews and a content analysis of key national journalism awards in Britain, Australia, and the United States. In doing so, this chapter analyses the development and consequences of this new model of transnational collaborative investigative journalism. By exam-ining a total of 30 years of peer-reviewed media awards, we can identify when award-winning newsroom collaborations began in these nations, their key story targets and outcomes. These findings are compared with interviews with journalists from outlets that undertake collaborative investigative journalism such as the *Boston Globe, ProPublica, The Washington Post, The New York Times, The Guardian,* the ICIJ, the ABC and Australia's Fairfax Media outlets, among others. By testing the theoretical framework in Chapter 3 and applying it to the findings here, we find a way to explain why watchdog reporting has been able to adapt to the new model of collaboration, which initially began as cross-media reporting and has developed into cross-national investigation. For some outlets, these collaborations allow news organisations committed to their democratic accountability role to continue as public watchdogs, notwithstanding newsroom cutbacks. By pooling resources, news outlets can continue to engage in expensive and time-consuming investigations, with some of these large-scale investigations attracting significant attention and potentially bolstering readership. It is therefore clear that being involved in these investigations may be purposeful for the outlet's brand development even if a commitment to democratic accountability is not a primary objective. The findings also shed light on how digital media technologies—arguably responsible for the 'journalism crisis'—paradoxically offer fresh opportunities for evidence-based journalism in the 21st century.

Concerns remain, however, about the future of investigative reporting due to limited resources within individual newsrooms. Clear signs that newsroom budget cuts are affecting investigative journalism include a measurable narrowing of the types, or genres, of investigative targets, and an emphasis on national or international investigations at the expense of local story investigations.

We begin by examining the backdrop for investigative reporting in the 21st century, including the rise of fake news and the shift to multi-newsroom collaborations. I briefly relate this to the theoretical model and then discuss the findings of the data and implications for investigative journalism's prospects in democracies.

Backdrop to 21st-Century Watchdog Reporting

The Rise of Fake News

There is nothing new about fake news. The 'Moon Hoax' of 1835 epitomised an early disregard for facts in the press. Orchestrated by Benjamin H. Day's *New York Sun,* the paper claimed to have observed life on the moon through a telescope. The paper later confessed to its readers about its deception, claiming it had all been good sport, as a way of 'diverting the public mind' from heavy debates around slavery (cited in Mott 1962, p. 226). Many mastheads of this time, collectively known as the penny press, had an elastic relationship with the truth, publishing sensationalist stories to attract and maintain readership (Conboy 2002; Hughes 1940; Mott 1962; Schudson 1978).

Moreover, the separation of objective 'facts' from subjective 'values' was not part of the journalistic ethic until World War I (Schudson 1978, p. 6). Even during the interwar period in 1922, Walter Lippmann (1922, p. 358) noted the partial and selective view of the world portrayed in the press, concluding that 'news and truth are not the same thing'. Throughout much of its modern history, the accuracy of news content has been both variable and contested.

But unlike these earlier times, the fake news stories of the 21st century can spread further and faster through digital technologies. The internet and computer algorithms make it easier for misinformation to travel like wildfire across the globe, whether deliberate (fake news) or not (sloppy reporting). This is of major concern to those sections of the public who value integrity and trust in their news sources. Since the election of US President Donald Trump, public apprehension has intensified about 'alternative facts', his 'war' on journalists, and false news (Solon 2016). This is a problem because at the same time that investigative journalism's economic viability is questioned, public confidence in the veracity of news is challenged by the explosion of fake news (Mitchell et al. 2016).

Public concern about fake news and trust in news matters because, as earlier chapters have outlined, inaccurate reporting has consequences for news media's perceived role to provide for a well-informed citizenry. Low media trust is particularly problematic during election campaigns when voters are best served by accurate information to inform their choice.

Of course, 'fake news' is an umbrella term that can include phenomena such as disinformation, post-truth, rumour, lies, misinformation, malicious information (mal-information), and satire. Analyses of any of these can focus on varying themes. At one end of the spectrum, there is false news presented as satire and humour; for example, satirical websites such as *The Onion* or late-night television such as *The Late Show with Stephen Colbert*. Our concern is on the use of the term 'fake news' as indicating 'news articles that are intentionally and verifiably false, and could mislead readers' (Allcott and Gentzkow 2017, p. 213). From this perspective, a significant theme in contemporary analyses of fake news centres on the ways in which it is damaging to society by contributing to the political polarisation of ideas via its influence on audience beliefs or even voting behaviours, and the stickiness of those beliefs (for more on the research in this field, see Bakir and McStay 2017; Mihailidis and Viotty 2017; Allcott and Gentzkow 2017; Cooke 2017).

Fake news rose to prominence following a series of false viral stories during the 2016 US election campaign arising out of Macedonia (Cvetkovska et al. 2018). The use of the term 'fake news' by the world's foremost political elite, the president of the United States, to undermine or denigrate a news outlet is an important development in the fake news landscape with implications for public trust in media.

At his first press conference as president-elect, Donald Trump attacked news organisations that had published unfavourable pieces about his alleged connections with Russia, including shouting, 'You are fake news!' at a CNN reporter, from whom he refused to take questions. The designation of news outlets as purveyors of fake news continued in the wake of this press conference via the president's Twitter feed, with CNN and *The New York Times* being frequent targets. This strategic weaponisation of fake news to delegitimise the news media potentially has significant implications for public trust in media. Even before Trump's use of the term, a 2016 US Pew Research Center report found 88 per cent of Americans believed fake news confuses the public about basic facts (Mitchell et al. 2016). This language is now pervasive; 'post-truth' and 'fake news' were declared words of the year for 2016 by the Oxford English Dictionary and Macquarie Dictionary, respectively.

Inaccurate reporting is also linked to falling trust in media. For example, public evaluations of news outlets' performances on accuracy, fairness, and independence in the United States fell to record lows between 1985 and 2013. The percentage of participants who said news outlets 'get their facts straight' fell from 55 per cent to 26 per cent; those who believed they 'deal fairly with all sides' dropped from 34 per cent to 19 per cent; the perceived 'independence' of outlets and their reporting also fell from 37 per cent to 20 per cent. Yet when asked about the media's watchdog role, and more specifically if the press were able to 'keep leaders from doing things that shouldn't be done', responses were higher than anticipated and had actually improved by one percentage point since 1985, to 68 per cent in 2013 (Dimock et al. 2013). This suggests that the public do believe credible watchdog reporting provides a check on the excesses of government and powerful private interests; or as Schudson (2008) has identified, it is a means to deter those in power from engaging in wrongdoing. In this sense, evidence-based journalism such as investigative reporting can help retain public trust in the media and thus, I argue, serves as a counterexample to fake news that diminishes public trust in news. For this reason alone, evidence-based investigative reporting's survival in difficult economic times is important.

From Single to Multiple Newsroom Investigations

Inspired by investigative examples like the Kim Philby spy affair in Britain in the 1960s and Watergate in the early 1970s, discussed earlier in this book, the 1970s saw a significant rise in the number and status of investigative journalists in newsrooms across the globe (Henningham 1990). It was considered a high tide for watchdog reporting in Australia, Britain, the United States, and elsewhere with many specialist investigative reporting units springing up in newsrooms (Carson 2013). Yet, these units were typically fiercely competitive and independent of one another. Media organisations competed to outclass each other with their exclusive investigative stories. Prestigious journalism awards were prized acknowledgements of this competitive environment. Charles Lewis (2016, interview with author, 31 August), a one-time judge of the Goldsmith Prize for Investigative Reporting at the Shorenstein Center at Harvard University, said of the more than 100 entries he judged, each one 'was every newspaper's proudest moment'.

However, as outlined in Chapter 3, proponents of a political economy perspective have long argued that news media's commercial interests can impede its public interest functions. Rather than offering a check on power, they counter that media produce the 'news fit to print' to uphold interests of capital and elites (Herman and Chomsky 2002). Accordingly, concentrated media ownership structures and profit-making motives were thought to result in neglect of costly investigative journalism (Curran 2005, p. 225). Digital media technologies that enable the viral spread of fake news provide a timely reappraisal of political economic theories of the media because they challenge the media's normative fourth estate functions.

This chapter continues the theoretical discussion begun in Chapter 3. While each of the existing theoretical streams of chaos and control were typically regarded as oppositional, I argue that this is not the case with investigative journalism. James T. Hamilton's (2016) findings from a cost-benefit analysis of investigative reporting's public outcomes also highlights that investigative journalism is valuable on both normative and economic grounds. Hamilton's work is salient here because it gives weight to my alternative framework whereby investigative journalism's role in democratic accountability can sit alongside a political economy perspective. In Chapter 3 it was conceptualised that the chaos and control paradigms belong on a spectrum rather than poles apart, with capacity for overlap. In this virtual shared space, investigative reporting endures.

This framework helps us to understand why once competitive media outlets will put their rivalry on hold and share resources in relation to investigative reporting. As part of a bigger whole attention is given to the mastheads that participate in investigative collaborations, and it strengthens their reputations as quality providers of investigative reporting. Thus the same conditions that allow for the viral spread of fake news—internet connectivity and many-to-many digital networks—are also responsible for a decisive shift in investigative reporting practice from highly competitive single-newsroom investigation to a new collaborative model of multiple newsrooms (and countries) sharing information to expose wrongdoing. As the Panama and Paradise Papers examples showed, collaborative investigative reporting is now possible on a global scale. Lewis (2016, interview with the author, 31 August) explains that without collaboration, no single newsroom could parse the big data available to us in the digital age:

> [The Panama Papers] is a pinnacle moment in the history of journalism itself, in the world. No question. But what is fascinating about it is that none of those [single] papers are big enough, strong enough, have enough people to cover the whole world, understandably. No one can cover that. But by involving journalists who have specialty knowledge about their countries and their politicians and their leading business people and all these subjects, that's how you can cover it and you couldn't do it with a single newspaper. No single paper could ever do it.

Further, the ICIJ is just one example of 106 non-profit investigative reporting organisations in 47 countries driving the new model of global investigative journalism (Kaplan 2013). The transition of quality investigations originating from single newsrooms to collaborations with multiple journalists and outlets, and their characteristics, is now examined.

Applying the Operative Definition

This chapter takes a comparative approach, focusing on award-winning investigative journalism in three liberal democracies. I analyse exemplar journalism in select categories of the oldest peer-reviewed national journalism awards in each country: Australia (Walkley Awards, established 1956), Britain (British Press Awards, established 1962, renamed Press Awards in 2010) and the United States (Pulitzer Prizes, established 1917). The awards were selected because each has prestige within its respective journalism communities and attracts hundreds of entries each year.[2] As media have changed, so have the categories. For this reason, only categories that remain consistent over a ten-year period (2007 to 2016) and are relevant to investigative reporting were selected for analysis (see Table 5.1).[3]

The time frame of 2007–16 resulted in data from 180 awards from categories that were expected to capture investigative collaborations. Of course, some collaborations do not win awards, and some quality collaborations may have occurred too early to be captured here. Investigative journalism might also be found in categories that were not analysed. The purpose here is not to be exhaustive but to detect trends in investigative reporting over time. The rationale for analysing these particular national awards for researching journalistic collaborations, as opposed to others, was to ensure a comparative and systematic approach using awards that are recognised by the journalism community as exemplary in comparable democracies.

I use the same operative definition (see Table 2.1) and collection method of finding stories as I did in Chapter 4 in the Australian Walkley

Awards analysis. In each case, the award-winning journalism was located on the national awards' websites. Once the title and author were identified, LexisNexis and Factiva database searches of news articles were often required to find the full story or story series that won the award to conduct further evaluation. The questions answered in this chapter are:

1. What press outlets win awards for investigative journalism, and has this changed over time as the economic landscape for media has altered?
2. What are the common targets in the investigative stories? Have they changed over time?
3. When did journalistic collaborations start appearing in the awards? What other characteristics can be observed about the investigative stories over time?

Table 5.1 The Award Categories and Number of Investigative Stories Identified Across Three Countries From 2007 to 2016

Country	Name of categories 2007–16	Investigative	Non-investigative	Total	%
United States	Explanatory, *Public Service, Investigative Reporting, Local, National	33	23	56	59
Britain (of the year)	Campaign; *Scoop; *Digital Journalist; *Young Journalist; *Journalist; *Cudlipp Award; *Business and Finance Journalist; Science and Health Journalist	36	31	67	54
Australia	*Print News Report; Newspaper Feature Writing; Best Digital Journalism; *Business Journalism; *Investigative Journalism; *Sport Journalism; *Gold Walkley; Print/Text News Report; Feature Writing Long; Feature Writing Short; Multimedia Storytelling; Scoop of the Year	31	26	57	54
Totals		100	80	180	

Source: Author using data from Australian Walkley Awards, British Press Awards, and US Pulitzer Prizes for journalism.

*Category names survive over time.

Note: N = 180, story duplicates removed. For comparative purposes, operative definition applied to print stories only.

The Press Still Matters

The first observation from the data is that the role of the traditional press in producing investigative journalism remains important this century, notwithstanding significant newsroom cost-cutting and masthead closures. Two of the three awards (Pulitzer Prizes and Press Awards) specifically honour the press and online journalism, so it is a moot point about how the quantum of press investigative journalism compared to other media platforms in these countries.

Although the Australian Walkley Awards include *all* media, newspapers (print and online) continued to produce more award-winning investigative reporting than radio and television in the studied time frame. But increasingly, award-winning stories were being told across platforms and through collaborations between television and print. In Australia, a cross-media collaboration—in this instance between a newspaper and a television program—collected the prestigious Gold Walkley for the first time in 2014. Collaborating teams also won the 'investigative journalism' award twice, in 2014 and 2016. Until 2014, the 'old model' of single-newsroom investigations in competition with one another prevailed. This turning point from single-newsroom investigations to cross-media investigations for award-winning investigative journalism is a significant change.

All three countries' awards reveal that the old established mastheads continue to win awards in the digital age for their investigative reporting (see Figures 5.1, 5.5,and 5.6). Mastheads such as *The New York Times, The Wall Street Journal,* and *The Washington Post* are still prominent producers of US award-winning investigative reporting this century. In Britain, *The Guardian* and Rupert Murdoch's *The Times* and *The Sunday Times*—the first British paper to establish 'Insight', a dedicated investigative unit, in the 1960s—remain key providers of investigative reporting (see Figure 5.1).

We can see that *The Guardian* has been recognised for its quality investigative reporting in all three countries (see Figures 5.1, 5.5, and 5.6), demonstrating that its ambition for global expansion has *not* compromised its watchdog role. Also of note, tabloid-style newspapers in Australia—unlike their British counterparts such as the *Daily Mail*—rarely produce award-winning investigative journalism. In other words, award-winning investigative journalism largely remains the domain of Australia's elite mastheads rather than tabloid newspapers. As discussed earlier, Australia's broadsheet-style papers such as *The Australian, The Age,* and *The Sydney Morning Herald* (*SMH*) have a tradition of investigative reporting and have appointed dedicated watchdog reporting teams. Further, these investigative units in the broadsheet-style papers were largely unscathed after several rounds of newsroom cutbacks this century.

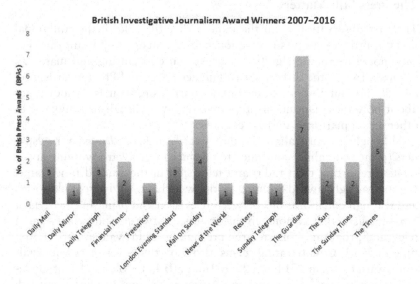

Figure 5.1 British Publishers of Award-Winning Watchdog Reporting, 2007–16
Source: Author using data from the British Press Awards
Note: n = 36

Former ABC managing director and a former Fairfax editor-in-chief, Mark Scott (2010, interview with the author, 19 August), argued that companies that undertake investigative journalism do so because of its value to their brand name and, as a consequence, investigative journalism by Australian media organisations has been subsidised by other forms of reporting that attracts readers and advertising. *The Washington Post*'s Jeff Leen (2016, interview with author, 30 August) adds to this point:

> *The Washington Post* still believes that investigative reporting is part of its brand. *The Washington Post* achieved an international brand through investigative reporting, through Watergate. And it, sort of, built its reputation on that and so investigative reporting is very important to us it's part of our DNA. . . . And, so, that's a big commitment in terms of resources and it shows you that they're willing to spend . . . put their money where their mouth is in terms of the most difficult, risky journalism that you can do in the public service.

These expert views suggest marketing is not antithetical to the liberal democratic functions of news media. However, traditional media's financial challenges have forced outlets to adapt and to find other ways to produce investigative journalism in the harsher political economic environment. In some cases this has provided new opportunities for watchdog reporting, such as cross-media collaborations and use of digital tools to tell stories, but also fresh challenges.

Investigative Journalism's Challenges

The loss of thousands of journalism jobs and masthead closures in recent decades have been well documented. As outlined in Chapter 1, the key trends include traditional media ownership consolidation; journalism job losses (e.g. 20,000 US journalism jobs over 20 years); masthead closures (e.g. 126 fewer US mastheads since 2004), and multinational online competitors such as Google and Facebook dominating digital advertising revenues and becoming the primary sites for sections of news audiences to get their news (Mitchell and Holcomb 2016). These trends extend to developed economies beyond the United States.

Yet, the data shows the impact of these extraordinary changes to the media landscape on award-winning watchdog reporting is more nuanced. On one hand, collaborations and new digital tools have meant that the quality and quantity of watchdog reporting has endured. Figure 5.2 shows that, of the studied awards, more stories were passing the operative definition (outlined in Chapter 2) of investigative reporting than ten years earlier. But the types of investigations and story targets of those investigations do change over time, and some of this change provides cause for concern.

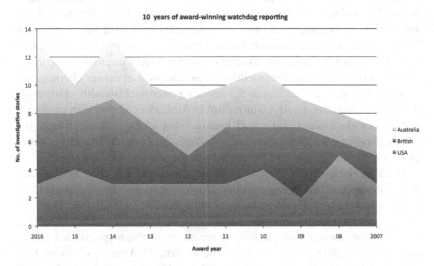

Figure 5.2 Number of Stories Passing the Definition of Investigative Reporting in Three Countries, 2007–16

Source: Authors using data from the British Press Awards, Pulitzer Prizes and Walkley Awards

Note: n = 100

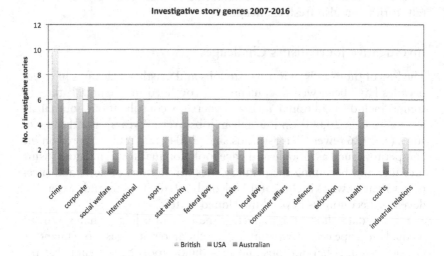

Figure 5.3 Investigative Story Targets in Three Countries, 2007–16

Source: Authors using data from the British Press Awards, Pulitzer Prizes and Walkley Awards

Note: n = 100

Narrowing of Story Targets

Following the GFC, there has been an increase in corporate and business focused award-winning investigative journalism in each country studied (see Figure 5.3). This suggests greater journalistic scrutiny of these sectors than in times past. This is a positive development, as earlier research had found that there was a conspicuous absence of corporate investigative reporting in Australia prior to the global meltdown, as discussed in earlier chapters. Of concern, however, is that Figure 5.3 reveals a narrower breadth of topics of award-winning investigative journalism in Australia compared to the larger markets of the United States and Britain. This might be indicative of the highly concentrated press ownership in Australia compared to larger numbers of daily mastheads and proprietors in Britain and the United States.

Even in these larger Anglo-American markets, the data shows that there has been a fall in the number of investigations that focus on local politics and industrial relations issues between 2007 and 2016. This is the case for all the studied countries and might be indicative of the shrinking state of newsrooms and the loss of reporters in these specialised policy areas. Lewis (2016, interview with the author, 31 August) observes that many quality American newspapers select which investigations they will pursue depending on how well read they think the stories will be:

> They're into eyeballs and they're into subscriptions and hits and, of course, that helps advertising and lots of other things and I understand

the reasons for all of that. I totally do. But there are just an awful lot of subjects they're just not going to undertake.

The *Boston Globe*'s award-winning Spotlight editor, Walter Robinson (2016, interview with the author, 25 September) argues that this is also true of specialised, 'beat' reporting, which has particularly suffered because of newsroom cutbacks.

> There are so many important junctures in life where there is no journalistic surveillance going on. There are too many journalistic communities in the United States now where the newspaper doesn't have the reporter to cover the city council, the school committee, the mayor's office . . . we have about half the number of reporters that we had in the late 1990s you can't possibly contend that you are doing the same level or depth of reporting. Too much stuff is just slipping through too many cracks.

In Australia, ABC investigative journalist Linton Besser (2017, interview with the author, 16 March) observed an inverse relationship between a dearth of local reporting and the resourcing of investigative journalism, particularly as the focus had broadened to national and international stories.

> I think a big problem for society and for its relationship with journalism is the lack of local reporting. There is a dearth of good local reporting now. That is what has died. I don't think investigative journalism has died at all since newspapers have run out of money. It's where they're pumping money in; I mean the small amounts they've got. And they're promoting it, and it's like their last brand thing that they're trying to do, is to say 'hey, we're important and we're alive'.

That said, Besser also found that the standard time allocated (nine weeks) to deliver an investigative story for ABC television's premium investigative program, *Four Corners*, made it difficult to pursue certain types of stories, which might explain why story targets were less diverse in Australia: 'I don't pitch things internally that I don't think I can land', he said.

> Going back from broadcast, three weeks is editing, three weeks is filming (so that's six weeks), one week is writing a shooting script, so you have two weeks' research time at *Four Corners*'. You have to make the story stand up in two weeks. And that includes that dilemma of getting people on camera, and they've all got to be booked in to be filmed in this block of time that you've got a crew . . . there's never enough time.

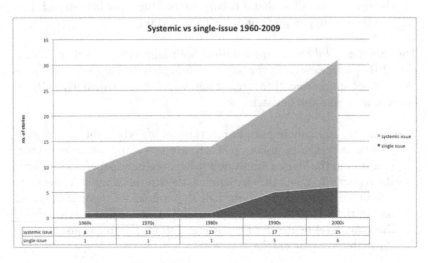

Figure 5.4 Australian Walkley-Winning Investigative Stories: Systemic Issue
Versus Single Issue, 1960s–2000s

Source: Author using data from Walkley awards 1956-2011

Notes: N = 187 investigative stories; n = 101 passing investigative test

Systemic Compared to Single-Issue Investigations

Another small but discernible trend in the Australian data is a shift back
toward single-issue investigation. The longitudinal data of the Australian
Walkley Awards, gathered for Chapter 4 over five full decades of award-
winning investigative journalism, shows a minor resurgence in single-
issue investigative reporting after the 1980s (see Figure 5.4). This is telling
because it is when profitability of Australia's traditional media began to
decline. A reason why a detectable increase in single-issue investigative
stories is appearing might be that, broadly speaking, these are simpler
stories, requiring fewer editorial resources to pursue. For example, investigating an unscrupulous doctor might require a few patient case studies,
which is a simpler exercise and less time-consuming than finding compelling evidence to demonstrate a broken health system that might take
many case studies and considerable time. Yet award-winning investigative stories by their nature generally are the result of putting in extra time
and effort compared to other investigative journalism that does not win
awards. Indeed, the Walkley story count over time still strongly prefer-
ences systemic reporting, as it is more likely to have a societal impact,
which draws the story to the attention of Walkley judges and is part of
the judging criteria. For this reason, it is unremarkable that two thirds
of Walkley Award–winning stories examined from 1956 to 2011 (127
stories out of 187) were about systemic issues.

However, at this time, there is no great cause for alarm. The emerging capacity to tell global stories in collaborative efforts with others and the use of data journalism to interrogate large amounts of information like never before suggest a more durable commitment using new digital tools (see below) to tackle systemic-issue investigative journalism. The concern here is directed more toward local watchdog journalism, where adaptations such as cross-media collaboration might not be possible locally as journalists are thin on the ground.

That said, *The Guardian*'s former Data Projects editor, Helena Bengtsson (2016, interview with the author, 24 September), and the *Boston Globe*'s Walter Robinson (2016, interview with the author, 25 September) predict that the internet and open source databases of local authorities will make it possible to do local journalism better with fewer resources than before. Bengtsson says 'we should be able to localise things in another way and give local journalists the tools to do more unique journalism'. Robinson adds that some of this local digging work is already being shared with readers:

> There are all of these tools, some of which we use and don't use enough and could use better. And then there are the ones that our readers are using, we're doing a lot of crowdsourcing to get good stories.

Award-Winning Collaborators

Newsroom adaptations in the form of cross-newsroom collaborations became evident in the US awards data from 2004. Michael Schudson and Leonard Downie Jr, writing about US newspapers in 2009 (n.p.), predicted other changes too. They wrote:

> The remaining economically viable newspapers—with much smaller staffs, revenues, and profits—will try to do many things at once: publish in print and digitally, seek new ways to attract audiences and advertisers, invent new products and revenue streams, and find new partners to help them produce high-quality news at lower cost.

In Australia, 'new partners' first began within media companies by outlets owned by the same investment group. For example, *The Age* and *The Sydney Morning Herald*, both owned by Fairfax Media (taken over by Nine in late 2018), began collaborating on investigative stories in 2009 and winning awards for their efforts. Three years later, the Australian data shows this developed into cross-media collaboration, with the first award-winning collaboration between traditionally competing media companies, the public broadcaster (the ABC) and Fairfax in 2012. *The Age*'s Nick McKenzie and Richard Baker partnered with McKenzie's former employer, the ABC, to use the medium of television to tell what had been a series of press stories about the Australian Reserve Bank's subsidiary companies linked to bribery allegations to secure print money-making contracts abroad. This trend of combining print with television investigation strengthens over time.

The ABC's Linton Besser (2017, interview with the author, 16 March) says that in his experience, combining print with television stories tends to increase the audience share and the story's impact. 'Television captures an audience in a way that the printed word just doesn't', he said. Besser also observed that front-page newspaper investigative stories have less impact than in the past, making it more important to collaborate with other media to attract attention. 'A very big [print] story is so subsumed so quickly by the news cycle that it just doesn't have the traction it used to have', he said.

The data supports Besser's argument. Journalists were taking advantage of working together from print and television to tell an investigative story across both media and online. Between 2014 and 2016, six Australian cross-newsroom collaborations, including with a non-media academic partner (*SMH* with journalism students at the University of Technology, Sydney) produced award-winning investigative reporting (see Figure 5.5). The collaboration with academia established an Australian-first database of political gifts that Australia's federal politicians received from big business and lobby groups. The database revealed thousands of free trips and junkets from powerful vested interests. These included 82 tickets to football grand finals, more than 100 overseas flights, and accommodation offered by a host of donors including mining billionaire Andrew Forrest's Fortescue Metals Group; the Australian airline, Qantas; and the Kingdom of Morocco. These cross-media and non-media partnerships show the prescience of Downie and Schudson's (2009) forecasts.

Award-winning collaborative investigative journalism was apparent several years earlier in the United States, but it did not become more familiar to newsrooms until the second decade of this century. For example, in 2004, *The New York Times*' David Barstow, with PBS *Frontline* and the Canadian Broadcasting Corporation (CBC), won the public service Pulitzer Prize for exposing the deaths and injuries of American workers when employers broke safety rules. Such cross-media collaborations dramatically increased from 2010 with non-profit organisations such as *ProPublica* teaming up with various partners to produce Pulitzer Prize–winning investigative journalism. This includes *ProPublica* working with *The New York Times Magazine* in 2010 to trace the devastating consequences of local hospital workers' decisions when cut off by Hurricane Katrina's floodwaters. *ProPublica* also partnered with another non-profit, *The Marshall Project*, to tell the harrowing stories of rape victims who had been failed by law enforcement agencies. What can be observed in this select sample of award categories is that through such collaborations *ProPublica*, which only began reporting in 2008, is matching very

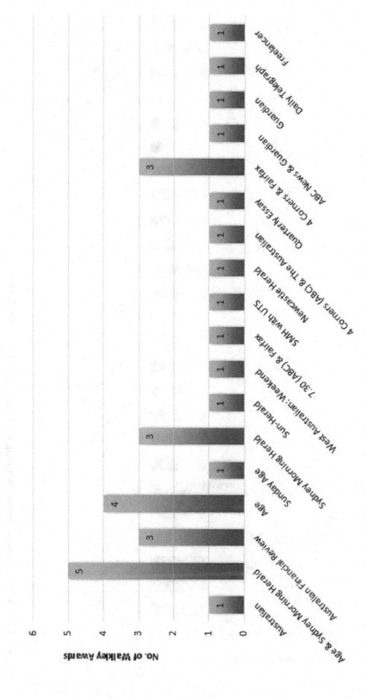

Figure 5.5 Australian Publishers of Award-Winning Watchdog Reporting, 2007–16

Source: Author using data from Walkley awards (2007–2016); n=31 passing investigative test

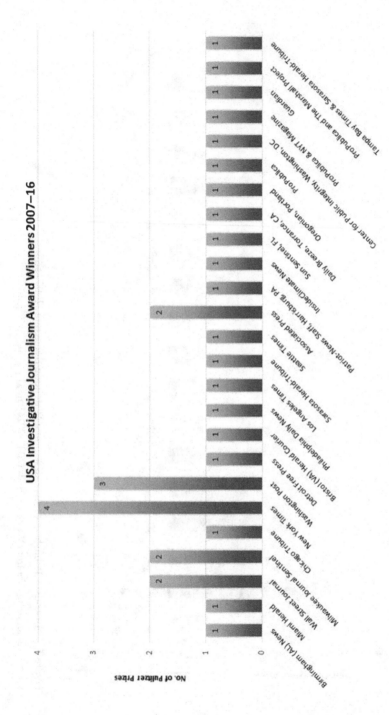

Figure 5.6 US Publishers of Award-Winning Watchdog Reporting, 2007–16

Source: Authors using data from the Pulitzer Prizes

Note: n = 33

established newspapers in producing award-winning quality investigative reporting. In this analysis, it won three awards, the same number as *The Washington Post* and one fewer than *The New York Times*. As can be seen in Figure 5.6, other non-profit journalism outlets were also winning Pulitzers for their investigative journalism, including *inside climate news* (in 2013 for revealing a major oil spill, the 'Dilbit Disaster'), and the Center for Public Integrity in 2014 (for exposing what the coal industry knew but failed to reveal about black lung disease affecting miners).

Lewis, who co-founded the Institute for Nonprofit News, argues that non-profit news outlets are filling some of the void left by cutbacks to commercial media outlets to keep communities informed (see Chapter 7). In some instances these new news outlets have formed partnerships with the remaining traditional news providers to do investigative work. Lewis states:

> We lost half of our commercial journalists and communities all over the United States. So that's why foundations and individuals and others all jumped in. That's why they all began partnering with broadcast stations with NPR, National Public Radio stations, and they started creating the small collaborations, partnerships, in each market. I've watched how that has evolved in places like Boston and Wisconsin and San Diego and Ashville, North Carolina, Western North Carolina, all kinds of places. I find it inspiring beyond words.
>
> (Lewis 2016, interview with the author, 31 August)

Yet, these cross-media collaborative trends are barely observable in the British Press Awards.[4] The only awarded case in the studied time frame was the collaborative effort of *The Guardian*'s Ewen MacAskill working with US investigative reporter Glenn Greenwald and freelance documentary maker Laura Poitras on the National Security Agency (NSA) leaks. Together, they told the story of 'Edward Snowden: The Whistleblower Behind the NSA Surveillance Revelations'. This story was the largest data leak of its time, involving tens of thousands of documents, later surpassed by the Panama Papers and then the Paradise Papers in 2017 (which involved 13.4 million documents). The NSA leaks led to data collaborations in all of the studied countries. The subsequent investigative reporting was recognised in each countries' awards: in Australia (ABC News with *The Guardian* in 2014) and in the United States (*The Washington Post*, a joint winner with *The Guardian* for the public service Pulitzer Prize in 2014). The ICIJ's Panama Papers, another transnational collaborative effort, was a winner in the 2017 Pulitzer Prizes, and its Australian partners were finalists in the 2016 Australian Walkley Awards.

These award-winning collaborations follow the mass data dumps of *WikiLeaks* (see Chapter 6). *WikiLeaks* and the Snowden leaks were important transitional steps toward producing highly coordinated large-scale trans-border journalism collaborations, such as the ICIJ's Paradise Papers and its 2018 medical stories collectively titled the 'Implant Files'. This transitional step from the *WikiLeaks* model to the NSA and ICIJ collaborative models is detailed in the next chapter.

Different Forms of Collaboration

Managing editor of *ProPublica*, Robin Fields, says collaboration occurs in various ways beyond journalists working on the same project. It also involves collaboration with other disciplines such as computer science and organisations like philanthropic foundations that financially support the journalism. Since its beginnings in 2007–08, *ProPublica* has partnered with about 160 media outlets, including media throughout the United States and in Europe (*ProPublica* 2017).

Fields said the people involved in different aspects of a story, whether it be data analysis or making phone calls and verifying facts, are brought in early to contribute to the entire process. She said collaborations, whether with a large newsroom like *The New York Times* or a non-profit, have succeeded because they share a common purpose.

> We agree on most things from the outset. Occasionally we will have vigorous and significant conversation about these things but I can't think of a case where we have had to throw up our hands and walk away. We have had the luxury of working with some of the best journalists in the world and if everybody around that table wants it to succeed, and thinks it is important and worthwhile and worth digging in and pushing forward on then I don't think you are going to let fairly superficial differences—write the lede this way—undermine your greater purpose.
>
> (Fields 2016, interview with the author, 6 September)

She observed that when *ProPublica* was first established, partnering with established media was useful for leveraging their institutional power and audience reach. But as the digital newsroom matured, *ProPublica*'s platform developed stronger connections directly with the public and less in need of this leverage.

Similarly, at the ICIJ, Hamish Boland-Rudder said that the ICIJ develops story materials for its journalistic partners to assist in telling global stories on topics such as tax rorting. 'We have a dual mission of serving audiences, and serving our partnership network', he said. Collaboration occurs in researching and telling the overarching story, but also during the process of developing digital news products:

> If I can't do something, I find someone that I know who can, within the network, which is great. The [Panama Papers] 'Stairway to Tax

Heaven' game was in collaboration with *Le Monde*, they pretty much did the design, and all the back-end work for it. We provided a reporter, editor and legal and fact checking services, as well as concept help all the way through. And that's how a lot of things end up working.

(Boland-Rudder 2016, interview with the author, 29 August)

Boland-Rudder said financial partners get involved too, such as the Pulitzer Center, by contributing financial support and assisting with story distribution. Thus we see that collaboration comes in many different forms and is filling the void where traditional news outlets can no longer operate alone.

Going Digital: New Tools for Investigative Journalists

Each of the national awards has changed its categories over time to accommodate change in journalism's methods for storytelling and for reaching audiences. This is most obvious with experimentation in the naming of online, digital, and multimedia categories around the turn of the 21st century. However, award-winning digital journalism did not really gain traction until 2006–07. By 2009, crowdsourcing information through databases and social media was being recognised as an innovative form of gathering data for investigative reporting. And by 2016, social media was firmly embedded in award-winning storytelling to reach audiences beyond the masthead's own.

David Barstow (2016, interview with the author, 5 May) argues that investigative reporting is of a higher quality than ever before because of the new digital tools and collaborations available to journalists:

> The very best investigative reporting is a cut above what used to be the best. At the highest levels it's in part because we have a whole bunch of new tools, our ability to interrogate data, our ability to display original documents, to embed original documents online, digital presentations, our growing sophistication with graphics, growing sophistication with how to integrate all of the different forms of story-telling.

The Walkley Awards were the first to introduce an 'electronic journalism' award in 1998. This quickly changed to the more apt 'online journalism' category the next year. It was again renamed to best 'digital journalism' in 2012; after that, it was transformed to a 'multimedia award' in 2014. Similarly, the British Press Awards introduced an online award in 2000, which disappeared after 2002 for four years and then reappeared in 2007, titled 'digital journalist of the year'. It was relabelled a 'digital innovation award' in 2009 and then renamed to 'Digital (scoop of the year) Award' in 2016. The Pulitzer Prizes, rather than change the name of categories, change the description of the eligibility to include online content in 2006. By 2011, the wording significantly altered to include stories using 'any available journalistic tool including text reporting, videos, databases, multimedia or interactive presentations or any combination of those formats, in print or online or both'. In the last few years this has been shortened to simply state: 'any available journalistic tool'.

These changes are important and reflect how journalists are using the affordances of the digital age to investigate in different ways. They also acknowledge that journalism is no longer limited to a single production platform. *ProPublica*'s Robin Fields (2016, interview with the author, 6 September) said data and data reporters are an integral part of their team:

> We would consider our data journalists, our news app developers, our social media platform folks, they are all journalists and they are all operating as reporters in various ways. When they collaborate with traditional reporters on projects, they don't do so passively as if they were mere technicians. That's one of the real differences of approach that we increasingly have believed in.

Similarly, the ICIJ considers its data analysts and software developers to be a key part of the journalism team. ICIJ journalist and web production journalist Hamish Boland-Rudder (2016, interview with author, 29 August) said the data team in 2016 made up 50 per cent of the ICIJ in-house staff.

> We've hired strategically, so that it's a very broad skill set. We have a front-end developer, we also have a data analyst who's a programmer, we've got a specialist scraper . . . they're all approaching the data from journalistic backgrounds, generally, which means they're coming at it from a perspective of what do we need to do to allow journalists to crack into this data?

Boland-Rudder (2016, interview with author, 29 August) said a challenge for the ICIJ was to tell global stories to many different local audiences and to work with media partners to do that effectively. This involved innovative ways to tell stories, including developing online games, videos, quizzes as well as traditional forms of written storytelling.

> We have to come up with [media] products that speak to a very global audience. Which means, all age groups, a lot of different languages, all sorts of different demographics. But our primary distribution network is through our partners. So, it has to be something that can be run just as easily on an Austrian tabloid news website, as it can on a public broadcaster in Australia. We don't always hit the mark, with

every single product. A lot of partners take them or leave them as they need to, but generally we have found pretty good success.

Platform Neutrality

The ICIJ's efforts to tell global stories, be they about economic inequality such as tax avoidance or an absence of medical oversight such as in the 'Implant Files', highlight another change in journalism from the 20th to 21st century: the story largely determines the medium rather than the platform determining how the story is told, as was the convention of the past. *The Sydney Morning Herald's* investigative reporter Kate McClymont (2017, interview with the author, 16 March) argues that with so many different ways to present an investigation, the art of storytelling and of thinking creatively about how to tell the story, whether it be print, podcast, or interactive visualisation, has become more important. In this way, practitioners have become more platform-agnostic than ever when it comes to telling their stories.

> I think that the digitalisation of the media has made all of us, even investigative journalists, realise the importance of telling a story. It's no good to, you know, put in ten company names. You have to tell a compelling story. I think that it's just one of those fabulous things now that there are so many ways you could make a story interesting. Also, you can divert readers off in to little byways by connecting to a previous story . . . those things are really important now and I think that perhaps in the past we didn't appreciate it enough.

The Australian editor of *The Guardian*, Lenore Taylor (2017, interview with the author, 6 July), agreed that journalists need to 'be much more aware and alive to telling stories, other than using just words'. They need to think about how they should be using 'visuals, using data, using graphics, using other ways of storytelling intertwined with words', she said.

In the United States since 2006, the Pulitzer Prizes have produced innovative digital investigative projects, which coincide with the eligibility criteria changes of award categories. In 2009, for example, the *Las Vegas Sun* used video, interactives, and documents to reveal that construction workers were dying at a rate of one every six weeks on building sites along the Las Vegas Strip. Among the 2012 winning entries, the New Orleans *Times-Picayune* used a blog to visually tell the story of the devastation of Hurricane Katrina. In 2012, *The Seattle Times* won the Pulitzer for employing data journalism using 'computerised analysis of death certificates, hospitalisation records and poverty data'. It found Washington State used methadone to treat chronic pain patients that led to 99 deaths, disproportionally in the poorer areas of the state.

While data journalism has been around for several decades, particularly in the United States, in the digital age these tools are being used to provide evidence for readers to verify stories for themselves. For example, for a 2016 National Pulitzer Prize–winning story, *The Washington Post* created a national database with interactive graphics to illustrate how often police shoot to kill and that few were held to account for thousands of deaths.

Sweden's Sveriges Television's Helena Bengtsson (2016, interview with the author, 24 September) explains the rise of data journalism in investigative reporting:

> For the first 10 years I was the strange girl in the corner doing Excel. There were very people in Sweden in all of Europe . . . doing data journalism, or computer assisted reporting as we called it back then. Not until 2010/11 did it really take off. The US has had a solid database interest since early 1990s . . . but even in the US in 2010 something happened, and it exploded. Visualisations really took speed then, you got different tools to work with and all of a sudden, the developer community started to get interested in that.

Crowdsourcing Stories

Other award-winning developments identified in the data include making the audience centre stage in both storytelling (gathering information) and dissemination of the reportage through social media sharing. In Britain, for example, *The Guardian* has used crowdsourcing on several investigations, its most famous involving the uploading of half a million documents in 2009 to allow its readers to scrutinise politicians' work-related expenses. While it was scooped on the MP expenses story by its rival *Daily Telegraph*, it did win 'reporter of the year' award in 2009 for another crowdsourcing story. Paul Lewis used Twitter and closed-circuit television (CCTV) footage to crowdsource information to show that a newspaper street seller, Ian Tomlinson, died during the G20 protests when he was pushed to the ground by a police officer. Police initially denied this version of events until the data showed otherwise and the officer, Simon Harwood, was prosecuted for manslaughter. He was found not guilty but was sacked from the police force for gross misconduct. Similarly, in Australia, Linton Besser was awarded the 2010 investigative journalism Walkley Award for exposing the Department of Defence's spending of millions of dollars on luxury items unrelated to its defence role. The *SMH* built a database to invite the public to trawl through more than 70,000 defence contracts and report anomalies. In the United States, the *Tampa Bay Times*, in collaboration with the *Herald-Tribune* in Florida, was awarded for its multimedia storytelling techniques that invited readers to interact through social media by using preselected quotes to quickly tweet by clicking on them. The ICIJ also uses social media more for disseminating stories than for gathering information. Hamish Boland-Rudder (2016, interview with the author, 29 August) explains:

> Social media does play a part in the investigative reporting, there
> may be a historic Facebook post from a source here or there that
> could be interesting. But, primarily for us it's dissemination, and I'm
> the first to say; we need to put a lot more resource into it.

Through these examples we see how social media extends the capacity for journalists to find information quickly, share stories, and include its readers in these processes. Thus, what we see is that the same social media tools that allow 'fake news' unprecedented reach are also be used by investigative reporters to instead interrogate claims and provide evidence in news stories.

Conclusion

The transition from single-newsroom investigative journalism to collaborations; the use of multimedia, data, and crowdsourcing in storytelling; and the continued prominence of established mastheads with institutional power suggest that despite challenging economic conditions that have triggered significant industry restructure, quality investigative journalism has not been lost in the digital age. Rather, the cross-national research in this chapter suggests that the industry has adapted to these changing conditions through developing innovative approaches to investigative work that enables journalists to fulfil their monitorial function in society and to promote their brands, albeit as a collective, by producing groundbreaking global stories. Specifically, this chapter has focused on collaboration—across outlets, media formats, and borders, and with non-media partners like academia—as a means to mitigate the pressures journalists face to produce quality investigative reporting. There are obvious benefits to working collaboratively for the reporters involved: the sharing of costs and information; increased story reach and a strengthened ability to set the news agenda; and the potential for more comprehensive or complex reporting on a grander, even global scale like the Panama Papers. In this way, investigative collaborations can be seen as a powerful antidote to declining revenues and falling journalist numbers as we move deeper into the 21st century. Moreover, while decades of scholarship have established the important watchdog role played by investigative journalism, in a 'post-truth' era featuring declining trust in media, quality investigative work that serves the public may be increasingly vital to preserve both public trust and editorial quality. Collaborations exemplify one way to sustain this journalistic role.

However, collaborative work does come with associated costs. This research suggests that a rise in collaborative journalism may be associated with a drop in the diversity of investigative story genres over time, particularly in the Australian context where news media ownership is very concentrated and there are fewer outlets. Collaboration is also associated with higher levels of syndication, which has the dual outcomes of increasing story reach but simultaneously decreasing media diversity. The shift in investigative practice from a more pluralistic investigative journalism marked by rivalry between single outlets towards larger-scale, cross-outlet, and transnational collaborative work potentially brings with it a drop in inter-media competition, although the diversity of winners represented across the three national awards examined here to date suggests a healthy breadth of quality investigative work. Local investigation might also come at the expense of national and transnational investigations as watchdog reporting scales up. Yet, despite these actual or potential drawbacks to the rise in collaborative investigate journalism, the findings in this chapter demonstrate that collaboration provides a novel way for news media to negate challenging structural changes within the industry, while still producing detailed and valuable journalism in the public interest. Further, the Australian data signalled a small but detectable rise in single-issue investigations, perhaps at the expense of systemic inquiry, and collaboration is a way forward to negate this regressive trend. Indeed, the slight rise in the total number of investigative winners across the time period under examination further indicates that investigative journalism continues to be produced and celebrated into the digital age. It also shows, as theoretically argued in Chapter 3, and as Hamilton (2016) has identified, the public interest function of journalism and its political economic objectives need not be mutually exclusive. Collaboration represents a useful tool for journalists to continue to do investigative work that serves as a critical aspect of their normative functions *and* supports their 'quality' branding claims. This chapter finds that while digital disruption has led to formidable challenges for newsrooms and the public sphere, particularly in the form of revenue losses and fake news, it also heralds unprecedented opportunities for large-scale collaborative investigative journalism. The next chapter explores in more detail the role of data in journalism and use of digital technologies that assist collaboration, and how these developments can mitigate some of the challenges to media freedom in democracies in contemporary times.

Notes

1. This chapter was based on a journal article: Andrea Carson & Kate Farhall (2018) Understanding Collaborative Investigative Journalism in a 'Post-Truth' Age, *Journalism Studies*, 19:13, 1899–1911, https://doi.org/10.1080/14616 70X.2018.1494515. It has been revised and updated and presented here with the permission of the co-author and publisher.
2. In 2017, the Press Awards had 30 categories and averages 600 entries (print and online). The Walkley Awards offered 34 categories (across all media) and

averaged 1,400 entries. The Pulitzers had 14 journalism awards (print and online) and averaged 1,100 entries.
3. Further data were gathered from the year 2000 for the Pulitzers and since the inception of the Walkleys in 1956. This larger database is useful for understanding benchmarks for reporting trends over time and is used in this chapter as a reference tool.
4. The British Journalism Awards—established in 2012 in response to the Leveson Inquiry—were not studied here but the awards did honour the BBC and *The Guardian* in 2017 for its reporting of the Panama Papers.

References

Allcott, H & Gentzkow, M 2017, 'Social media and fake news in the 2016 election', *Journal of Economic Perspectives*, 31(2), 211–36.

Bakir, V & McStay, A 2017, 'Fake news and the economy of emotions: Problems, causes, solutions', *Digital Journalism*, 6(2), 154–75.

Carson A 2013, '*Investigative Journalism, the Public Sphere and Democracy:* The watchdog role of Australian broadsheets in the digital age' PhD diss., University of Melbourne, accessed 1 December 2013, from https://minerva-access.unimelb.edu.au/handle/11343/38200.

Carson A & Farhall, K 2018, 'Understanding collaborative investigative journalism in a "post-truth" age', *Journalism Studies*, 19(13), 1899–1911.

Conboy, M 2002, *The Press and Popular Culture*, Sage, London.

Cooke, N A 2017, 'Post-truth, truthiness, and alternative facts: Information behavior and critical information consumption for a new age', *Library Quarterly*, 87(3), 211–21.

Curran, J 2005, *Media and Power*, Routledge, London.

Cvetkovska, S, Belford, A, Silverman, C & Lester Feder, J 2018, 'The secret players behind Macedonia's fake news sites', *OCCRP*, 18 July, accessed 15 February 2019, from www.occrp.org/en/spooksandspin/the-secret-players-behind-mace donias-fake-news-sites.

Dimock, M, Doherty, C & Tyson, A 2013, 'Amid criticism, support for media's 'watchdog' role stands out', *Pew Research Center*, accessed 5 March 2016, from http://assets.pewresearch.org/wp-content/uploads/sites/5/legacy-pdf/8-8-2013% 20Media%20Attitudes%20Release.pdf.

Downie, L Jr & Schudson, M 2009, 'The reconstruction of American journalism', *Columbia Journalism Review*, Accessed 1 May 2013, from https://archives.cjr.org/reconstruction/the_reconstruction_of_american.php

Hamilton, JT 2016, *Democracy's Detectives: The Economics of Investigative Journalism*, Harvard University Press, Cambridge.

Henningham, J 1990, *Issues in Australian Journalism*, Longman Cheshire Pty Limited, Melbourne.

Herman, ES & Chomsky, N 2002, *Manufacturing Consent: The Political Economy of the Mass Media*, Pantheon, New York.

Hughes, HM 1940, *News and the Human Interest Story*, University of Chicago Press, Chicago.

Kaplan, D 2013, *Global Investigative Journalism: Strategies for Support*, Center for International Media Assistance, Washington.

Lippmann, W 1922, *Public Opinion*, Harcourt, New York.

Mihailidis, P & Viotty, S 2017, 'Spreadable spectacle in digital culture: Civic expression, fake news and the role of media literacies in "post-fact" society', *American Behavioral Scientist*, 61(4), 441–54.

Mitchell, A & Holcomb, J 2016, 'State of the news media 2016', *Pew Research Center*, June, accessed 1 March 2017, from https://assets.pewresearch.org/wp-content/uploads/sites/13/2016/06/30143308/state-of-the-news-media-report-2016-final.pdf.

Mitchell, A, Holcomb, J & Barthel, M 2016, 'Many Americans believe fake news is sowing confusion', *Pew Research Centre*, 15 December, accessed 1 March 2017, from https://www.journalism.org/2016/12/15/many-americans-believe-fake-news-is-sowing-confusion/.

Mitchell A, Gottfried, J, Barthel, M & Shearer, E 2016, 'The modern news consumer: News attitudes and practices in the digital age', *Pew Research Center*, 7 July, accessed 1 March 2017, from https://www.journalism.org/2016/07/07/the-modern-news-consumer/.

Mott, FL 1962, *American Journalism: A History, 1690–1960*, Macmillan, New York.

Schudson, M 1978, *Discovering the News: A Social History of American Newspapers*, Basic Books, New York.

Schudson, M 2008, *Why Democracies Need an Unlovable Press*, Polity Press, Cambridge.

Solon, O 2016, 'Facebook's failure: Did fake news and polarized politics get Trump elected?', *The Guardian*, November 11.

6 New Frontiers
Big Data, Leaks, and Large-Scale Investigative Journalism

> Investigative journalism is where the heart of innovation has happened in journalism. We have the engagement of people now who are skillful in data and computer science encryption technology methods. There are not enough of them, but we have that now as a part of this field which we didn't have before.
>
> (Emily Bell 2017, interview with the author, 14 March)

Introduction

Words are basic tools of journalism, but numbers tell stories too. In the 21st century, technology has given journalists unprecedented ability to inform their stories through ready access to numbers and data. Computers, the internet, and smartphones have become primary tools of journalistic research.

As technologies have advanced, we have gained easy access to big data along with invaluable tools for more comprehensive and precise analysis of datasets. Thus, we have easier and more accessible pathways to understanding our social and physical environments through the collection and analysis of data. Investigative journalists, and investigative journalism, have been major beneficiaries of these advances. And if we accept the maxim that investigative journalism is a force for good in a democratic society, then it follows that society has benefitted from such advances in technology as well, at least in this context. Indeed, Sir Tim Berners-Lee, inventor of the World Wide Web, says data-driven journalism is the future. 'These are the people whose jobs are to interpret what government is doing to the people. [It's] going to be about poring over data and equipping yourself with the tools to analyse it and picking out what's interesting' (cited in Hughes 2013, p. 43).

The focus of this chapter is largely positive, examining how investigative journalists use mass data leaks and digital tools to collaborate and expose abuses of power. I also consider how big data can have negative impacts such as breaching privacy through mass data surveillance, which can hamper press freedom.

This chapter begins with a short history of data journalism, including its roots in computer-assisted reporting (CAR), and progresses to comparative case studies of the three most famous mega data leaks in recent journalism history: *WikiLeaks*, Edward Snowden's National Security Agency (NSA) revelations, and the International Consortium of Investigative Journalism's (ICIJ) Panama Papers. These examples reveal emblematic shifts in uses of data and different models of transnational investigative collaborations. I show the extent to which the organisation of collaborative investigative journalism is changing and highlight mainstream media's role in supporting (and criticising) these large-scale investigations during a transformative period for news media.

I do not examine methods of data journalism in detail; rather, the aim is to explain why big data is a new frontier for investigative journalism, which increasingly utilises social science research methods to expose wrongdoing in the public interest. The comparative cases all use large, secret datasets as their primary *source* and mobilise global networks of journalists (and media organisations) as their *method* to produce investigative news stories. Understanding the evolution of this global model is important because of the capacity for investigative journalism to promote transparency and strengthen democratic accountability in times of declining levels of press freedom and media resources.

This emerging global media watchdog model is not without challenges. They include shifting legal and political paradigms and technology enabling greater surveillance of journalists (and the whistleblowers who inform them), as well as diminishing funding to support investigations. The next section briefly details some of these challenges before moving on to examine how data, digital technologies, and collaboration provide new opportunities for global watchdog journalism.

21st-Century Challenges to the Media's Right to Know

Since the terrorist attacks in the United States on 11 September 2001, an international debate has intensified involving trade-offs between national security, the value of individual privacy, and the media's right to know. While these debates remain active, many democratic countries in Europe, North American, Australia, and elsewhere have tightened or remade laws to enable greater state surveillance, greater limits on media freedom, and the prosecution of whistleblowers in the name of fighting terrorism (for detailed analyses, see Lyon 2015; Greenwald 2014; Lidberg and Muller 2018). Australia's former independent national security legislation monitor, Bret Walker (2016), argued that in this context governments had developed an instinct to 'conceal and not to reveal'. Walker, whose oversight role was abolished when the Australian government strengthened its counterterrorism laws in 2014, cited Australia 'with more laws than any other in the name of counter-terrorism'. Lynch et al. (2015, p. 3) counted

64 separate pieces of anti-terrorism legislation at the end of 2014, mostly influenced by Britain's counterterrorism initiatives. These have expanded state power to bolster national security intelligence agencies and increase the capacity for democratic governments to limit public interest reporting (Pearson and Fernandez 2018, p. 64).

Authoritarian states also have leveraged heightened national security concerns to crack down on journalistic activity. Australian foreign correspondent Peter Greste experienced first-hand what can happen to reporters if they do not follow the official government line. Greste spent 400 days in an Egyptian jail in 2014 after he and two of his *Al Jazeera* colleagues were accused by the Egyptian government of spreading false news and supporting the blacklisted Muslim Brotherhood. A year after his prison release following a presidential decree, Greste said: 'Once you use the T word [terrorism] governments get away with things they normally would not' (Greste 2016).

On anti-terrorism, Australia has followed a similar approach to liberal democracies that share intelligence in the Five Eyes group: United Kingdom, United States, Canada, New Zealand, and Australia (Lidberg and Muller 2018). Critics like journalist Glenn Greenwald (2014, p. 210) argue anti-terrorist measures have occurred in a political environment whereby established news institutions too often abdicate their roles as watchdogs. Instead they become subservient to their governments in the name of fighting terrorism. Universally, media freedom has been eroded post-9/11.

The World Press Freedom Index reflects this tightening of media freedom across every continent, most notably in democratic Europe. The index identified that Malta, the Czech Republic, Serbia, and Slovakia had recorded four of the five biggest deteriorations in media freedom across the globe in 2018 (Reporters without Borders 2018).

Reporters without Borders, an international non-profit organisation dedicated to journalistic freedom, counted a record 80 journalist deaths in 2018 in connection with their work, while hundreds more were detained or imprisoned (Reporters without Borders 2018). Of the reporters killed, half were deliberately targeted by forces opposed to media freedom. The widely publicised murder of *Washington Post* columnist Jamal Khashoggi by Saudi operatives in Turkey in October 2018 was one tragic example of the contemporary dangers of practising certain types of journalism.

Notably, the United States dropped from 43rd to 45th in the Reporters without Borders world rankings in 2018. This was largely attributed to President Donald Trump's open hostility towards journalists and his frequent use of the term 'fake news' to try to delegitimise their work. The report authors argued this political behaviour was having a contagion effect across the globe. They wrote: 'More and more democratically-elected leaders no longer see the media as part of democracy's essential underpinning, but as an adversary to which they openly display their aversion'.

Freedom House came to similar conclusions in its 2017 press freedom report, in which it said press freedom had declined to its lowest levels in 13 years, with only 13 per cent of the world's press now considered free. It also singled out the US president for making a weapon out of the 'fake news' label and for labelling the news media as the 'enemies of the people'—a phrase of former Soviet dictator Joseph Stalin. In its press freedom rankings, Freedom House placed the United States at 23rd, one place behind Australia and two places ahead of Britain. While each of these Five Eye countries is considered to have a free media overall, each has extended its state security apparatus in ways that cause concern for the practice of investigative journalism this century.

One example of this is the British Parliament's passing of the Investigatory Powers Act 2016, dubbed the Snoopers' Charter, which permits the 'bulk hack' of computers, networks, mobile devices, servers, and interference of software to extract information by the state's police forces and intelligence services. While a warrant is required and the Investigatory Powers Commissioner (IPC) oversees the use of these investigatory powers (Burgess 2017), this law has the capacity to compromise journalists' sources because reporters would not know if they were being watched, which could 'discourage investigative journalism' (Freedom House 2017). In 2018, the UK high court ruled that the legislation violated EU law. It was amended to include a definition of 'serious crime' as an act that could attract a 12-month jail term. Authorisation for access to data also needed approval by a judicial commissioner (Paterson 2018, p. 26). Civil rights groups argue the changes are inadequate for protecting rights to privacy and freedom of expression (Liberty 2018).

Another example is the Australian government's passage of the National Security Legislation Amendment Bill (No. 1) 2014, under which journalists and whistleblowers could face ten years in jail for reporting intelligence operations—with no public interest defence (Pearson 2014). This was amended in 2018 to allow journalists and their editors a capacity to argue a 'public interest' defense. Further, a 2015 law compelling telecommunication companies to store user metadata for two years could hamper journalists' interactions with sources. In 2016, federal police lawfully accessed (without a warrant) the communications metadata of *Guardian* Australia journalist Paul Farrell to hunt for his story's sources after he wrote about covert asylum seeker boat turn-backs in Indonesian waters (Farell 2017). Australian lawmakers in late 2018 cited heightened terrorism and criminal activity as the motivation for passing a law to compel technology companies to grant police and security agencies access to encrypted messages on platforms such as WhatsApp (BBC 2018).

In the United States, Edward Snowden revealed to the world, through National Security Agency (NSA) document leaks in 2013, how easy it was in the big data age for democratic governments to undertake mass surveillance of citizens without their knowledge. Surveillance is a major threat to investigative journalists. Snowden's release of restricted documents belonging to the UK's signal intelligence agency, Government Communications Headquarters (GCHQ), proved media watchdogs around the globe were being watched. The agency harvested emails of journalists from the BBC, Reuters, *The Guardian, The New York Times, Le Monde, The Sun*, NBC, and *The Washington Post*. One leaked report outlining a GCHQ security assessment listed 'investigative journalists' as a threat alongside terrorists and hackers (Ball 2015). President Barack Obama eventually responded to the leaks by urging an end to the NSA's bulk data collection (Tiffen 2019).

Paterson (2018) argues investigative journalism cannot exist unless the public has confidence that journalists can protect their sources. He identifies three ways in which digital technologies are used to hinder the work of journalists: technologies that disclose an individual's physical location and movements, such as GPS trackers; technologies that undermine anonymity in public places, such as facial recognition technologies; and technologies that undermine the security of data as it is stored or communicated.

Investigative journalists have responded to these challenges by adapting their newsgathering methods. Australian ABC investigative reporter Linton Besser (2017, interview with the author, 16 March) said:

> If I'm calling a public servant, I don't use my phone or any phone connected with me, never use email, never do anything like that. I've got a relationship with one source, for instance, where we write letters to each other. But I can't even send my letters to his address; I've got to send them to a friend of his address, and not put his name on the envelope, but a made-up name.

On a story about cybersecurity, Besser left his mobile phone in his hotel room to prevent his physical movements being traced. Yet what concerns him most when researching sensitive stories is getting sources to understand the risks of disclosing secret state information.

> Sources don't actually understand. The problem is they call you. I got a call, it was a federal public servant wanting to blow the whistle on something. And I had to say to her, you can't call me. And, of course, she completely freaked out, realising what she'd done. I think now I've probably scared her off from ever doing it. And it was just the first call.
> (2017, interview with the author, 16 March)

Former investigative reporter Ross Coulthart (2011, interview with the author, 28 December) said a hostile legal environment meant reporters needed institutional media support:

> Unfortunately, the [Australian] defamation laws are prohibitive, and it is frightening to run a legal case, you know it's probably about a

quarter of a million (dollars) to defend yourself for one week. . . . I wouldn't dream of doing a story, publishing a story as a freelancer unless I was given an indemnity by the organisation that publishes it.

The Evolution of Data Journalism

Data journalism has existed as a genre of reporting since the 1990s, an era when it was more likely to be referred to as computer-assisted reporting (CAR). The tradition of using computers to assist with reporting originated in the United States in the late 1960s, and initially grew slowly before a milestone in 1989 with the establishment of the National Institute for Computer-Assisted Reporting (Hewett 2013, p. 3). An early example of CAR for investigative reporting was when *Miami Herald* reporter Philip Meyer used a mainframe computer to analyse the educational backgrounds of rioters in Detroit (Hughes 2013, p. 44). After completing a Nieman Fellowship at Harvard, Meyer was interested in applying the scientific method to journalism and would go on to promote the use of statistical methods in reporting in his 1973 book *Precision Journalism* (Hewett 2013, p. 6). Meyer found college students were as likely as high school dropouts to have participated in the riots, allowing him to draw public attention to the bigger story of racial prejudice and inequality.

The term CAR had outlived its usefulness by the third millennium, when Meyer urged peers to abandon it: 'CAR is an embarrassing reminder that we are entering the twenty-first century as the only profession in which computer users feel the need to call attention to themselves', he wrote (1999, p. 4). Data journalism gained momentum in the 1990s, with some US mastheads employing investigative journalists who had become experienced data reporters (Hewett 2013, p. 5). Among them were the former executive director of Investigators Reporters and Editors (IRE), Brant Houston, and another was US/UK journalist Heather Brooke, who found Britain lagged the United States in availability of public datasets (Hewett 2013, p. 6).

The first training centre for data journalism in Britain, the Centre for Investigative Journalism, was established in 2003 and run by US investigative reporter Gavin MacFadyen (Hewett 2013, p. 4). By the mid-2000s journalism educators at tertiary institutions on both sides of the Atlantic were beginning to offer data journalism subjects and courses. British journalists began campaigning for greater access to public data through the 'free our data campaign' and using freedom of information requests when it was not easily accessible (Hewett 2013, p. 11). Hewett observed that even as late as 2008, other than in areas like business reporting, many British journalists were not using data analysis. By 2010, the power of data was highlighted when *The Guardian* collaborated with *WikiLeaks* to report on secret classified US military files that would tell the true cost of lost civilian lives in the wars in Afghanistan and Iraq.

In Australia, we see a somewhat different picture on the uptake of data journalism. Wright and Doyle's (2018) study of Australian data journalism found it was uncommon in newsrooms until about 2011. Of the small number of journalists (nine) who regularly undertook data journalism, most were self-taught with different ideas about what it was. Significant cutbacks to Australia's major newsrooms in 2012 (see Chapter 1) curbed the practice of data journalism. There were fewer ambitious crowdsourced projects and more simpler stories using data for explanatory (rather than exploratory) storytelling (Wright and Doyle 2018, p. 10). Some data specialists had their roles diluted to include duties not involving data. Funding for professional training was also uncommon. Yet, Wright and Doyle (2018) found a keenness for data journalism existed, with reporters collaborating to advance skills within their news organisation (Fairfax Media) and externally with non-profit organisations (*The Guardian* Australia). Collaboration is an important theme for the endurance of investigative journalism in this book, and the thin practice of data journalism in Australia is partly overcome through collaboration.

Data Technologies and Methods

The annual data journalism awards founded by the Global Editors Network (GEN) in 2012 highlight the increasing extent to which journalists worldwide are using data and new technologies such as virtual reality (VR) and artificial intelligence (AI) methods such as machine learning and natural language processing in their reporting. In 2017, the awards received 630 entries (up from 471 entries in 2016) from 58 countries, representing five continents (Global Editors Network (GEN) 2018). About a quarter of these entries were for investigations. As expected from the historical development of data journalism, the United States has dominated the entries with 142 submissions, almost double the number from Britain with 75, Canada 29, Germany 23, Brazil 17, France 15, Spain 14, and Australia 13 (Global Editors Network (GEN) 2016). Studies show collaboration is a critical feature of the award entries. Most entries averaged five authors, and one third had external partners (Loosen et al. 2017, p. 8).

The entries reveal the range of skills acquired by investigative journalists, from basic data analysis for reporting to advanced statistical analysis, augmented reality storytelling, and the use of machine learning. Many use software for visualising and mapping data using digital tools including Tableau, Gephi, OutWit Hub, Google Fusion Tables, and NodeXL. Journalists also trawl data to find people in stories using free search tools like Picodash, YouTube DataViewer, and reverse image programs like TinEye (Carson 2016).

Social network analysis (SNA) from data scrapping of social media sites might be best placed to show who is influential in shaping political opinion online. Databases can be open to crowdsourcing campaigns to use the power of numbers to overcome time-intensive tasks. The largest example to date was 'Electionland'. Led by *ProPublica*, it involved 1,100 journalists and students working together to map the growing problem of voter suppression during the 2016 US presidential election, and the 2018 midterm elections. It used social media verification techniques to expose acts of voter suppression, yielding hundreds of stories each day. The impact was quick: many voters denied access to the ballot had their rights restored in several states.

As will be shown in the following case studies, combining big data analysis with collaboration enables journalists to continue to overcome some of the challenges to the media's right to expose wrongdoing on a global scale. But it also presents ethical questions about the merits of redacting information to protect individual privacy and the consequences of radical transparency, which involves actions and approaches that radically increase the openness of organisational processes and data.

WikiLeaks

WikiLeaks, founded by Australian Julian Assange, is an important case study in the development of a 'connective publishing' model of investigative journalism using data, data journalism, and collaboration. Dreyfus and Hrafnsson (2013) define connective publishing as a model for collaborative publishing between media outlets whereby individual publishers in each country are connected with a larger whole. In the case of *WikiLeaks*' largest data dump, 'Cablegate' in 2010, the whole was the archive of US diplomatic cables.

Published six years before the Panama Papers, at 1.73 gigabytes, Cablegate was the largest leak in the history of journalism since the leak of the Pentagon Papers in 1971 (Greenberg 2016). By comparison, the Panama Papers was a hundred times bigger.

To publish Cablegate, *WikiLeaks* worked with a handful of established media partners including *The Guardian*. *WikiLeaks* expanded its offering to other media outlets shortly after the first stories appeared. At its peak, it had 89 media organisations from 50 nations trawling through its classified files to find stories relevant to each organisation's country of origin (Dreyfus and Hrafnsson 2013, p. 41). This was an early example of connective publishing, using data journalism in collaboration with traditional media to tell a global story (of international diplomacy) with local news angles made possible by the involvement of reporters from different nations. It was not to last. The relationships between Assange and his media partners, and between some of his media partners, faltered. However, the build-up to and publication of Cablegate provided important lessons about the various forms that large-scale collaborative investigation could take.

WikiLeaks' move towards a connective publishing model was an important precursor to understanding the 2016 Panama Papers publishing model. Both Cablegate and the Panama Papers involved collaboration with established media, and relied on various custom-made digital tools to parse (or technically analyse) enormous databases to find pertinent local stories involving a global narrative that challenged power. But they also differed in important ways. Power networks within the *WikiLeaks* model were less diffuse and more contested, as revealed by the eventual partnership collapses, compared to the ICIJ (Panama Papers) and NSA partnerships. There was also ambiguity about Assange's role: Was he a source or a journalistic partner? This was further complicated by Assange's attitudes towards redaction of sensitive material and his preference for radical transparency or 'sunshine' journalism. This conflicted with established media outlets that saw their roles as gatekeepers with the responsibility to make 'careful choices about responsibly publishing the material we considered to be of public interest' (Rusbridger 2018, p. 250) Assange's initial approach to data, and by extension data journalism, supported sunshine journalism, where the original documents on which a story are based are provided in full, usually online, and unredacted (Dreyfus and Hrafnsson 2013, 41). The ICIJ and its partners, and *The Guardian* and others' use of the NSA leaks, did not follow this more radical approach to data.

Why Involve Mainstream Media?

Assange had no difficulty attracting leaks when he first began publishing online in 2006. So why did he change *WikiLeaks* from a lone wolf operation, publishing raw data, to one involving media organisations in producing journalistic stories from the data? Or, to use the words of Australian media proprietor Eric Beecher, why move from being a warehouse to a retailer? Beecher, who believes the activities of *WikiLeaks* were not journalism, argued:

> They are an electronic warehouse. They make it very, very easy for anyone who has information to deposit that information anonymously into their warehouse. Once it is in the warehouse, they have a distribution system and they take it off the shelf and decide what to do with it.
>
> (Beecher 2011, interview with the author, 15 February)

Australian academic Robert Manne, who corresponded with Assange when he was a largely unknown computer hacker, provides some of the answer for why Assange sought media partnerships. Assange had revealed many internationally significant events between 2006 and 2009 in the developing world. These included an Islamist assassination order from Somalia, widespread corruption and killings in Kenya, an oil spill in Peru, and dumping of toxic waste off the Ivory Coast by the Trafigura Group, among other atrocities (Manne 2011, p. 229).

In established democracies, *WikiLeaks* also revealed tax avoidance by Swiss Bank Julius Baer; American intelligence insights on the battle of Fallujah; Australia's internet censorship lists; Britain's 'Climategate' emails, alleging misconduct within the climate science community; and the unusual lending practices of the Icelandic bank Kaupthing weeks before the Icelandic financial collapse (Manne 2011, p. 229).

These were significant revelations. Yet Assange, according to Manne and others (Poterfield 2012), felt his leaks were not receiving the global coverage they deserved. Assange blamed the political and economic priorities of the established media and their overriding commercial imperatives. He wrote of his frustrations to his volunteers:

> WikiLeaks' unreported material is only the most visible wave on an ocean of truth rotting in draws [sic] of the fourth estate, waiting for a lobby to subsidize its revelation into a profitable endeavour.
>
> (Manne 2011, p. 220)

Assange's long-held contemptuous view of commercial media as vehicles for capitalism, a political economy perspective, conflicted somewhat with his recognition of their value to his enterprise: that his leaks had greater impact after receiving mainstream coverage. *The Guardian*'s stories about *WikiLeaks*' Kenyan revelations in 2007 were a prime example of how mainstream media coverage could increase the reach and impact of *WikiLeaks* (Poterfield 2012, p. 57). Perhaps mindful of this, Assange began establishing formal relations with mainstream media.

WikiLeaks as Investigative Journalism?

Academics and journalists have engaged in spirited debate about whether *WikiLeaks*' revelations could, or should, be defined as investigative reporting. Scholars Terry Flew and Jason Wilson (2012) argued that *WikiLeaks*' revelations constituted investigative reporting because they disclosed information that others sought to keep hidden (Flew and Wilson 2012, p. 175). The late Evan Whitton, a prominent Australian investigative journalist (2012), agreed that *WikiLeaks* was investigative reporting because, using the most basic definition, 'it exposed wrongdoing' (Whitton 2012, interview with the author, 8 February). In 2011, the Australian Walkley Board concurred. It awarded *WikiLeaks* the prize for most outstanding contribution to Australian journalism for delivering an 'avalanche of inconvenient truths' (Walkley Foundation 2012).

But Ross Coulthart disagreed with the assessment of *WikiLeaks* as journalism: 'I have got very strong views about this and I disagreed with the Walkley [Board] giving Julian Assange a journalism award. I feel very, very strongly that Julian Assange is a source' (Coulthart 2011).

The involvement of the established press unquestionably changed the style and presentation of the stories exposed by the *WikiLeaks* source documents. The verification and context added to the source information and transformed the leaks from raw data (information) to journalism. At this point, many of those stories began to fit within the operative definition of investigative journalism used in this book (see Chapter 2). Journalists researched the background information for story context and sought interviews with relevant figures to verify details in the leaks. The institutional media also expanded the audience reach of stories. For example, the staggered release of the 250,000 diplomatic files that formed Cablegate on 29 November 2010 drew more than four million unique viewers to *The Guardian*'s website. At the time, it was *The Guardian*'s largest single day of traffic ever (Ellison 2011).

From 'Collateral Murder' to 'Cablegate'

In April 2010 *WikiLeaks* released a classified US military video taken in July 2007 from an Apache helicopter during the Iraq War (*WikiLeaks* 2011). Assange labelled the video 'Collateral Murder', and its contents were shocking. The footage showed US soldiers in Baghdad indiscriminately firing on civilians, including two Reuters news wire staff. It bears witness to the killings of a dozen people, including a man attempting to help the injured, and the wounding of his two children (*WikiLeaks* 2011a). The audio revealed US soldiers laughing in the aircraft (*WikiLeaks* 2011b). At the time, the Pentagon covered up the event (Dreyfus and Hrafnsson 2013, p. 39). The US military concluded that 'the actions of the soldiers were in accordance with the law of armed conflict and its own "Rules of Engagement"' (*WikiLeaks* 2011a). Assange presented 'Collateral Murder' first at the National Press Club in Washington, DC, and followed up with an appearance on *The Colbert Report* (Ellison 2011). In doing so, he had another powerful experience of what mainstream media coverage could do for the reach and impact of stories contained within the *WikiLeaks*' data warehouse.

Assange had the world's attention and more leaks to offer. Three months after 'Collateral Murder', in July 2010, *WikiLeaks* co-published with mainstream media the 'Afghan War Diary, 2004–2010'. It teamed up with four established mainstream media outlets, including *The New York Times*, *The Guardian* newspaper and Channel 4 television in Britain, and Germany's weekly newspaper *Der Spiegel* (Ellison 2011). After *WikiLeaks*' second (Iraq files) and third tranche of documents (Cablegate), it added more names to its stable of publishing partnerships: France's *Le Monde* and Spain's *El País* newspapers; television stations *Al Jazeera* (Doha) and Swedish public broadcaster SVT; London's non-profit

Bureau of Investigative Journalism; and non-media partners such as the non-governmental organisation (NGO) Iraq Body Count and Public Interest Lawyers (Dreyfus and Hrafnsson 2013, p. 40).

'The Afghan War Diary, 2004–2010' consisted of more than 76,000 documents written by coalition soldiers about the war. These leaks were provided to *WikiLeaks* by junior US intelligence analyst Private Chelsea (formerly Bradley) Manning, who was arrested in Iraq in May 2010 and was convicted of violations of the US Espionage Act in 2013. In one of his final acts as president, Barack Obama commuted her sentence from 35 years to 7 years.

In October 2010, *WikiLeaks* released the 'Iraq War logs', another of Manning's secret downloads. It consisted of almost 400,000 classified documents about the war from 2004 to 2009, as told by US soldiers, but this time with many names redacted (*WikiLeaks* 2011b). The Iraq War logs showed the civilian death count was perhaps 15,000 higher than officially recorded (Dreyfus and Hrafnsson 2013, p. 40).

These various examples reveal how Assange during 2010 shifted his 'sunshine journalism' lone-wolf model to a connective publishing model. He moved to this cooperative publishing model for several reasons. He had attracted considerable criticism for not redacting what many considered life-endangering information in earlier leaks. His defenders pointed out that, as the head of a small non-profit organisation, he did not have the resources to sift through vast amounts of data to identify the stories that needed redaction. He also needed local expertise to fully appreciate the importance of stories to audiences in different countries (Dreyfus and Hrafnsson 2013, p. 41). Finally, media partnerships with respected outlets generated greater audience reach and public impact.

Leonard Downie Jr and Michael Schudson (2009, p. 11) observed that when investigative journalism was pursued collaboratively with an 'institutional authority' (in this case traditional media with *WikiLeaks*), it guaranteed 'that the work of newsrooms could not be easily ignored'. Institutional collaborations were valuable for these types of public interest stories because they could offer support through money, logistics, and legal services, and heighten audience reach and impact (Schudson and Downie 2009, p. 11). This assessment of the value of working with established media organisations fits with *WikiLeaks*' publishing trajectory, at least up until the point before the partnerships with *The Guardian* and other media ended.

The Breakdown of the WikiLeaks Collaborations

The breakdown occurred for a number of reasons, including disagreements about redaction (Assange continued to publish unredacted material on the website) and personal conflicts involving Assange (see Lundberg 2011; Rusbridger 2018). A catalyst for the breakdown came in February

2011 when *Guardian* journalists David Leigh and Luke Harding published *WikiLeaks: Inside Julian Assange's War on Secrecy*, in which Leigh inadvertently published the encryption key Assange had given him (Mackey et al. 2011). *WikiLeaks* decided to publish the remaining trove of the diplomatic cables unredacted, arguing the cables were already in the public realm because of the security lapse. Assange was heavily criticised for the decision, particularly by his former media partners. According to *The Guardian*, the released unredacted data included more than 1,000 cables containing names of individual activists and 150 whistle-blowers, putting them potentially at risk of harm. *Guardian* journalist James Ball (2015) asserted: 'The decision to publish by Julian Assange was his, and his alone'.

There is an important ongoing debate about Assange's model of radical transparency compared to the mediatisation of big data leaks as evidenced in the cases that follow. These involve journalists applying their professional judgements about what to publish and how it can be published, with context and responsibility, to minimise harm. In 2016, Assange added heat to this debate when DC Leaks (later found to be a Russian-sponsored website) and *WikiLeaks* (weeks later) released 100,000 hacked emails from Hillary Clinton's presidential campaign. The leaks included off-the-record interactions with media and financial and donor information, and revealed the Democratic National Committee's unprofessional lack of neutrality towards the Bernie Sanders campaign. DC Leaks also included lawmakers' personal phone numbers. Followed up by mainstream media, the leaks disrupted Clinton's campaign and communications, requiring contact details to be changed. Clinton, who won the popular vote, partially blamed the leaks for her election loss (Estepa 2017). Assange responded on his website:

> The First Amendment does not privilege old media, with its corporate advertisers and dependencies on incumbent power factions, over WikiLeaks' model of scientific journalism or an individual's decision to inform their friends on social media. The First Amendment unapologetically nurtures the democratization of knowledge. With the Internet, it has reached its full potential.

But with gestures of ultimate transparency come questions of responsibility. Until the issue of redaction is resolved, the tension between transparency and responsibility will persist. Hypothetically, if lives were lost due to the unfiltered publication of names of bystanders and whistleblowers in a radical disclosure, who would be accountable? While it is not the objective here to apply a normative standard, it is important to consider the issue of responsibility within a framework of global collaborative investigative journalism and big data leaks. The early and later examples of *WikiLeaks*, where context and verification are absent, do not fit the operative definition of investigative journalism laid out in Chapter 2. Some of the stories arising from the Iraq and Afghan war logs and Cable-gate files, which utilised journalists to apply investigative skills to verify the raw data, do fit the operative definition and are formative examples of the connective publishing model that has subsequently been broad-ened and deepened by the ICIJ.

Edward Snowden and the NSA Files

In 2013, while working as a contractor for the US National Security Agency, Edward Snowden handed over 58,000 secret documents to investigative journalist Glenn Greenwald and independent documentary filmmaker Laura Poitras (Lyon 2015, p. 17). Snowden is an interesting case study, not least because, unlike Assange, he saw himself as a whistle-blower, not a journalist. But like Assange, he recognised the potential of journalists to achieve maximum public impact and, although possessing the technical skills to release the information himself, he chose not to.

The leaked NSA documents exposed details of three alarming trends: democratic governments were engaging in mass surveillance of their own citizens without their consent; corporations were sharing data about their customers with governments in return for government contracts; and through mobile phone usage and social media participation, citizens were unwittingly providing the NSA and its collaborators with troves of data about themselves.

Greenwald recalled that after seeing the first few documents he knew immediately that he required 'substantial institutional support to do this reporting. This meant involving *The Guardian* . . .' (Greenwald 2014, p. 21).

The Cost of Whistle-Blowing

As Downie and Schudson (2009) predicted about media institutional col-laboration, *The Guardian*'s involvement ensured the story reached a wide audience, although publishing came at a cost for those involved. Like Assange, Snowden was labelled a traitor. He too went into exile (in Rus-sia). Greenwald (2014, p. 218) recalled how his own personal life was trawled through, and he was variously labelled an activist or a polemi-cist rather than a journalist by other journalists. At one point his part-ner, David Marinda, was detained at Britain's Heathrow Airport under Terrorism Act of 2000 powers (Greenwald 2014, p. 242). *The Guard-ian* was threatened with prosecution if it did not destroy computer hard drives and files about GCHQ in Britain (Greenwald 2014, p. 239). These intimidations speak to the difficult reporting environment in the post-9/11 security context discussed at the beginning of this chapter. They also speak to the chaos-control framework outlined in Chapter 3, which, I argue, helps explain why investigative journalism is pursued in the digital age. Some commercial media rivals, including *The Daily Mail* and *The Sun*, were highly critical of *The Guardian*. *The Daily Mail* editorialised that *The Guardian* had helped to produce a 'handbook' for terrorists (Glover 2013). Other commercial outlets, including *The New York Times*, embraced the exposure of state surveillance practices and pursued the story. Sitting in between the philosophical divide—pitting considerations of national security and deference to institutional secrecy against transparency and the public's right to know—was *The Washington Post*. Having won a Pulitzer Prize for publishing the Snowden leaks in 2014, its board editorialised two years later that Snowden should not be pardoned but instead face a criminal trial (*The Washington Post*, 2016). The ambivalence of some legacy media reveals their different motivations for engaging or not engaging with the story, as expected under the chaos-control framework. As Tiffen (2019) concludes, it also shows legacy media no longer monopolise the debate.

The widespread reportage of the leaks, however, achieved what Snowden wished for: greater state transparency. In a letter to Greenwald, Snowden wrote that his purpose was to 'fight to keep the spirit of the press alive and the internet free. I have been to the darkest corners of government, and what they fear is light' (Greenwald 2014, p. 32). In May 2016, Greenwald, who by then had left *The Guardian* and co-founded online global media outlet *The Intercept*, made available Snowden's leaks in a series of uploads, the first being 166 articles of the NSA's internal newsletter, *SIDtoday*. Greenwald urged the public to trawl through the documents, much in the way that *The Guardian* offered its readers details of MPs' expenses as a way to unearth stories (see Chapter 5). As Ryle did at the ICIJ, Greenwald stated that *The Intercept* team redacted some documents 'consistent with the requirements of our agreement with Snowden in a bid to prevent serious harm to innocent individuals' (*The Intercept* 2016). As shown in the previous chapter, crowdsourcing uses the power of human numbers to complete time-intensive tasks to dig deeper into the data. In this way, the audience is invited to be both a consumer and producer of news content in the digital age.

The Panama Papers

The Panama Papers episode began when a whistleblower describing himself as 'John Doe' contacted investigative journalist Bastian Obermayer at the German newspaper *Süddeutsche Zeitung* in late 2014 with the simple message: 'Hello. This is John Doe. Interested in data?' Obermayer responded: 'We're very interested' (Levy 2016).

More than a year later, on the first Sunday of April in 2016, news began to break through traditional and social media that a global network of journalists had forensically sifted through 11.5 million leaked files to expose the offshore financial links of prominent figures including world leaders, celebrities, sporting heroes, and criminals. The investigation was coordinated by the ICIJ, and was dubbed the Panama Papers in reference to the Panama-based law firm, Mossack Fonseca, from which the documents originated. The size of the leak—it included documents held by Mossack Fonseca spanning 40 years—was unprecedented, as was the collaboration of almost 400 journalists representing more than 100 media organisations, working in 21 languages from 80 countries. The code of silence among the reporters was astonishing. For 12 months they had quietly analysed the 2.6 terabytes of leaked data that included emails, financial spreadsheets, passports, and corporate records of more than 200,000 companies, foundations, and trusts. In these files they identified the secret owners of bank accounts and the labyrinth of shell companies hiding funds in 21 offshore tax havens, including Nevada, Hong Kong, and the British Virgin Islands.

While size of the leak was extraordinary, the revelation that super-rich celebrities and leaders of corrupt nations—including Bashar al-Assad of Syria, Russia's Vladimir Putin, and Chinese Communist leaders—were sending trillions of dollars offshore to hide their wealth and avoid tax was less so. To be expected were their attempts to block media coverage, as China had attempted to do, or to deny it as a Western conspiracy, as was Putin's approach. The Russian president, speaking at a media conference in April 2016 in St Petersburg, said the papers were an attempt to destabilise Russia and that although his own name was not found in the files, journalists had smeared the reputations of his 'friends and acquaintances' whose names were listed (Luhn and Harding 2016).

While many of the powerful targets of the Panama Papers predictably tried to block media coverage, what was atypical in this case was that their usual tactics—such as violence, intimidation, censorship, or legal manoeuvres—could not shut down what quickly became a global news story. Transparency theorists label these types of leaks 'radical disclosure'. In this case, a revelatory action by autonomous actors disrupted power relations and its effect was to reconfigure the visibility of incumbent organisations without their consent. It was achieved through 'socio-technical relations' that enable mass digital data and simultaneous reach across the globe (Heemsbergen 2016, p. 144). Just as the mainstream media could not monopolise the debate, nor could the powerful.

The story received coverage in almost every nation. The 11 million documents from a four-decade archive contained interesting and powerful names from many places across the world. Through digital dissemination the story had global coverage, but also, importantly, local appeal or 'newsworthiness'. ICIJ Director Gerard Ryle explained that recruiting journalists locally was important for understanding and conveying the local and global significance of the story:

We saw a lot of data, for instance, from Iceland pretty early on, but we didn't know we had the Prime Minister. It took an Icelandic journalist to come on board for us to realise that a lot of the names we were looking at were actually linked to the collapse of the financial system in Iceland and of course in the end we found three pretty major politicians, including the Prime Minister. So, you have the advantage of numbers and you have the advantage of local knowledge in a way that you would never be able to do that from your own newsroom in one country or, just from, you know, if you're working in one organisation.

(Ryle 2016, interview with the author, 23 September)

The ICIJ through its media partners 'retailed' the wholesale information in the papers as news stories, verified and tailored to be relevant to local audiences while telling a global story of economic inequality. This model extends the connective publishing model of *WikiLeaks*, which was highly critical of the ICIJ's selective approach. Assange tweeted in April 2016: 'The latest, entirely bogus, excuse for the lucrative privatization of #PanamaPapers archive: source protection'. Others, such as British Prime Minister David Cameron, himself named in the archives, also urged the ICIJ to fully release the data to assist authorities to investigate tax evasion and other wrongdoing (DW 2016). The ICIJ responded that it would not make available the full database because this was the most responsible way to protect the initial source of the leak and innocent bystanders named in the data (DW 2016).

On 10 May 2016, the ICIJ released parts of the data archive online for the public to explore aspects of the data and find untold connections. Ryle (*Media Watch* 2016), however, differentiates between the Panama Papers reporting and public use of its database from *WikiLeaks*' data dumps:

We work very differently to *WikiLeaks*. When we get information like this, we believe that you need to apply journalism ethics and journalism practice to the documents, and what's inside the documents, and put context around what we have seen. We don't publish all of the documents. That is our basic business model. We give them to the journalists and we let them find the stories and then report on it. . . . We are now the alternative to *WikiLeaks*. It is a different model.

Cultural Chaos: The Power of Global Journalism

The Panama Papers is an example of 'cultural chaos at its most progressive and democratising', according to McNair (2016, n.p.). Certainly, the chaos model accounts for the demonstrable limited exercise of elites' control of public messaging because of interruptions to global information flows from sources such as mass disclosures made possible by digital technologies and collaboration.

With the Panama Papers, despots and elites could not make the adverse stories about themselves disappear. Equally, democratic leaders, who had during the global financial crisis of 2007–09 criticised banks and espoused the need for their populations to embrace austerity measures by sharing in their nation's tax burden, could not hide their own hypocrisy on tax avoidance, as revealed in the data. High-profile democratic leaders embarrassed by the anonymous leak included Sigmundur Davíð Gunnlaugsson, who was forced to resign as Iceland's prime minister after it was revealed he and his wife hid millions of dollars in a shell company purchased from Mossack Fonseca. Herman and Chomsky's (2002) propaganda model of news media, which underscores the power of capital and elites to filter the news fit to print, was undermined in this case by the scale of the network journalism, and challenged by journalists' use of digital technologies to investigate the mass data dumps and to break these stories simultaneously across the globe.

One of the more visible aspects of the chaos paradigm for journalism is the technology-driven dissolution of spatial boundaries of time and space so that audiences are no longer limited by time or geography as they once were (McNair 2006, p. 4). This alteration of time and space is true for newsmakers also. It is reflected in journalists' ability to collaborate with others beyond their physical place—across borders—but also to be more flexible in their creative spaces that were once limited or defined by platform or professional organisation. The ICIJ used adapted and custom technologies to bring together hundreds of journalists, some without professional organisational affiliations, across the globe with different skillsets to tell the story of the Panama Papers on a global scale across all media platforms: broadcast, print, and digital. It then used social media to disseminate the stories further and invite the audience to participate by exploring the database.

The ICIJ's data and research unit head, Mar Cabra, said this mass exposure and reach was made possible through technology, collaboration, and trust. Unlike the unstable power structure of the *WikiLeaks* collaboration, the ICIJ treated all participants as equals. 'Technology helped us collaborate across borders, get a virtual newsroom and share for a year in secret', Cabra (2016) explained. 'All documents were shared with everybody. We called it radical sharing'. Cabra said the technology enabled the team to work together, but trust in one another was the glue that made it successful. 'It is important to understand that everything we did was fuelled by trust. And without trust we would not have been able to achieve such a big investigation'.

Cabra said working on the Panama Papers taught her three important lessons about investigative journalism:

> Global massive leaks, electronic leaks, are the new normal. Global collaboration is the only way to deal with them. And that data

journalism is here to stay, it is not a trend, it is something that can help us do better investigative journalism.

(Cabra 2016)

However, Ryle (*Media Watch* 2016) cautions that global investigative stories are a specific genre. 'You've got to have a very global story to be able to pull this off and they're very hard to find' (*Media Watch* 2016).

The three case studies examined in this chapter reveal the emergence of a pattern of combining data and collaboration to undertake large-scale investigative reporting. For *WikiLeaks*, initially, the power of leaked government data seemed enough to disrupt and transform global power structures. However, in a highly fragmented media environment, *WikiLeaks* did not get the attention it sought to produce the outcomes it envisaged. *WikiLeaks* then moved to the connective publishing model and partnered with institutional media organisations. But the power diffusion—perhaps a proxy for a lack of trust or mutual respect—was unstable within the network structure. What ensued were fundamental disagreements about mediatisation played out publicly with the debates over redaction and editorial care versus the public's right to know. Yet, *WikiLeaks* was the first to show that cross-border media collaborations were possible for reporting globally significant stories.

Snowden, at the outset, had decided mediatisation—handing the story over to journalists—was the best way to achieve exposure for information in the NSA leaks. This was more of a traditional source-journalist relationship. With the release of the Panama Papers in 2016, the connective publishing model was strengthened and deepened by the ICIJ. Power was more diffuse within the network and all participants regarded as equals (Cabra 2016). The organisation recognised the value of the cultural power of media organisations, and the positive gatekeeping role of professional journalists to be sense-makers. It had a common publishing purpose and was able to diffuse power across its network. In doing so, the ICIJ not only enabled journalists to leverage the institutional power of their employer institutions but also to distinguish themselves as journalists, with individual agency, connected to a much larger whole.

Conclusion

This chapter examined the value of connecting large-scale data with large-scale investigative collaborations in the 21st century to critique global power and its injustices. Beginning with *WikiLeaks*, the comparative cases showed how big data leaks developed from: a sunshine model of radical transparency, to an early connective form of media outlets working together, to the ICIJ's highly coordinated connective network of reporters.

While social science techniques to interpret data have been employed by journalists for investigating stories since the 1960s, the use of big data in journalism did not rapidly develop until the second decade of this century. The mass collaborations required professional journalists and their media organisations working together with data specialists using digital technologies to unveil the secrets contained in the data. In an era of politicians attacking media reporting as 'fake news', global investigative journalism has emerged as a counter example, whereby information is verified and localised by individual journalists and its audience impact is leveraged through the institutional authority of established media organisations. This model is able to produce investigative journalism that bridges the local and global nexus to provide evidence-based public interest stories that 'could not be easily ignored,' as alluded to earlier by Downie and Schudson (2009, p. 11).

Certainly, investigative journalism has other challenges this century. Political and legal obstacles include governments restricting media freedoms in the name of national security, and with a propensity to 'conceal rather than reveal' information. And established media businesses have lost significant revenues as advertising has shifted online.

Yet, the new forms of global collaborative investigative journalism that have emerged are disruptive to established political, economic, and social orders. Some examples of this disruption have been positive, while others, such as the Russian and *WikiLeaks* data dumps during an election campaign, arguably have not. The impact of the Panama Papers has been well documented, with billions of dollars in lost taxes recouped, criminal charges laid, and notable political and elite figures losing their professional roles and status in society. The NSA leaks and the *WikiLeaks* war logs revealed the extent of the surveillance state in democracies and the number of civilian deaths owed to war, respectively. These examples show that the news 'fit to print' can no longer be fully controlled by political elites or those with vast capital. But, *they* also illuminate the need to marry this power with responsibility, particularly in some of the *WikiLeaks'* examples. They underscore the democratising power of data and the technology-driven dissolution of spatial boundaries to engender an emergent global public sphere to highlight global problems. Large-scale collaborative investigative reporting has indeed shown the power of numbers to tell human stories of global significance in new ways.

References

Ball, J 2015, 'GCHQ captured emails of journalists from top international media', *The Guardian*, January 20, accessed 11 May 2016, from www.theguardian.com/uk-news/2015/jan/19/gchq-intercepted-emails-journalists-ny-times-bbc-guardian-le-monde-reuters-nbc-washington-post.

BBC 2018, 'Australia data encryption laws explained', *BBC News*, 7 December, accessed 7 December 2018, from www.bbc.com/news/world-australia-46463029.

Burgess, M 2017, 'What is the IP act and how will it affect you?' *Wired*, accessed 6 January 2019, from www.wired.co.uk/article/ip-bill-law-details-passed.

Cabra, M 2016, 'The Panama Papers: Lessons learned and the road ahead', *Uncovering Asia*, 23 September, Global Investigative Journalism Network Conference, Kathmandu, Nepal.

Carson, A 2016, 'How investigative journalists are using social media to uncover the truth', *The Conversation*, 18 October, accessed 18 October 2016, from https://theconversation.com/how-investigative-journalists-are-using-social-media-to-uncover-the-truth-66393.

Downie, L Jr & Schudson, M 2009, 'The reconstruction of American journalism', *Columbia Journalism Review*, 19.

Dreyfus, S & Hrafnsson, K 2013, '*WikiLeaks* and two new models for investigative journalism', in S Tanner & N Richardson (eds), *Journalism Research and Investigation in a Digital World*, pp. 39–46. Oxford University Press, South Melbourne.

DW 2016, 'From Germany to the US, authorities want access to Panama Papers', *DW*, 22 April, accessed 1 May 2016, from www.dw.com/en/from-germany-to-the-us-authorities-want-access-to-panama-papers/a-19209191.

Ellison, S 2011, 'The man who spilled the secrets', *Vanity Fair*, 6 January, accessed 12 May 2016, from www.vanityfair.com/news/2011/02/the-guardian-201102.

Estepa, J 2017, 'Hillary Clinton blames Comey, WikiLeaks for 2016 election loss', *USA Today*, 2 May, accessed 2 May 2017, from www.usatoday.com/story/news/politics/onpolitics/2017/05/02/hillary-clinton-blames-comey-wikileaks-2016-election-loss/101203972/.

Flew, T & Wilson J 2012, '*WikiLeaks* and the challenge of the "fifth estate"', in M Ricketson (ed), *Australian Journalism Today*, Palgrave Macmillan, Melbourne.

Farell, P 2017, 'Australia's government muddles its way through to hide details of boat turnbacks', *The Guardian*, 3 April, accessed 3 April 2017, from www.theguardian.com/australia-news/2017/apr/03/australias-government-muddles-its-way-through-to-hide-details-of-boat-turnbacks.

Freedom House 2017, 'Freedom of the press', accessed 5 January 2018, from https://freedomhouse.org/report/freedom-press/freedom-press-2017.

Global Editors Network (GEN) 2016, 'Data journalism awards 2016', accessed 18 May 2016, from www.globaleditorsnetwork.org/programmes/data-journalism-awards/.

Global Editors Network (GEN) 2018, 'Data journalism awards', accessed 5 January 2019, from https://datajournalismawards.org/.

Glover, S 2013, 'Stupendous arrogance: By risking lives, I say again, the *Guardian* is floundering far out of its depth in realms where no newspaper should venture', *Daily Mail Australia*, 10 October, accessed 5 May 2016, from www.dailymail.co.uk/debate/article-2451532/STEPHEN-GLOVER-By-risking-lives-The-Guardian-floundering-far-depth.html.

Greenberg, A 2016, 'How reporters pulled off the Panama Papers, the biggest leak in whistleblower history', *Wired*, 4 April, accessed 5 April 2016, from www.wired.com/2016/04/reporters-pulled-off-panama-papers-biggest-leak-whistleblower-history/.

Greenwald, G 2014, *No Place to Hide*, Metropolitan Books Henry Holt and Company, New York.

Greste, P 2016, 'Too terrified to speak', Panel discussion at the 40th Australian Press Council Conference, Sydney, May 4–5.

Heemsbergen, L 2016, 'From radical transparency to radical disclosure: Reconfiguring (in)voluntary transparency through the management of visibilities', *International Journal of Communication*, 10, 138–51.

Herman, ES & N Chomsky 2002, *Manufacturing Consent: The Political Economy of the Mass Media*, Pantheon, New York.

Hewett, J 2013, 'Learning in progress: From computer-assisted reporting to data journalism, via freedom of information, open data and more', in J Mair, RL Keeble with P Bradshaw & T Beleaga (eds), *Data Journalism: Mapping the Future*, Abramis Academic Publishing, Suffolk.

Hughes, N 2013, 'A beginner's guide to data journalism and data mining/scraping': In *Data Journalism: Mapping the Future*, in J Mair, RL Keeble with P Bradshaw & T Beleaga (eds), *Data Journalism: Mapping the Future*, Abramis Academic Publishing, Suffolk.

The Intercept 2016, 'The intercept is broadening access to the Snowden archive: Here's why', *The Intercept*, 17 May, accessed 17 May 2016, from https://theintercept.com/2016/05/16/the-intercept-is-broadening-access-to-the-snowden-archive-heres-why/.

Levy, M 2016, '"Interested in data"': Panama Papers leak began with message from "John Doe"', *Sydney Morning Herald*, 6 April, accessed 10 May 2016, from www.smh.com.au/business/banking-and-finance/interested-in-data-panama-papers-leak-began-with-message-from-john-doe-20160405-gnzd0i.html#ixzz48z4RwPjQ.

Liberty 2018, 'Stand up to power', *Liberty*, assessed 6 December 2016, from www.libertyhumanrights.org.uk/.

Lidberg, J & Muller, D 2018, *In the Name of Security—Secrecy, Surveillance and Journalism*, Anthem Press, London.

Luhn, A & Harding, L 2016, 'Putin dismisses panama papers as an attempt to destabilise Russia', 7 April, accessed 9 May 2016, from www.theguardian.com/news/2016/apr/07/putin-dismisses-panama-papers-as-an-attempt-to-destabilise-russia.

Lundberg, K 2011, 'Friend or foe? WikiLeaks and the Guardian', *The Journalism School Knight Case Studies*, 11(41), 1–22, accessed 1 May 2016, from http://ccnmtl.columbia.edu/projects/caseconsortium/casestudies/70/casestudy/www/layout/case_id_70.html.

Loosen, W, Reimer, J & Silva-Schmidt, FD 2017, 'Data-driven reporting: An ongoing (r)evolution? An analysis of projects nominated for the data journalism awards 2013–2016', *Journalism*, doi:10.1177/1464884917735691.

Lynch, A, McGarrity, N & Williams, G 2015, *Inside Australia's Anti-terrorism Laws and Trials*, NewSouth, Sydney.

Lyon, D 2015, *Surveillance After Snowden*, Polity, Cambridge.

Mackey, R, Harris, J, Somaiya, R & Kulish, N 2011, 'All leaked U.S. cables were made available online as WikiLeaks splintered', *The Lede*, 1 September, accessed 5 May 2016, from https://thelede.blogs.nytimes.com/2011/09/01/all-leaked-u-s-cables-were-made-available-online-as-wikileaks-splintered/.

Manne, R 2011, *Making Trouble*, Black Inc Agenda, Melbourne.

McNair, B 2006, *Cultural Chaos: Journalism, News and Power in a Globalised World*, Routledge, London.

McNair, B 2016, 'The leakers of panama', *The Conversation*, 6 April, accessed 10 April 2016, from https://theconversation.com/the-leakers-of-panama-57334.

Media Watch 2016, 'Interview with Gerard Ryle', ICIJ, *ABC*, 4 April, accessed 2 May 2016, from www.abc.net.au/mediawatch/episodes/interview-with-gerard-ryle-icij/9973010.

Meyer, P 1999, 'The future of CAR: Declare victory and get out', in P Nora (ed), *When Words and Nerds Collide: Reflections on the Development of Computer Assisted Reporting*, Poynter Institute for Media Studies, Florida.

Paterson, M 2018, 'The public privacy conundrum—anonymity and the law in an era of mass surveillance', in J Lidberg & D Muller (eds), *In the Name of Security—Secrecy, Surveillance and Journalism*, pp. 15–32 Anthem Press, London.

Pearson, M 2014, 'Journalists face jail for reporting intelligence operations: With no public interest defence', *Journlaw*, 3 October, accessed 15 May 2016, from https://journlaw.com/2014/10/03/journalistsfacejailforreportingintelligence operationswithnopublicinterestdefence/.

Pearson, M & Fernandez, J 2018, 'Surveillance and national security "hyper-legislation": Calibrating restraints on rights with a freedom of expression threshold', in J Lidberg & D Muller (eds), *In the Name of Security—Secrecy, Surveillance and Journalism*, pp. 51–76, Anthem Press, London.

Poterfield, J 2012, *Julian Assange and WikiLeaks*, Rosen Publishing Group, New York.

Reporters without Borders 2018, 'US falls in world press freedom index', accessed 4 December 2018, from https://rsf.org/en/rsf-index-2018-hatred-journalism-threatens-democracies.

Rusbridger, A 2018, *Breaking News: The Remaking of Journalism and Why It Matters Now*, Canongate, London.

Tiffen, R 2019, 'The era of mega-leaks', in AK Schapals, A Bruns & B McNair (eds), *Digitizing Democracy*, Routledge, New York.

The Walkley Foundation 2012, 'Walkley winners announced', *The Walkley Foundation*, 27 November, accessed 2 January 2012, from www.walkleys.com/news/5131/.

Walker, B 2016, 'Too terrified to speak', Panel discussion at the 40th Australian Press Council Conference, Sydney, May 4–5.

Washington Post 2016, 'No pardon for Edward Snowden', *Washington Post*, 17 September, accessed 8 December 2018, from www.washingtonpost.com/opinions/edward-snowden-doesnt-deserve-a-pardon/2016/09/17/ec04d448-7c2e-11e6-ac8e-cf8e0dd91dc7_story.html?utm_term=.28128e881230.

WikiLeaks 2011a, 'Collateral murder', *WikiLeaks*, accessed 4 May 2016, from https://collateralmurder.wikileaks.org.

WikiLeaks 2011b, 'The Guantanamo files: David Michael Hicks, Mamdouh Ibrahim Ahmed Habib', *WikiLeaks*, accessed 4 May 2016, from www.wikileaks.org.

Wright, S & Doyle, K 2018, 'The evolution of data journalism: A case study of Australia', *Journalism Studies*, doi:10.1080/146167OX.2018.1539343.

7 Bankrolling Journalism to Support Investigative Reporting

> You can spend weeks doing a story and it might be up on your website for two hours, that is really disappointing. But it's interesting that we're getting the feedback from our editors that they now realise that they're the stories that they've got to promote more. The credibility of your masthead is now becoming the big selling point.
>
> (Kate McClymont 2017, *Sydney Morning Herald* investigative reporter, interview with the author, 16 March)

Introduction

Former *Sydney Morning Herald* editor Eric Beecher tells the story of how in 2004 the Fairfax board rejected his forecast that classified advertising would be lost to online competitors. One board member, holding up a copy of Fairfax's hefty Saturday papers, responded: 'I don't ever want anyone coming into this boardroom again, and telling us that people will buy houses or cars, or look for jobs, without *this*, dropping the bundle on the table with a thud' (Beecher 2011, interview with the author, 12 May).

Beecher foresaw the disruption the internet would cause to newspapers' business model. Like many media companies, Fairfax failed to grasp early the opportunities to invest in online job, real estate, and car sales websites that would experience enormous growth in the digital age.

It was an almost universal underestimation. As Ken Doctor, former vice president at Knight Ridder Digital, observed, newspaper publishers 'had no idea how much the internet would change ad spending and they didn't realise that ad inventory on the internet was infinite' (Levine 2011, p. 114).

As we saw in Chapter 1, the economic problems for traditional media lay with a business model built around analogue advertising welded to journalism. In the mid-20th century, Marshall McLuhan prophesied that 'the classified ads (and stock market quotations) are the bedrock of the press. Should an alternative source of easy access to such diverse daily information be found, the press will fold' (1964/1994, p. 207). In the century to follow, this major source of revenue began to dry up as advertisers migrated online, decoupling advertising from editorial content. Clay

Shirky (2014) described it as the 'slow divorce between advertising and editorial'. Further, digital metrics provided by technology platforms like Google and Facebook, which told advertisers how many people clicked on individual ads, thus allowing more accurate targeting of key demographics, proved potent and unmatchable.

Technology platforms do not produce news; rather, they aggregate it and influence what audiences see. While the platforms allow publishers to reach larger audiences than before, they can also diminish the visibility of the traditional publishers' brands as the main vehicles for news (Bell and Owen 2017). David Eun, Google's former vice president of content partnerships, summed up traditional media's chief problem:

> Traditional media was about bringing the audience to where you decided the content was going to be . . . the new media, it is not about bringing the audience to where the content is. It's about taking the content to where the audiences are. And the audiences are all over the web.
>
> (cited in Auletta 2010, p. 257)

This directional change between the audience and the media does not mean the end of journalism or investigative journalism. People are still hungry for news, but they are less willing to pay for it online, especially when there is so much available for free. But as the opening quote from Kate McClymont suggests, there is a developing consensus that audiences will pay for unique quality news, which is what good investigative journalism is.

A sustainable media business model is particularly important to produce quality investigative journalism, which tends to be costlier than other forms of reporting. In the second decade of the 21st century, no single replacement funding model has emerged to sustain investigative journalism. Rather, several models have evolved, and in some cases a combination of funding models is being used to generate the funds to underwrite newsrooms and support investigative reporting.

Investigative editor in charge of *The Washington Post*'s dedicated investigative units Jeff Leen (2016, interview with the author, 30 August) put it this way:

> Even in the darkest scenario, if nobody ever finds a business model and everything crashes and burns, a thousand flowers will spring out of the ashes and something will grow into something that will deliver investigative reporting because people want it. I think you're seeing a little bit of that now with all these non-profits and all these websites and everybody trying something different and there's a lot of hit and miss and people haven't figured it out. But I think that the human drive to know and to expose wrong doing is not going to go away.

In the United States, philanthropic funding of non-profit media organisations is a growing revenue source that has revitalised investigative journalism (Birnbauer 2017). However, as discussed below, this option is less viable in countries without a highly developed philanthropic culture or tax breaks for donations to fund journalism.

This chapter provides an overview of some of the different revenue models for journalism. Owing to the nascent nature of these models, conclusions on their efficacy for sustaining newsrooms are tentative. For similar reasons, scholarly literature is somewhat limited, and so industry reports and interviews with media experts figure more prominently here than in other chapters. I capture a range of 21st-century funding models that are not specific to investigative journalism per se but provide revenue to fund newsroom activities including watchdog reporting. I conclude that the future business model for small digital native newsrooms is likely a hybrid one, relying on multiple revenue streams *without* involving paywalls. But for traditional outlets, especially those in larger markets, or those that produce specialist content such as financial news, a paywall model is a likely first choice. We start with the digital paywall for this reason.

Digital Paywall Models

Soft Versus Hard Paywalls

Paywall models broadly fall into two categories: 'soft' and 'hard'. Hard paywalls prevent free access to online news content (beyond a few paragraphs of lead stories) such as *The Times* of London and *The Wall Street Journal* (*WSJ*). Most have free introductory offers or significant discounts for new customers such as the *WSJ*'s US$1 for two months (at the time of writing).

Soft paywall options allow limited viewing of full articles without charge. With the 'metered' model, the number is capped typically between 5 and 30 articles a month. The soft paywall is designed to keep internet traffic flowing to a newspaper's website, which is important for audience metrics used for attracting advertisers, and to entice readers to pay for more online access beyond the free sample.

A variant of the soft model is the noble paywall, also called the 'freemium' or 'leaky' paywall. It provides some free content, but not for stories with premium value for which editors judge consumers are more likely to pay. Premium stories might be those written by a popular columnist or belong to a popular section like information technology or business.

My earlier research (Carson 2015) made five findings about paywalls and print newspapers that still hold in early 2019. These were (1) one size does not fit all; (2) metered paywalls are more widely used by newspapers than other forms; (3) digital-only subscriptions are rising (and are generally cheaper than print) but also serve to cannibalise print subscription revenue; (4) consumers are more likely to pay for hard-to-get (niche) content and quality reporting; and (5) having a (soft) paywall does not necessarily limit audience reach if the masthead's reputation is substantial. *The New York Times* (*NYT*), for example, has a monthly online unique audience of almost 100 million, and *The Washington Post* has 92 million unique views online per month (comScore data cited in Doctor 2017). This metric tells us how many different individuals visit a site over time and as such quantifies the size of the unduplicated audience that a site reaches. I elaborate on these five points below.

Finding the 'Sweet Spot': One Size Does Not Fit All

The paywall experiment began in 1997 with the Rupert Murdoch–owned *WSJ*, a financial masthead. The UK's *Financial Times* was another early adopter. It put a subscription model in place in 2002, but revised it to a metered paywall in 2007. Murdoch extended the paywall to the centuries-old London *Times* newspaper in 2010, charging readers to access general news online. A year later, in 2011, Murdoch's *The Australian* also adopted a hard paywall.

The *WSJ* and *The Times* models have been tweaked to allow readers to access a few sentences of stories before being asked to subscribe. Murdoch's *The Australian* switched to a noble, allowing a few articles to get through the paywall to pique the interest of non-subscribers, while Murdoch's Australian tabloid the *Herald Sun* converted from a hard to a metered paywall to abate a 20 per cent drop in online traffic shortly after the paywall was introduced in 2012 (Hawthorne 2012). The *Herald Sun* has since adopted a noble model. With the adoption of paywalls, we see a degree of experimentation by newspapers to find the right model to fit their content and desired audience.

Australia's first newspaper to use a hard paywall was a financial masthead, Fairfax's *Australian Financial Review*, in 2006 (Simons 2007, p. 140). It significantly adjusted pricing on three occasions—without great subscriber success. Five years later, it abandoned the hard paywall for a noble model like *The Australian*'s. At the time, in 2011, *AFR* CEO Brett Clegg revealed the number of digital subscribers barely exceeded 6,000 (Burrowes 2011). Even with price discounting, the *AFR* remains among the world's most expensive paywalls at about A$20 a week for its premium model in 2019, which also includes hardcopy subscription (weekdays only). Unlike the British and American markets, Australia does not have a large population base to support a hard paywall market for general news, particularly when competitors like public broadcaster the ABC and new commercial entrants such as *The Guardian* provide general news without a paywall.

It is harder for tabloids to get readers to pay for general news content. Typically, tabloid readers belong to a lower socio-economic demographic and may not be inclined to pay for general news content that can be freely found elsewhere. While Australia's *Herald Sun* relaxed its paywall access, Murdoch's *The Sun* newspaper in Britain adopted a hard paywall in 2013, only to abandon it in 2015, after which online traffic grew 26 per cent (Myllylahti 2016).

This story of experimentation extends across Britain, the United States, and Australia. In 2011, the *NYT* reintroduced a paywall after a failed attempt in 2005. On the second occasion, it chose a metered paywall rather than a 'freemium' model. In 2012, the *NYT* halved its free articles from 20 to 10 and then to 5 in late 2017 to entice readers to pay. It has had great success, with more than four million digital and print subscribers combined worldwide (New York Times Company [NYTC] 2018). In its third quarterly report of 2018, the NYTC noted that some of its paywall revenue specifically funded investigative journalism. It singled out the efforts of three reporters that produced a 14,000-word account on the suspect tax schemes of US President Donald Trump and his family (NYTC 2018).

Paywalls are popular choices for legacy newspapers. The American Press Institute (2016) found that 79 per cent of US newspapers with a circulation above 50,000 had some form of paywall. Most opted for a metered model (63 per cent), 12 per cent chose a noble or freemium model, while only 3 per cent erected a hard paywall. My earlier research (Carson 2015) found that most of Australia's daily newspapers had a paywall by 2013—the year following large-scale Australian journalism job cuts and conversion of several Fairfax broadsheets to tabloid-size newspapers. The year 2012 saw more paywalls implemented in the three studied countries of Australia, Britain, and United States than in any other single year. This uptick sharply contradicted Arianna Huffington's (2009) earlier predictions that 'the paywall is history'. As noted in Chapter 1, 2012 was a particularly difficult year for newspapers in Australia, and erecting paywalls was a key response to this financial nadir for print.

These examples suggest that experimenting with paywall prices and models has been necessary for media companies to find the best fit for their size, brand, news content, and market population. A hard paywall can work for a newspaper like the *WSJ* because of its financial content, which is hard to find for free elsewhere. Financial mastheads can also lure subscribers with exclusive financial data and tools to interact with share prices online (Carson 2015).

In finding the right subscription model, publishers are searching for a 'sweet spot', or what Australian news publisher Alan Kohler (2010, interview with the author, 5 October) described as the balance between 'maximising clicks on a story with creating a brand that has a set of values'. Publishers want readers to pay for journalism, yet they also need enough website traffic to serve digital advertisers' needs regarding audience demographics and volume. For general news providers, the 'sweet spot' is often a metered paywall because it does not stifle non-paying online traffic flow. Some publications, like *The Guardian* and *Daily Mail*, reject the paywall altogether, preferring to maximise audience reach on a global scale to attract advertisers.

The Reuters Institute at the University of Oxford has found that hard paywalls curb website traffic flows significantly compared to metered models (Newman and Levy 2013, p. 92). The difference was an 85–95 per cent reduction in web traffic in the initial months compared to 5–15 per cent loss of digital traffic using a metered paywall. A noble paywall reduced web traffic by about a third (Nakashima 2012). Losing digital traffic can be a significant issue for newspapers—unless the resulting subscription revenue outstrips advertising revenue. But few papers other than *The New York Times* have yet achieved this.

The Challenges for Paywall Models

While digital subscription is becoming an important revenue source for the industry, even successful paywalls—including those of *The New York Times, Financial Times*, and *The Wall Street Journal*—do not wholly cover lost advertising revenue. Certainly, the growth of paywalls points to a shift in readers' willingness to pay for journalism online. Since the election of Donald Trump, a spike in readers subscribing to quality mastheads has meant *The Washington Post, Los Angeles Times*, and *NYT* have been able to hire more journalists (Doctor 2018). Yet these established mastheads remain economically vulnerable, particularly where falls in advertising revenue outstrip growth in subscription revenue. The *NYT*, for example, has grown its digital subscriber base to three million (four million with print), and digital and hardcopy subscriptions have surpassed advertising revenues. Yet the *NYT*'s total revenues were declining because of a fall in print advertising (NYTC 2018). Likewise, the *WSJ* has 2.2 million subscribers (58 per cent are digital), but in 2018 relied on cover and subscription price increases so that its parent company, News Corporation, could offset a A$44 million fall in its third quarter advertising revenues (News Corp 2018).

Pickard and Williams (2014) came to a similar finding about the commercial vulnerability of newspapers at a time when digital subscriptions were growing. They analysed the paywalls at the *Arkansas Democrat-Gazette*, the *Dallas Morning News*, and *The New York Times* and found that while each had enjoyed varying levels of success, the paywalls themselves were unable to offset losses in overall advertising revenue over time. Doctor (2017) also raises questions about smaller papers behind paywalls, pointing out that they have worked well for national papers but mastheads like *The Baltimore Sun, The Sacramento Bee*, or the *Arizona Republic*, with readership one-fifth to one-twentieth that size, would struggle. Similarly, Felle (2016) argued that erecting paywalls was a challenge for smaller players because regional and local newspapers have little or no prospect of having enough subscribers to make them profitable. As a result, many smaller papers are reliant on their print editions to bring in money and their websites to create an online presence, and build their brands and market share. Like my earlier study (Carson 2015), Felle (2016) concluded that the newspaper paywall works better for affluent readerships, and specialist news brands such as business titles, where content is exclusive and in demand.

Against this evidence, Australia's newspaper duopoly of Fairfax Media and News Corp introduced paywalls to some of its regional town publications in 2016, arguing that readers would pay for their unique local content online (Samios 2018). Given the highly concentrated newspaper ownership in Australia, and with little other competition (except the public broadcaster), this might prove to be true, although the new owner of the regional Fairfax mastheads, Antony Catalano, has expressed doubts.

Digital-Only Newsrooms

A different picture emerges, however, when the gaze is turned to the viability of paywalls for digital-only start-up newsrooms. To study what the future newsroom looked like in Australia, my colleague and I interviewed editors from seven of Australia's digital-only newsrooms: *HuffPost, BuzzFeed, The Guardian, the Daily Review, Mumbrella, Crikey,* and *Junkee*. Only *Crikey*, the oldest of the digital only newsrooms, used a paywall (Carson and Muller 2017). Each of these digital news entrants appeared after 2012, when print newspapers were at their height of cost-cutting. *Crikey* began publishing in 2000 behind a freemium paywall model. None of the other online publications had intentions to install a paywall because of concerns it would limit online traffic. Rather, they have diversified revenue streams by introducing public events, digital advertising, native advertising, donations, and corporate consultancies (Carson and Muller 2017).

Tim Duggan, the publisher of *Junkee*, an online youth news website, said he would not consider using paywalls as part of its business model.

> I don't love them. I understand them, in some media, but I think for our audience, which is under 35-year olds, they are used to getting their content for free now. We need to figure out what our business model is that provides them free content.
>
> (2017, interview with the author, 12 July)

At *Mumbrella*, a media and marketing news site, founder Tim Burrowes said paywalls would not work for his site for two reasons. First, the advertisers they attract pay a premium to advertise to *Mumbrella*'s audience. The high digital advertising rate meant *Mumbrella* was 'fairly sustainable' without a paywall. Second, more than half of its revenue came from organised events, meaning it was important to have 'daily conversations with a mass audience to tell them about our events', said Burrowes (2017, interview with the author, 11 July).

Burrowes says if he ran a different media business, he might consider a paywall:

> Paywalls work where your boss is paying for it. So, a subscription to *The Australian* or maybe a subscription to *Crikey*. It's probably that the boss, or the taxman, is paying for it so they work. I think that's why, you know, when you look at things like, the *Daily Telegraph* or the *Herald Sun* or whatever, maybe it doesn't go as well because that's harder to justify as a business expense.
> (2017, interview with the author, 11 July)

The Guardian Australia relied on a mix of digital advertising, donations or voluntary subscriptions, and philanthropy. Its editor, Lenore Taylor, explained:

> We would vastly prefer our journalism to be open to everybody. And there's a great thing about having, effectively, it's a voluntary paywall, so asking for people to pay for what they read, is that it remains open to everyone and you're rewarded the most for the best that you do. So, it's like a built-in alignment between editorial excellence and financial reward because people are going to be more inspired to give you money if you've done something that they really like. We've never said never to a pay wall. We're working with this model and at the moment it's going fabulously.
> (Taylor 2017, interview with the author, 6 July)

The new news media outlets' concerns that erecting a paywall would limit audience reach align with studies showing a reluctance from citizens to pay for news.

Paying for News?

For example, Deloitte's Sixth Annual Media Consumer Survey found 90 per cent of the 2,000 Australians responding to an online survey did not pay for online news (2017, p. 26). When they did pay, they said they did it to get in-depth news or because they trusted the brand. This supports the earlier findings that quality brands and unique content are more likely to succeed with a paywall model.

Just over half of the respondents relied on traditional media for news (55 per cent) except for millennials (50 per cent), who tend to get their news online (Deloitte 2017, p. 25). A Danish study (Kammer et al. 2015) found younger people were willing to pay for online subscriptions, but only if they could combine content from different news providers, allowing them to individualise their news products. This fits with David Eun's earlier observation that in the digital age news must come to the audience, not vice versa.

Another study concluded that media organisations would find it more difficult selling online subscriptions for the same price as printed editions (Atasoy and Morewedge 2017). This was because US consumers placed more value on physical goods than on digital products. Media, such as a paperback book, a printed photograph, or a DVD, when digitised lost some of its value to buyers. A key driver of this 'value' loss was that digital goods do not engender the same feeling of ownership that physical goods do.

Easy access to free news also discouraged consumers from paying for news online. A Reuters study of news consumers' attitudes to paying for news in four countries (United Kingdom, United States, Finland, and Spain) found people were prepared to pay for 'quality' news (Newman 2017a). Quality referred to different attributes including accuracy and impartiality of reporting, breadth and depth of coverage, or an engaging writing style. When people paid for online news, it was for reasons including that they were familiar with the brand, it was part of their daily habit, or their print subscription had automatically transferred to online. Supporting a news organisation that had an alternative editorial stance to the mainstream media was another motivation for paying. Fletcher and Nielson (2017) found those who paid for printed news were more likely to pay for online news. But only a minority of readers paid for online news. This is important research to note because it provides insight into what publishers need to do to get readers to pay for news, and part of that equation is quality and unique reporting such as investigative journalism.

Kate McClymont (2017, interview with the author, 16 March) has observed that:

> The time for investigative journalism could not be better and it's because of the 'Trump effect'. I think the 'Trump effect' has meant that people are—not everyone—willing to read and believe credible sources now more than ever before.

This might be true, but reading and paying for content are separate concerns. BBC media director Amol Rajan (2018) argued that, given the rise of Google and Facebook to a position of dominance in the global digital advertising market, and because they could change algorithms that affected what users saw in their newsfeeds without warning, newspaper organisations could no longer rely on consistency of advertising revenue and were better off relying on revenue from audience subscriptions.

In response, Google and Facebook have developed tools to assist publishers in attracting more subscribers to their digital mastheads. Google sells digital newspapers on its iKiosk, giving publishers 85 per cent of the revenue generated (Christian 2018). Google's news initiative (Linares 2018) also included a 'Subscribe with Google' tool that allowed users to subscribe to a newspaper or digital site with their own Google account. A part of Google Analytics, it includes a Consumer Insight tool with a 'Propensity to Subscribe' signal. This allowed news organisations to analyse, through machine learning, the flow of users to its site to identify those readers most likely to subscribe.

As part of its 'Journalism Project', Facebook also worked with news publishers to develop strategies to increase news subscriptions. Through Facebook's 'Instant Articles', readers see a subscription link to the publisher's website when they hit the paywall, making it easier for them to subscribe. However, these initiatives do not change the reality that almost all the growth (99 per cent) in digital advertising revenue in the United States went to Google or Facebook in 2016 (Newman 2017b).

The *Boston Globe*'s editor-at-large Walter Robinson (2016, interview with the author, 25 September) says the *Globe* is focused on stories that readers cannot get from free services:

> We're shedding the old label of 'paper of record' and Brian McGrory's phase for what we're becoming is we're becoming the 'paper of necessity' and that gets right at our sweet spot. Our readers want stories that hold powerful institutions accountable. Our readers want investigative reporting. Our readers want stories they can't get anywhere else. And if you give them all that, they pay for it.

Paywall Alternatives? The Hybrid Business Model

New offerings of home-grown and overseas digital news media proliferated in Australia after the 2012 job cuts at traditional commercial news outlets. Among the new entrants capitalising on this period of turbulence for traditional media were *Global Mail* (2012), *Junkee* (2012), *The New Daily* (2013), the *Daily Mail* Australia (2015), *HuffPost* (2015), *The Guardian* Australia (2013), *BuzzFeed* (2014), *Vice* (2014), SBS *Viceland* (2016), and *The New York Times Australia* (2017). A few digital newsrooms arrived before this critical tipping point in 2012, including *Crikey* (2000), *New Matilda* (2004), *Pedestrian TV* (2005), *Mamamia* (2007), *Mumbrella* (2008), *The Conversation* (2010), and *Hoopla* (2011). The success of these sites is mixed, revealing the precariousness of finding a sustainable funding model in the digital age. The most successful are those with a diverse revenue model that is adaptable to changes in market conditions at short notice.

We found that of the seven newsrooms studied, all relied on a hybrid model to fund their newsrooms (Carson and Muller 2017). No single revenue-raising activity was enough to meet newsroom expenses. Types of revenue activities varied between outlets, but advertising still played an important role for each. To survive in the highly competitive digital market for news, outlets needed to be responsive to market changes and swiftly shift revenue-raising activities accordingly. *Junkee*'s Tim Duggan (2017, interview with the author, 12 July) observed that the advantage of the hybrid model was its flexibility:

> If we see that native [advertising] is going up, and that display [advertising] is going down, it allows us to put more energy into the areas of revenue that are most going to impact on us. So, by having five or six different revenue models, it's the only way of surviving and thriving, in 2017, as a media company.

Hoopla (a news site focused on and targeting women) and the *Global Mail* (a long-form and investigative journalism site) are two Australian digital news media start-ups that did not survive. The *Global Mail* dissolved when it lost its major philanthropic funding support. *Hoopla* tried to implement a paywall when it could not attract enough advertisers, but the changes came too late. Its founder Wendy Harmer said at the time:

> In the face of enormous and radical change in the online space, we are unable to keep operating in our present form. This is the reality we've been grappling with for some time.
>
> (Levy 2015)

A lesson learned from these examples is the need for a diverse revenue stream that can respond to changed market conditions; too much reliance on one revenue stream can leave a digital newsroom vulnerable. For example, Australia's *HuffPost* and the arts-focused *Daily Review* have both struggled. *HuffPost* lost substantial revenue when its partnership with Fairfax Media fell apart in late 2017. The *Daily Review* has tried to adapt but is heavily reliant on the niche Australian arts community as its main audience. And *BuzzFeed*, after five years of local growth, was forced to shed half its Australian newsroom staff (11 individuals) in early 2019. This followed company headquarters' global announcement that it was shedding 200 staff. *BuzzFeed*'s changed fortunes were attributed in part to lost social media traffic after Facebook changed its news feed algorithm in 2018 (Ingram 2019).

Meanwhile, other digital entrants have grown significantly since their arrival in the Australian news market. In most cases, outlets have doubled or tripled staffing levels and are returning a profit (Carson and Muller 2017, p. 3). The largest newsroom is *The Guardian* Australia, which swelled from a few local hirings to 90 staff at last count. Some (*Mumbrella*, *BuzzFeed*, *Crikey*, and *The Guardian*) do investigative journalism because they regard it as important to their brand and/or for reasons of accountability. Tim Burrowes said it was a necessary investment for his brand:

> It will cost us a fair bit of money and we'll get decent traffic for it, but not enough to cover the cost directly. But what it does is it just adds to your kudos and your credibility. It shows that we take the industry seriously and we do this stuff.
>
> (2017, interview with the author, July 11)

Where digital-only newsrooms differ from traditional media is breadth of news coverage. Digital editors know their reporting strengths. They produce stories that align with these areas. Their focus is more narrow than traditional newsrooms. And they use data analytics in real time to better understand their core audience to refine their story focus. Digital reporters largely abandoned the 'old model' of storytelling that was considered 'impartial' and relied on the 'inverted pyramid', whereby basic facts of 'who', 'what', 'when' and 'where' came first and finer details followed. Rather, digital newsrooms emphasise storytelling with a narrative *and* a viewpoint. *Junkee*'s Tim Duggan explained:

> We insert tone, and opinion, and attitude into it; and that, I think, is the part where it differs. So, we're not trying to be impartial, we think that we know who our audience is, which is young Australians. Most of them are a bit progressive and we write for them.
>
> (2017, interview with the author, July 12)

Social media platforms, particularly Facebook, are essential for reaching bigger audiences and for allowing them to engage in conversations. A story's shareability was a key criterion in editors' news judgements. For this reason, any changes to shareability can have significant consequences for digital news providers—as evidenced by *BuzzFeed*'s job losses. Our study found that digital-only newsrooms were generally smaller, nimbler, and less hierarchical than their 20th-century predecessors (Carson and Muller 2017, p. 3). We also found that journalists were skilled at telling stories across all platforms and that the story largely determined the platform selected to tell it. Video, however, featured prominently. This was because it is a highly attractive medium to advertisers and audiences alike. It is readily shared on social media, and is mobile-friendly (p. 4). To understand how the hybrid business model is working in Australia, its component revenue streams are now explored in more detail.

Advertising

Newspapers' overall share of the advertising market is declining (see Chapter 1). Also problematic for newspapers is that digital advertising unit prices (and revenues) are much lower than they once were for print. Not only do newspapers get less money for digital advertising, their share of it is also being eroded by other online competitors. In Australia, total annual advertising spend is expected to be $17.2 billion in 2019 (Cameron 2018). More than half (54.9 per cent) will be spent on digital advertising. Print is expected to get a 9.8 per cent overall share of the advertising pie.

In the USA, the Pew Research Center found that total US newspaper advertising revenue was falling. In 2017 was US$16.5 billion, down 19 per cent from 2015 (Pew Research Center 2018).

As newspaper advertising revenue share has fallen, media companies have attempted to adapt to decrease their reliance on it. In 2005 *The New York Times* drew 68 per cent of its revenue from advertising; by 2017 advertising's share had slumped to just 37 per cent. *The Wall Street Journal*'s parent Dow Jones also gets just a third of its revenue from advertising (Carson and Muller 2017, p. 8).

While digital advertising is a growing market, most digital news media companies have been unable to get a sufficient share to wholly sustain their journalism, so other methods are needed to finance their newsroom operations. The advantage of digital media companies' multi-pronged approach for raising revenues—the hybrid model—is that it spreads the risk and the reward. Advertising remains an important part of the revenue mix. It is generally employed in several ways: classified ads, online display or banner ads, and native advertising, in both text and video form. The most lucrative of these is native advertising.

Native Advertising and Studio Work

Broadly defined, native advertising matches the page content, design, and platform behaviour of the website in which it appears. Native advertising is designed to make the consumer feel that the ad *belongs* on the site. The US Interactive Advertising Bureau (IAB) identified six forms of native advertising (see Box 7.1).

Junkee uses a mix of advertising on its websites that include traditional banner ads and native advertising. Its native ads were a 'massive part of our revenue', Duggan said. Native advertising is divided into written native and video native. 'Video native is an even larger part of that revenue', said Duggan (2017, interview with the author, July 12).

An advantage for *Junkee* is that its content speaks to a specific audience—young Australians aged 18–35. So *Junkee* says it is able to charge a premium to advertisers to reach a target audience. Duggan explained:

> Brands want to speak to young Australians, and find it hard to get them elsewhere. So, our [cost per thousand impressions or CPMs,] the rate that we can charge an advertiser to get to that audience, is quite high. And it is across the whole youth space. So, us, *Pedestrian*, and *BuzzFeed*, all have similar CPMs.
>
> (2017, interview with the author, July 12)

Box 7.1 Types of Native Advertising

In-feed ads. Usually written in story form. The advertisement has been written by or in partnership with the publisher to match the surrounding stories. Commonly used disclosure language for in-feed ads include 'advertisement' or 'promoted' or 'sponsored content'.

Paid search units. Usually found above the organic search results. It looks exactly like the surrounding results (except for its disclosure aspects).

Recommendation widgets. Usually an ad or paid content link that is delivered via a 'widget' that resembles other widgets used on the website.

In-ad with native element units. This ad looks like a standard ad that contains contextually relevant content. It should have clearly defined borders so as not to be confused with normal page content. It may link to another page.

Custom. Examples of native advertising that do not fit into the above categories.

The *Daily Review*'s initial business model relied on display advertising from the Australian arts sector. *Review* owner Raymond Gill said he planned to sell advertising as a yearly packaged deal—such as a gold or platinum package—to major organisations like art galleries and opera companies. He achieved early successes with advertising in the first year, then sponsors disappeared. With not enough advertising revenue, he tried native advertising. This involved doing reviews of shows such as the stage hit *Matilda* for sponsors (Gill 2016, interview with the author, 11 August).

Native and traditional advertising is also an important revenue stream for *Mumbrella*. It displays ads on its website, in its emailed newsletters, and at its events. It sends one EDM (electronic direct mail) sponsored by a commercial partner each week.

Junkee works with clients to help them to develop their own social media through its *Junkee* Studio. It is modelled on overseas outlets such as *The New York Times*' Brand Studio, *Vice*'s Virtue, and *The Guardian*'s Guardian Labs (Carson and Muller 2017).

As a form of native advertising, Guardian Labs (2017) describes itself as 'the branded content arm of *The Guardian*. We create the most engaging and influential stories that connect brands to a progressive audience'. The media outlet used a range of digital and multimedia storytelling 'products'. These included written editorial, visual journalism, mobile experiences, video and audio, and live events. Its partners have included Nespresso, Spotify, Hyundai, Vulcan, Airbnb, eBay, and Vodaphone.

Junkee Studio has a long-term native advertising partnership with the airline Qantas, called AWOL. It also works with Westpac, producing an online publication, *The Cusp*. Duggan explains that both Westpac and Qantas were established, credible brands, but brands that had 'trouble speaking to millennials'. Duggan says:

> We identified the best way of doing that was, kind of, creating sub-brands that catered to what we knew young people were into. So, *AWOL* is like a sub-brand of Qantas, essentially, where we talk about travel and trying to give people FOMO (fear of missing out) to go off and travel the world. And *The Cusp* is also based out of our research, which showed us that three of the biggest concerns of the young Australians were: my career, my money, and my health and wellbeing.
>
> (T. Duggan 2017, interview with the author, 12 July)

Using the example of *The Cusp*, most young people access it through Facebook.

Junkee would not survive without *Junkee* Studio, Duggan stated.

Declaring Native Advertising

An ongoing debate about native advertising is whether to declare to readers that it is paid editorial. 'We think everyone wins when you declare it as loud and proud as you can', said Duggan (2017, interview with author, July 12). But it is not always so straightforward. *Junkee* Studio, for example, derives income by doing contract work to create content for third-party brands on the clients' websites and Facebook pages, which they have no obligation to declare.

At *HuffPost* Australia, native content is transparent. Former editor-in-chief Tory Maguire contended that native content could elevate consumers' regard for a brand:

> We've done some analysis about their view of the brands, who was behind it, when they read a piece of our content that's sponsored by a particular brand and they're attitude towards that brand always improves after being exposed to content on our website that that brand has sponsored.
>
> (Maguire 2017, interview with the author, 12 May)

Ray Gill said he experienced pushback from clients when he declared native advertising as advertising: 'There's a lot of muddled thinking around it. I thought I wanted to, and on some we did. The advertisers hated it', he said (2017, interview with the author, 11 August).

But real-life experience shows that readers do not always differentiate between editorial and sponsored content. For example, in 2016 the

British advertising regulator criticised *BuzzFeed* in the United Kingdom for publishing a 'listicle' sponsored by dye manufacturer Dylon that did not sufficiently disclose it was sponsored content (Ingram 2016). This is problematic because it blurs the lines between advertising and news. This may add to public confusion about what is news and what is not. At worst, it can fuel scepticism and distrust about news that is perceived as primarily a vehicle for advertising, or indistinguishable from advertising.

Databases

Some outlets profit by building and selling databases to customers. *Mumbrella* developed the Source, a database to match various brands to the advertising agency they belong to. The database is available to companies through subscription. It is a revenue solution that also informs the site's journalism.

> When our reporters are writing about when an [advertising] account changes or how an agency is doing, they've got the Source then as a resource, in its own right, to look at what other accounts the agency has.
>
> (Burrowes 2017, interview with the author, July 11)

Events

Hosting events is also a profitable activity for some digital-only media companies. *The Guardian, Daily Review, Mumbrella,* and *Junkee* all host large public events. *BuzzFeed* hosts events in the United States, but not in Australia. *Junkee* runs 'Video Junkee', a video festival. It also hosts 'Junket', which Duggan describes as 'an influencer un-conference' (2017, interview with the author, July 12). *The Guardian* offers ticketed events to hear prominent Australian speakers being interviewed by *Guardian* editor Lenore Taylor. As part of building a reader community, which is important for sustaining revenue flows, *Guardian* subscribers receive discounted rates.

Burrowes says events constitute 'more than half of [*Mumbrella*'s] business model' (2017, interview the author, July 11). Of the 30 events they host each year, their key attraction is a three-day media and marketing conference in Sydney, '*Mumbrella 360*', which sells 3,000 tickets. Ticket prices vary depending on the function but can be up to A$2,500 per person for *Mumbrella 360*. Other events include major industry awards, breakfast gatherings, and training and industry summits.

The Daily Review turned to events to bolster lacklustre advertising revenues. These included drama workshops with actors on Netflix's hit political drama, *House of Cards,* and creative writing workshops with international renowned playwright Joanna Murray-Smith. Attracting audiences to the masterclasses was not a problem for *The Daily Review*, but drawing sufficient revenue was challenging. Faced with hard choices, Gill downsized his operations and shed staff (2017, interview with the author, 11 August).

New Media Products

Through its own data research in 2017, *Junkee* found that Australian youth thought differently about the world compared to youth surveyed five years earlier. 'The Gen Z's are a lot more optimistic than their older brothers and sisters', Duggan said. From these findings, *Junkee* Media launched a new digital site, *Punkee*, aimed at this younger age bracket (15- to 22-year-olds). Its focus was pop and media culture.

Similarly, *Mumbrella* launched new products based on its audience and advertisers' needs. These included specific industry summits for marketers and the public relations sector, industry awards, and conferences. It also provided a weekly newsletter for the public relations industry. This same formula of hosting awards and events is provided for the publishing industry. Burrowes explained that the journalism of *Mumbrella* offered the authority to host credible events and build audience trust within these niche professional communities. 'You're becoming a familiar brand with your readers so that they'll trust you that you know what you're talking about when the event comes along', said Burrowes (2017, interview with the author, July 11).

It is clear from the accounts of all these digital newsroom executives that they need multiple revenue streams—a hybrid model—to sustain their journalism. This is not without problems. Changes in markets can leave digital newsrooms vulnerable, as was seen with changes to *BuzzFeed's* reliance on audience share through social media spread. Further, native advertising offers its own set of ethical challenges for publishers if audiences cannot tell the difference between news and advertising. This might contribute to citizens' low levels of trust in news. The next sections focus on various forms of donations and micropayments to fund journalism.

Crowdfunding and Donations

The rise of crowdfunded journalism coincides with the growth of social media (Liu 2016). Easy access to online payment methods has also broadened options for revenue raising for media outlets. With the internet, anybody online, in any country, can sponsor journalism.

Success stories include the Dutch online journal *De Correspondent*, which raised US$2.6 million from more than 45,000 subscribers from 130 countries (*De Correspondent* 2019). It is the largest subscription-based news site in the Netherlands. It secured 19,000 members after its initial crowdfunding campaign in 2013 raised US$1.7 million (Pfauth 2017). Utilising social media platforms like Facebook to turn "likes" into members, it promised readers independence, diversity of news, quality stories, and an ad-free experience. The outlet said the fundraising successes meant it could expand its editorial team in 2019 (*De Correspondent* 2019).

Similarly, German website *Krautreporter* raised more than €1 million in 2014 by securing €60 commitments from 17,000 people (Doctor 2014). A simple WordPress blog in Spain named #NoHaceFaltaPapel was another crowdfunding success that developed into a publishing company, *El Espanol* (Johnson 2016). It used social platforms Instagram, Facebook, and Spotify and an email newsletter to drive support. The campaign raised US$3.1 million in two months from 5,500 supporters across the EU (Johnson 2016). In Switzerland, start-up digital magazine *Republik* raised more than 2.6 million francs by crowdsourcing funds, as well as 3.5 million francs from investors (Langley 2017). It also offered ad-free journalism that promised to 'reinforce democracy'.

In Australia, political website *Crikey* launched its 'Crikey Digs' campaign in March 2018 to fund the reporting of an undisclosed 'nationally and globally important' story. It passed its initial target of A$15,000 within three days of being launched. After passing the initial target, it extended the goal to A$20,000 (Wallbank 2018).

A year later, with undisclosed funds from individual investors John B. Fairfax and Cameron O'Reilly, *Crikey* announced it would expand its newsroom by about a dozen full-time reporters to pursue investigative or 'inquiry' journalism. It called for reporters to apply who have 'a distaste for spin and managed news; a passion for independent journalism untainted by corporate influence and ideological agendas; a mind open to original and unconventional ideas' (Beecher 2019). To sustain newsroom funding, it will rely on a subscription model (Duke 2019). Here, we see a direct link between developing a revenue stream and investigative journalism.

Analysis by the US Pew Research Center found journalism-related projects were commonly crowdfunded using the website Kickstarter, and a significant proportion promised to do investigative reporting. More than 600 journalism projects were funded this way, amassing US$6.3 million between 2009 and 2015 (Vogt and Mitchell 2016). A quarter of raised funds went to established media organisations and to longer form journalism including investigative reporting (Vogt and Mitchell 2016).

A negative aspect of crowdfunding is that many journalists were uncomfortable embracing entrepreneurial techniques and marketing their work to attract finance. One study recorded that the amount of work involved in organising a journalism funding campaign was like having a second full-time job (Hunter 2016).

Philanthropy

The philanthropy model has been deployed extensively in the United States to fund non-profit media organisations in response to the rise of fake news and polarised politics following the election of Donald Trump. This phenomenon is comprehensively covered in Bill Birnbauer's book *The Rise of Nonprofit Investigative Journalism in the United States* (2018), so I limit the discussion to a few cases.

In the United States, *ProPublica*, the Center for Investigative Reporting, the Center for Public Integrity, and First Look Media, which supports Glenn Greenwald's *The Intercept*, are all committed to investigative journalism and supported by major foundations and individual donors (Sievers and Schneider 2017).

Philanthropy has also stepped in to support local journalism with funding for independent non-profit local online newspapers, including the *Voice of San Diego, VTDigger, MinnPost, Honolulu Civil Beat*, and *Denverite* (Dubb 2018).

The Charleston Gazette-Mail, which was heading into a Chapter 11 bankruptcy in the United States, was saved by philanthropic support from the social entrepreneur journalism outfit 'Report for America' and investigative newsroom *ProPublica* (Westphal 2018). It was among seven news organisations subsidised by *ProPublica*. Other non-profits funding journalism include the Nieman Foundation, based at Harvard University; the Democracy Fund, founded by eBay founder and billionaire Pierre Omidyar; the News Integrity Initiative, a US$14 million fund at New York's City University to support journalism and its collaborators; and the Lenfest Institute for Journalism, founded in 2016 by cable television entrepreneur H. F. (Gerry) Lenfest to find new models for sustaining journalism.

Britain's *Guardian* launched a non-profit venture in the United States (at Theguardian.org) to raise money to support its journalism (Moses 2017). The non-profit has raised US$6 million since its launch in 2016 and attracts tax-exempt status. The Skoll Foundation donated funds to support coverage of climate change, Humanity United gave money to cover slavery, and Conrad N. Hilton Foundation supported reporting on early childhood development. Philanthropic support made up about US$4.9 million of the company's US$276 million in revenue in 2017 (Tsang 2017).

See Box 7.2 for other philanthropic examples.

Box 7.2   Examples of UK Philanthropists Funding Journalism in the Digital Age

Wincott Foundation aims to improve financial journalism. It provides annual awards, research grants.

Sigrid Rausing Trust, which provides grants towards research, journalism, and reporting in areas of international conflict.

Steven Bloch Image of Disability Charitable Trust also aims to promote understanding of disability through arts and journalism.

M. J. Samuel Charitable Trust provides a grant for fact-checking in journalism.

Marjorie Deane Financial Journalism Foundation provides financial assistance for students and interns in financial and economic journalism.

Lorana Sullivan UK Foundation provides education, training, and awards to improve the standards of investigative, business, and financial journalism.

JJ Charitable Trust provides a grant for the International Broadcasting Trust.

Indigo Trust provides grants for citizen journalism, digital technology, data journalism, especially for local media in Africa to develop civil society.

David Astor Journalism Awards Trust provides professional development support for young African journalists.

In Australia, where tax deductibility for journalism is very limited, philanthropic journalism is relatively underdeveloped. But times might be changing. Philanthropist Judith Neilson announced in late 2018 that she would fund a $100m institute for Australian journalism. While the Susan McKinnon Foundation announced in 2019 that it will provide AU$400,000 for specialist reporting work on questions of governance and accountability as part of the *Guardian* Civic Journalism Initiative Trust, with the University of Melbourne and the Guardian Australia. Exception is the academic online digest *The Conversation*, which publishes timely research by academics and is edited by journalists in a news style for a general audience. It is registered as a non-profit organisation and has tax-deductibility status owing to its 'educational' qualities. It also receives funding from the university sector.

The Conversation business model promotes republication of its articles through a creative commons license, and it has had significant global success expanding to eight other countries including the United States, United Kingdom, Africa, France, Canada, Indonesia, New Zealand and Spain. The UK edition also has charitable status, with initial funding from 12 universities (Harrow and Pharoah 2017) and these philanthropic foundations: the Esmée Fairbairn Foundation, the Wellcome Trust, and Lloyd's Register Foundation. The African edition has funding from the Gates Foundation.

The Public Interest Journalism Foundation (Birnbauer 2017) has made recommendations to the Australian Parliament that the Australian Tax Office consider extending tax deductibility to public interest journalism to offset the shrinking newsrooms of traditional media this century. At the time of writing, the competition watchdog, the Australian Competition & Consumer Commission, was also investigating if tax deduction laws should be changed in Australia to provide incentives to produce journalism (ACCC 2018).

Another uncommon example of philanthropy funding journalism in Australia is *The Guardian*, which expanded its franchise to Australia in 2013 with an investment from the founder of travel website Wotif, Graeme Wood. It was Wood's second attempt at supporting public interest journalism in Australia. In 2012, Wood offered A$15 million to establish the non-profit *Global Mail*. Two years later he ceased funding the outlet, saying it had failed to reach audience targets, and it subsequently folded. The founder of the Center for Public Integrity, Charles Lewis, observed that reliance on one benefactor to financially support a media outlet's journalism could make it more vulnerable to failure:

> The one challenge when a group has enough money from one donor is that you have to begin, very quickly, as soon as possible, to find other donors because donors are wonderful, sometimes they're very generous and they're also pretty notoriously fickle.
> (Lewis 2016, interview with the author, 31 August)

This is not the case with *The Guardian*, which has a diversified revenue model that includes reader contributions. Editor-in-chief Katharine Viner said the success of *The Guardian*'s voluntary subscriber model in the United States, United Kingdom, and Australia was driven by readers responding to original reporting, including investigative reporting: 'It just shows all along what people value . . . people want those people held to account, they want the powerful to be challenged', she said (Dodd et al. 2018).

The Guardian Media Group is also financially supported by advertising and a trust fund established in 1936 by John Scott, the owner of the then *Manchester Guardian*. But like other newspapers in developed economies, it has had significant financial difficulties. In 2012, it was the third most read news website worldwide, yet it recorded an operating loss on its newspaper businesses of £54 million (*The Economist* 2012). This shows that good journalism is not synonymous with good business. After adapting its business model in 2016 to include reader donations, Viner expects the news organisation will 'break even' in mid-2019 for the first time since the 1990s. Viner said US readers tended to contribute one-off donations, whereas Australians made ongoing contributions: 'We have fantastic reader contributions [in Australia], proportionally more than anywhere else in the world'.

The non-profit news sector in the United States has become big business. A 2018 report estimated it collected US$350 million in total annual revenue to fund more than 200 newsrooms (Cross 2018). This is important because non-profits tend to focus on investigative journalism and analysis (Cross 2018). The Institute for Nonprofit News itself funds more than 100 US non-profit media organisations, including the International Consortium of Investigative Journalists.

A downside to philanthropic funding is that journalists can feel compelled to pursue stories of less news value but of great interest to financial supporters. To negate conflicts of interest arising from philanthropic funding, the American Press Institute (2016) has written guidelines for non-profits and philanthropic foundations when funding journalism. These require news organisations to have 'written policies that establish . . . principles of editorial independence, transparency and communication, which will be the starting point of any interaction with funders'. Philanthropists are required to 'be transparent [with the public] about the media they are funding, and they should expect media partners to report their sources of funding'. They should likewise 'articulate their motivations for funding journalism and explain what would constitute success in meeting their purposes'.

Another patron of sorts for 21st-century journalism has been the return of the press baron. The difference this century is that the 'barons' have come from other industries to 'rescue' old mastheads from economic hardship. Some of the most famous examples are listed in Box 7.3. The public interest concern here is that while these 'white knights' might reinvigorate old media companies, they might also be motivated to garner attention for their own political and economic agendas.

Micropayments

This decade-old concept involves charging website visitors a few cents (or less) for reading an online story using a viewer's PayPal account or equivalent. In exchange for the micropayment, the user expects an ad-free experience and faster connection to the website—because online advertising can take time to download and slow the internet speed. However, most news start-ups rejected micropayments until recently. Common arguments against micropayments included users' concerns about inadvertent overcharging, that users paid up front without knowing the quality of the article, and that much internet content was freely available without charge (Shirky 2000). Federman (2015) insists micropayments are doomed to fail because pricing becomes a race to the bottom.

But with advances in blockchain technologies making payment methods simpler, publishers' interest in this funding method has returned. Examples of its use include the Dutch online news platform Blendle, which aggregates articles from newspapers and magazines (Robinson 2017). Based on the Spotify model, users in its home market pay a €9.99 monthly fee for a selection of 20 articles per day. Most major Dutch newspapers

---

Box 7.3   Examples of Billionaire Buyers 'Rescuing' News Media Companies in the Digital Age

Amazon founder Jeff Bezos bought *The Washington Post* for US$250 million in 2013.

Marc Benioff, founder and CEO of Salesforce, and his wife bought *Time* magazine for US$190 million.

Jack Ma acquired the *South China Morning Post* through his Alibaba Group in 2015 for US$266 million.

John Henry, the billionaire owner of the Boston Red Sox and the Liverpool Football Club, bought the *Boston Globe* in 2013.

Las Vegas casino billionaire Sheldon Adelson purchased the *Las Vegas Review-Journal* in 2015 for US140 million.

Joe Mansueto, the chairman and chief executive of Chicago-based investment research firm Morningstar, bought *Inc.* and *Fast Company* in 2005.

Peter Barbey's investment company, Black Walnut Holdings, bought the *Village Voice* in 2015.

Los Angeles doctor and pharmaceutical billionaire Patrick Soon-Shiong's Nant Capital purchased the *Los Angeles Times* and *San Diego Union-Tribune* in 2018.

Warren Buffett's Berkshire Hathaway made a bet on the newspaper industry in 2012 with a US$142 million deal to buy Media General's 25 regional newspapers.

Russian billionaire Viktor Vekselberg's investment arm, Columbus Nova bought a minority stake in *Gawker* in January 2016 prior to *Gawker's* demise after a crippling legal case against it later that year.

Alexander Lebedev, Russian billionaire and former KGB agent stationed in London, bought *The Independent* and Independent on Sunday for £1 in 2010.

Bernard Arnault, who oversees an empire of 70 brands including Louis Vuitton and Sephora, bought France's financial paper *Les Echos* in 2007.

---

have signed up to Blendle on a "pay-per-article" basis. Articles typically cost €0.35 each. Revenue is split between titles and Blendle on a 70:30 ratio. Backed by the Axel Springer Group and *The New York Times*, it has expanded into the United States but was still in beta development at the time of writing. *The New York Times, The Wall Street Journal, The Washington Post,* and *Time* were among 22 US publishers to have partnered with Blendle.

The free London business newspaper *City A.M.* a uses micropayment technologies on its website, targeting readers who use ad blockers. It gives readers who use an ad blocker a choice: either an ad-free experience at the cost of £0.50 per day or whitelisting the site in their ad blocker, making ads visible again to increase ad revenue (Scott 2018). The Irish local newspaper *Limerick Leader* also employed micropayments to monetise its story archives. The newspaper offers readers access to past articles for a day. As technologies advance, this is a payment method to watch.

Conclusion

This chapter has examined different funding methods for media organisations—large and small, in print and online—to pay for journalism. A sustainable funding model is necessary if outlets are to undertake investigative reporting. The findings here are mixed. Aside from public broadcasters, there is no single solution for funding news this century. Rather, it is evident that experimentation, adaptation, and flexibility are necessary in the digital age to fund journalism and, by extension, investigative reporting. But there is also the growing idea that investigative journalism itself can drive audiences to a news outlet if it is quality reporting that, in the words of Walter Robinson, 'hold[s] powerful institutions accountable'.

Erecting paywalls is the most common adaptive mechanism employed by print mastheads in the second decade of this century to get online readers to pay for news. The most common type of paywall is a soft or porous model that does not stymie online traffic. This enables publishers to satisfy the needs of advertisers, who want maximum eyeballs to view their products, while also generating some subscription revenue. Some print mastheads, particularly tabloids, reject the paywall option altogether, instead preferring to use the internet's natural strength to expand their geographical reach to entice more digital advertisers. The negative of this approach is that it can incentivise clickbait stories to attract online traffic.

The soft paywall works best for quality or specialised mastheads that attract readers who are most able or willing to pay for a digital subscription. It enables print mastheads to transition from an analogue model to a digital environment while generating revenue from both advertisers and readers. Many outlets still produce print copies and get revenue from print advertising as well. However, newspapers' annual reports show that total revenue tends to be much lower than in more bullish times last century, which has necessitated cost-cutting to try to realign income with expenses. Another consequence is that some topical and geographical areas of reporting have suffered.

But contrary to popular predictions, investigative journalism has continued in the first two decades of this century. This has been enabled partly by established newsrooms adjusting to their changed economic circumstances and experimenting to find new revenue-raising methods. *The*

New York Times was among the first to receive more income from digital subscriptions than advertising after it implemented its metered paywall.

Smaller news organisations, however, have been disadvantaged by the paywall model because they have struggled to attract enough subscribers. Diversification of revenue is likely to be critical for their survival. In such cases, a combination of various revenue streams may include native advertising, events, new media products, client-based studio work, micropayments, crowdfunding, and philanthropic support. For non-profits, the rise of polarised politics with the election of US President Trump has seen a lift in donations to outlets that do investigative reporting. This suggests that audiences, including philanthropists, value quality investigations and will pay for it.

In the age of social media, it is likely that newspapers' proportion of total global advertising share will shrink further as technology giants like Facebook and Google continue to impress advertisers with their global reach, sophisticated algorithms, and capacity to use data to target consumers. In some countries this has prompted governments and their agencies to reconsider competition and tax laws to limit the impact of Google and Facebook on news providers. A hybrid funding model is one means for news outlets to guard against Marshall McLuhan's dark prophecy.

References

American Press Institute 2016, *How Digital Subscriptions Work at Newspapers Today*, American Press Institute, accessed 5 May 2018, from www.american pressinstitute.org/publications/reports/digital-subscriptions-today/.

Atasoy, O & Morewedge, C 2017, 'Customers won't pay as much for digital goods: And research explains why', *Harvard Business Review*, 22 December, accessed 1 May 2018, from https://hbr.org/2017/12/customers-wont-pay-as-much-for-digital-goods-and-research-explains-why.

Auletta, K 2010, *Googled: The End of the World as We Know It*, Penguin Books, New York.

Australian Competition and Consumer Commission [ACCC] 2018, *Digital Platforms Inquiry: Preliminary Report*, December, accessed 15 January 2019, from www.accc.gov.au/focus-areas/inquiries/digital-platforms-inquiry/preliminary-report.

Beecher, E 2019, 'Crikey is assembling a team of a dozen "inquiry journalists"', *Crikey*, 11 February, accessed 11 February 2019, from crikey.com.au.

Bell, E & Owen, T 2017, 'The platform press: How silicon valley reengineered journalism', *Tow Center for Digital Journalism*, 29 March, assessed 1 May 2018, from www.cjr.org/tow_center_reports/platform-press-how-silicon-valley-reengineered-journalism.php/.

Birnbauer, B 2017, 'Philanthropy is funding serious journalism in the US, it could work for Australia too', *The Conversation*, 16 June, accessed 16 June 2017, from https://theconversation.com/philanthropy-is-funding-serious-journalism-in-the-us-it-could-work-for-australia-too-79349.

Birnbauer, B 2018, *The Rise of Nonprofit Investigative Journalism in the United States*, Routledge, London.

Burrowes, T 2011, 'AFR cuts cost of pay wall', *Mumbrella*, 30 November, accessed 1 June 2012, from https://mumbrella.com.au/afr-cuts-cost-of-pay-wall-67091.

Cameron, M 2018, 'Report: Australian ad spend to tip $17bn in 2019', *CMO*, 3 December, accessed 22 May 2019, from https://www.cmo.com.au/article/650320/report-australian-ad-spend-tip-17bn-2019/

Carson, A 2015, 'Behind the newspaper paywall: Lessons in charging for online content: A comparative analysis of why Australian newspapers are stuck in the purgatorial space between digital and print', *Media, Culture & Society*, 37(7), 1022–41.

Carson, A & Muller, D 2017, *The Future Newsroom*, University of Melbourne, Melbourne, September, accessed 16 September 2017, from https://arts.unimelb.edu.au/__data/assets/pdf_file/0003/2517726/20913_FNReport_Sept2017_Web-Final.pdf.

Christian, R 2018, 'Google appeases newspapers, play store to sell subscriptions', *Channel News*, 19 March, accessed 1 May 2018, from www.channelnews.com.au/google-appeases-newspapers-play-store-to-sell-subscriptions/.

Cross, S 2018, 'INN Index: The State of Nonprofit News: 2018 Survey Report', *Institute for Nonprofit News*, accessed 4 January 2019, from https://inn.org/wp-content/uploads/2018/10/INN.Index2018FinalFullReport.pdf.

De Correspondent 2019, 'Get acquainted with our journalism', *De Correspondent*, accessed 10 February 2019, from https://decorrespondent.nl/.

Deloitte 2017, *Deloitte's Sixth Annual Media Consumer Survey*, Deloitte, accessed 1 May 2018, from https://www2.deloitte.com/content/dam/Deloitte/au/Documents/technology-media-telecommunications/deloitte-au-tmt-media-consumer-survey-2017-290818.pdf.

Doctor, K 2018, 'Newsonomics: 18 lessons for the news business from 2018', *Nieman Lab*, 19 December, accessed 28 December 2018, from www.niemanlab.org/2018/12/newsonomics-18-lessons-for-the-news-business-from-2018/.

Doctor, K 2017, 'Newsonomics: Our Peggy Lee moment: Is that all there is to reader revenue?', *Nieman Lab*, 26 September, accessed 28 December 2018, from www.niemanlab.org/2017/09/newsonomics-our-peggy-lee-moment-is-that-all-there-is-to-reader-revenue/.

Doctor, K 2014, 'The newsonomics of European crowds, funding new news', *Nieman Lab*, 26 June, accessed 1 May 2018, from www.niemanlab.org/2014/06/the-newsonomics-of-european-crowds-funding-new-news/.

Dodd, A, Carson, A & Ricketson, M 2018, 'Media files: Covering trump, funding news and the rise of impunity: The Guardian's Kath Viner on the big media stories of 2018', *The Conversation*, 6 December, accessed 6 December 2018, from https://theconversation.com/media-files-covering-trump-funding-news-and-the-rise-of-impunity-the-guardians-kath-viner-on-the-big-media-stories-of-2018-106540.

Dubb, S 2018, 'Nonprofits increasingly central to the future of the news', *NPQ*, 12 February, accessed 1 December 2018, from https://nonprofitquarterly.org/2018/02/12/nonprofits-increasingly-central-future-news/.

Duke, J 2019, 'Eric Beecher's Crikey to launch investigative reporting arm', *Sydney Morning Herald*, 11 February, accessed 11 February 2019, from www.smh.com.au/business/companies/eric-beecher-s-crikey-to-launch-investigative-reporting-arm-20190211-p50x0s.html.

The Economist 2012, 'Unguarded', *The Economist*, 1 December, accessed 1 December 2012, from www.economist.com/node/21563334.

Federman, W 2015, 'Micropayments for news articles are a terrible, horrible, no good, very bad idea', *Medium*, 26 April, accessed 1 February 2017, from https://medium.com/@wfederman/micropayments-for-news-articles-are-a-terrible-horrible-no-good-very-bad-idea-267930d95a3a.

Felle, T 2016, 'Are paywalls saving journalism?', *The Conversation*, 22 February, accessed 22 February 2016, from https://theconversation.com/are-paywalls-saving-journalism-53585.

Fletcher, R & Nielson, R 2017, 'Paying for online news: A comparative analysis of six countries', *Digital Journalism*, 5(9), 1173–91.

The Guardian Labs 2017, *The Guardian*, accessed 4 September 2017, from https://advertising.theguardian.com/au/labs.

Harrow, J & Pharoah, C 2017, *Philanthropic Journalism Funding in the UK*, European Journalism Centre, London, accessed 5 January 2018, from https://journalismfundersforum.com/uploads/downloads/jff_london_report.pdf.

Hawthorne, M 2012, 'Murdoch in step back from papers', *Sydney Morning Herald*, accessed 23 July 2012, from https://www.theguardian.com/media/2012/jun/28/news-corp-split-rupert-murdoch.

Huffington, A 2009, 'The paywall is history', *The Guardian*, 12 May, accessed 12 May 2009, from www.theguardian.com/commentisfree/2009/may/11/newspapers-web-media-pay-wall.

Hunter, A 2016, '"It's like having a second full-time job"', *Journalism Practice*, 10(2), 217–32.

Ingram, M 2016, 'BuzzFeed slammed by UK regulator for native ad', *Fortune*, 13 January, accessed 1 May 2018, from http://fortune.com/2016/01/13/buzzfeed-native-advertising/.

Ingram, M 2019, 'BuzzFeed cuts should mean the death of metric-obsessed media', *Columbia Journalism Review*, 31 January, accessed 1 February 2019, from www.cjr.org/the_media_today/buzzfeed-cuts-end-metrics.php.

Johnson, K 2016, 'Behind journalism's top crowdfunding campaign', *Global Investigative Journalism Network*, 30 May, accessed 1 February 2018, from https://gijn.org/2016/05/30/the-story-behind-and-tips-from-the-most-successful-crowdfunding-campaign-in-the-history-of-journalism/.

Kammer, A, Boeck, M, Hansen, J & Hauschildt, L 2015, 'The free-to-fee transition: Audiences' attitudes toward paying for online news', *Journal of Media Business Studies*, 12(2), 107–20.

Langley, A 2017, 'A startup that promises "no-bullshit journalism" nets serious cash', *Colombia Journalism Review*, 3 May, accessed 3 May 2017, from www.cjr.org/innovations/news-startup-crowdfunding-switzerland.php.

Levine, R 2011, *Freeride*, Doubleday, New York.

Levy, M 2015, 'The Hoopla to cease publication, says Wendy Harmer', *The Sydney Morning Herald*, 23 March, accessed 1 February 2017, from www.smh.com.au/business/companies/the-hoopla-to-cease-publication-says-wendy-harmer-20150323-1m5ehg.html.

Linares, C 2018, 'New Google tools will help journalists generate revenue, optimize their work and increase security', *Knight Center for Journalism in the Americas*, 18 April, accessed 18 April 2018, from https://knightcenter.utexas.edu/00-19796-new-google-tools-will-help-journalists-generate-revenue-optimize-their-work-and-increase-se.

Liu, L 2016, *A Comparative Study of Crowd-Funding Journalism in China, Taiwan and the UK*, Reuters Institute, accessed 5 January 2019, from https://reutersinstitute. politics.ox.ac.uk/our-research/comparative-study-crowd-funding-journalism-china-taiwan-and-uk.

Moses, L 2017, 'The Guardian launches a non-profit to funds its journalism', *Digiday*, 28 August, accessed 28 August 2017, from https://digiday.com/media/guardian-launches-nonprofit-fund-journalism/.

McLuhan, M 1964/1994, *Understanding Media: The Extensions of Man*, Routledge, London.

Myllylahti, M 2016, 'Why some newspaper paywalls are simply unsustainable', *The Conversation*, 26 May, accessed 26 May 2016, from https://theconversa tion.com/why-some-newspaper-paywalls-are-simply-unsustainable-59577.

Nakashima, R 2012, *Newspapers Erect Pay Walls in Hunt for New Revenue*, Associated Press, accessed 1 February 2014, from http://news.yahoo.com/newspapers-erect-pay-walls-hunt-revenue-174925369.html.

Newman, N 2017a, 'Attitudes to paying for online news', *Reuters Institute for the Study of Journalism*, University of Oxford, August, accessed 1 February 2019, from https://reutersinstitute.politics.ox.ac.uk/our-research/attitudes-paying-online-news.

Newman, N 2017b, *Journalism, Media, and Technology Trends and Predictions*, Reuters Institute for the Study of Journalism, accessed 1 August 2018, from https://reutersinstitute.politics.ox.ac.uk.

Newman, N & Levy, D 2013, *Reuters Institute Digital News Report 2013*, Reuter's Institute, University of Oxford, accessed 1 February 2014, from https://reutersinstitute.politics.ox.ac.uk/our-research/digital-news-report-2013.

News Corp 2018, *Quarterly Report*, News Corp, accessed 31 December 2018, from http://investors.newscorp.com/static-files/83f921f3-8899-4480-8a6c-d21 aa842a399.

New York Times Company 2018, 'The year in numbers: 2018', accessed 31 December 2018, from www.nytco.com/the-year-in-numbers-2018/.

Pew Research Center 2018, *Newspapers Fact Sheet*, Pew Research Center, accessed 31 December 2018, from www.journalism.org/fact-sheet/newspapers/.

Pfauth, EJ 2017, 'De correspondent now has 50,000 paying members', *Medium*, 22 January 2017, accessed 20 January 2018, from https://medium.com/de-correspondent/de-correspondent-50k-members-59d1005ec9d3

Pickard, V & Williams, A 2014, 'Salvation or folly?' *Digital Journalism*, 2(2), 195–213.

Rajan, A 2018, 'The tortoise and the share', *BBC.com*, 5 March, accessed 5 March 2018, from www.bbc.com/news/entertainment-arts-43230640.

Samios, Z 2018, 'Why News Corp's regional and local paywalls are holding strong', *Mumbrella*, 2 July, accessed 2 July 2018, from https://mumbrella.com.au/why-news-corps-regional-and-newslocal-paywalls-are-holding-strong-531378.

Scott, C 2018, 'City A.M. employs micropayments in the fight against ad blocking', *Journalism.co.uk*, 27 February, accessed 27 February 2018, from www.journalism. co.uk/news/city-a-m-employs-micropayments-in-the-fight-against-adblocking/ s2/a718088/.

Shirky, C 2000, 'The case against micropayments', *Openp2p*, accessed 21 November 2012, from https://web.archive.org/web/20180222082156/www.openp2 p.com/pub/a/p2p/2000/12/19/micropayments.html.

Shirky, C 2014, 'Last call: The end of the printed newspaper', *Medium.com*, 19 August, accessed 1 February 2019, from https://medium.com/@cshirky/last-call-c682f6471c70.

Sievers, B & Schneider, P 2017, 'Can philanthropy save the media?', *Can Philanthropy Save the Media?*, 20 March, accessed 20 March 2017, from https://gijn.org/2017/03/20/can-philanthropy-save-the-media/.

Simons, M 2007, *The Content Makers: Understanding the Media in Australia*, Penguin Books, Melbourne.

Tsang, A 2017, 'The Guardian sets up a nonprofit to support its journalism'. *The New York Times*, 28 August, accessed 1 May 2018, from https://www.nytimes.com/2017/08/28/business/media/guardian-non-profit-philanthropy.html

Vogt, N & Mitchell, A 2016, *Crowdfunded Journalism: A Small but Growing Addition to Publicly Driven Journalism*, Pew Research Center, 20 January, accessed 20 January 2016, from www.journalism.org/2016/01/20/crowd funded-journalism/.

Wallbank, P 2018, '*Crikey* successfully completes journalism crowdfunding campaign', *Crikey*, 11 April, accessed 11 April 2018, from https://mumbrella.com.au/crikey-successfully-completes-journalism-crowdfunding-campaign-510354.

Westphal, D 2018, 'Journalism's new patrons: Newspapers deepen embrace of philanthropy', *Colombia Journalism Review*, 8 February, accessed 1 December 2018, from www.cjr.org/local_news/newspapers-philanthropy.php

Conclusion

The Future of Investigative Journalism: Reasons for Optimism

The aim of this book has been to assess the current state and future prospects of investigative journalism in the context of profound changes to the operating environment of the news media since the late 20th century. The development of the internet and digital technologies have broken traditional media's monopolistic grip on advertising revenues and news audiences. As a result, media organisations that have historically been the main purveyors of investigate journalism are now financially chastened and, in many cases, struggling to survive. Despite these travails, and the attendant erosion of traditional media's former cultural dominance, research conducted for this book confirms legacy news organisations have adapted to the new environment in ways that have enabled investigate journalism to continue to exert major influence, as demonstrated in Chapters 4, 5, and 6 of this book. Increasingly, to maintain a focus on investigations and their watchdog role in a democracy in an era of tight editorial budgets, established media have been collaborating with other organisations and exploiting the emerging research potential of digital databases. In some instances, this has resulted in the generation of global investigative stories of major consequence that would not have been possible in the pre-digital age. Thus, amid an otherwise prevailing atmosphere of gloom in traditional media, radical developments and innovation in the practice of investigate journalism provide cause for optimism.

By any measure, the period since the mid-1990s, when the internet was commercialised and online networks began to flourish, has been devastating for traditional newsrooms across developed economies. It has been marked by mass editorial redundancies, masthead closures, and a flurry of acquisitions and mergers that have led to greater concentration of ownership of established titles, and arguably less diversity of news sources. Amid pervasive pessimism about the future of journalism generally, fears about the possible demise of investigative journalism gained currency (Kelley 2009; Halliday 2010), particularly as its principal exponents and sponsors were print newspapers, which were among the enterprises hit hardest by the digital revolution.

As this book records, pessimistic commentary about the future of investigative journalism peaked during the global financial crisis of 2007–09, which was a particularly difficult time for newsrooms in the Northern Hemisphere. The economic trough for newsrooms in Australia came a little later, in 2012, when there were mass job losses, closures of printing plants, conversion of broadsheets to tabloid size, and the introduction of paywalls. In the aftermath, Australians witnessed a gaggle of new online-only news entrants, predominantly local versions of global titles like *BuzzFeed, HuffPost, The New York Times*, and *Daily Mail*. As the end of the second decade of the century nears, the rate of decline of larger traditional newsrooms in the studied countries appears to have slowed, although changes to Australian media ownership laws have resulted in further consolidation of metropolitan media after Fairfax merged with television network Nine in 2018. It is unknown at this time what this will mean for the future of investigative reporting in Australia, but the lack of cultural synergies between the two merging partners has prompted some concern. However, the influx of philanthropic funding for investigative journalism in Australia; and decision of Private Media, owner of *Crikey*, to set up a newsroom of about a dozen reporters in 2019 dedicated to inquiry and investigative reporting gives greater confidence in investigative journalism's future in Australia. In the United States, a brighter picture has emerged with the *Los Angeles Times, The Washington Post*, and *The New York Times* (Doctor 2018) re-hiring journalists in 2017–18 with a focus on investigation. Book-length publications of empirical works such as James T. Hamilton's *Democracy's Detectives* (2016), Bill Birnbauer's *The Rise of Nonprofit Investigative Journalism in the United States* (2018), and Beth Knobel's *The Watchdog Still Barks* (2018) all find that despite significant financial challenges, previous predictions of investigative journalism's demise were premature.

This study, with its examination of the state of investigative journalism in Australia and across Europe and North America has a broader geographic scope than the aforementioned US studies. For more granular analysis, its focus was on empirical data and findings about the United States, United Kingdom, and Australia. This study included almost 50 original interviews with media experts, an analysis of four decades of Australian newspaper content (1971–2011), and longitudinal examination of the comparator countries' national journalism awards, in Australia's case traced over six decades. To befit the theoretical framework, I focused on similar countries with mature economies to examine the health and role of watchdog reporting in democracies in the internet era. This study, like the US studies, finds that investigative journalism has endured and in some respects thrived in the digital age. Investigative journalism was examined across all media platforms including digital-only newsrooms and outlets with varied funding models. But given print's historically central role in developing investigative journalism (outlined in Chapter 2), and for the purpose of exploring investigations in comparative detail, the primary focus was on newspapers and their contemporary digital platforms.

This book's earlier chapters examined the origins of watchdog reporting and how it has changed over time. Methods for identifying and evaluating investigative journalism were developed, along with a working definition of investigative journalism. I traced shifts in practice from highly rivalrous single-entity newsrooms to multi-newsroom collaboration. Some of these changes in practice have prompted a rethinking of media theories to help explain why investigative journalism can prosper in the 21st century.

Changes in the practice of investigative journalism are documented in this book, with examples such as the International Consortium of Investigative Journalists' (ICIJ) medical 'Implant Files' in 2018 and *ProPublica*'s crowdsourcing efforts to expose voter suppression in the 2016 and 2018 reporting of 'Electionland'. Yet there are also sobering trends that cannot be ignored when assessing investigative journalism's future. For this reason, and considering the further consolidation of established media in Australia, the prospects for investigative journalism are viewed here with cautious optimism. I now reflect on five major shifts in investigative journalism theory and practice emerging from the earlier chapters' findings, and consider watchdog reporting's ongoing challenges to fulfil its monitoring role in democratic societies. This chapter concludes by reflecting more broadly on how the political environment for investigative journalism can be reconsidered to better serve the democratic needs of citizens.

1. Reconceptualising Chaos and Control Theories

The book's theoretical framework revisits the chaos and control streams of media theory. They are conceived as existing on a continuum (rather than as opposites) to argue that editors have a range of motivations (some commercial, some philosophical) for pursuing investigative journalism. This framework provides a theoretical basis for understanding why investigative journalism endures in the digital age. It also helps us understand why editors largely quarantined watchdog reporting when faced with newsroom cutbacks. Some editors, like Australia's *Mumbrella* founder Tim Burrowes, regard investigative journalism as beneficial for a masthead's branding strategy and will make provisions to pursue it, even if it loses money in its own right (see Chapter 7). In other instances, newsrooms like *The Guardian*'s in Britain and Australia have adapted to difficult economic times by pooling resources with other media or non-media organisations for investigative collaborations. *WikiLeaks* has been a conspicuous player in this development. *The Guardian* editor-in-chief Kath Viner (Dodd et al. 2018, n.p.) said investigative journalism was appreciated by its readers, many of whom had responded accordingly with financial contributions: 'Our investigative work is what drives the most [financial] contributions', she said. Digital outlets like Yahoo News have also expanded into watchdog reporting, with Yahoo hiring experienced former *Newsweek* and NBC investigative reporter Michael Isikoff in 2014 in a bid to bolster the organisation's branding as a serious news website.

Investigative collaborations, including those coordinated by the ICIJ, have reached global scale, making use of digital technologies to expose transgressions that cross national boundaries. Investigations such as the Panama Papers and Paradise Papers exemplify the 'chaos model', where the dominant political classes and elites have been unable to shut down investigations of their misconduct—in these cases involving tax avoidance in offshore havens. Their usual means of controlling messages by use of litigation, public relations campaigns, or more illicit forms of intimidation failed because of the global spread of the evidence and audience. Some of these global investigations have resulted from autonomous individuals leaking secret mass data that revealed the perpetration of inequality or injustice against powerless victims, including taxpayers and the broader public. In this way, transnational investigative stories can expose global power flows and stand up for victims in ways not previously possible.

By considering chaos and control theories as existing on a scale, I explain how the political economy of the commercial media can provide a somewhat protective buffer to investigative journalism by confining editorial budget cuts to other reporting areas considered less critical to the organisations' broader objectives. By sustaining their investment in investigative journalism, traditional news organisations have continued to set news agendas and maintain a critical area of competitive advantage over, and differentiation from, other commercial media. This has enabled the perpetuation of 'quality' broadsheet branding strategies, which underpin the shift in emphasis by some media organisations to a reader subscription revenue model after the collapse of the traditional advertising base. The nurturing of investigative journalism also enables them to demonstrate the wider societal impact of their stories to sponsors, as evidenced in their annual reports (see Chapter 3). It is at this juncture between political economy and liberal democratic theories of the media that we can see how investigative journalism can continue to prosper.

Yet, for both economic and political reasons, there are limits to the types of investigative journalism that some media outlets will pursue. For example, as documented in Chapter 4, at various times in recent history there has been a conspicuous absence of corporate investigative reporting by commercial news organisations. This might be because it is expensive to target corporations with the financial reserves to litigate or, alternatively, because business journalists, particularly during boom times, have become too close to their subjects, behaving more like cheerleaders and supporters than objective observers and critics. The dearth of investigative business journalism before the GFC was highlighted in the Australian data and reported by others in the United States (Schiffrin 2014). Chapter 5 also showed that some non-business story topics were unlikely to be the subject of investigations. In Australia, these topics included local government, the courts, and industrial relations, among others. The neglect of such speciality news subjects for investigation might be indicative of reduced editorial resources and the resulting loss of expert 'beat' reporters who develop deep knowledge and contacts in local and specialised reporting areas over time. The Australian Media, Entertainment and Arts Alliance estimated that 3,000 journalism jobs were cut from Australia's largest media outlets from 2011 to 2017 (MEAA 2017, p. 6), while interviewees such as Linton Besser (2017, interview with the author, 16 March) in Australia and Walter Robinson (2016, interview with the author, 25 September) in the United States identified reporting gaps in specialised and local areas (Chapter 5). By contrast, given the reduced editorial budgets of recent times, investigative journalism has been most commonly practised in subject areas where efforts to substantiate alleged wrongdoing are likely to be realised in a relatively short time frame, and therefore at less cost to the organisation and early rewards. Subject areas that fit this contemporary austerity model include crime, national politics, and corporate stories *after* the global financial crisis of 2007–09.

Thus, the theoretical framework of this book helps explain the motivations for *why* investigative journalism is still pursued. The next section continues to reflect on the major themes arising out of the findings to address the question of *how* investigative journalism can endure, notwithstanding difficult financial times for media companies.

2. Experimentation and Adaptation in the 21st Century

Two words that best capture how newsrooms have sustained investigative journalism while undergoing waves of staff cutbacks are 'experimentation' and 'adaptation'. Adaptation began with significant changes to the presentation of investigative journalism in newspapers over time. Chapter 4 documents a gradual decline in long-term investigative series and a corresponding rise in the production of one-off revelations and 'big hit' stories. These changes were born out of necessity. As paid circulations of newspapers fell and audiences fragmented, attempts to bolster story impact and widen a masthead's readership led to greater promotion of stories on front pages, and more frequent use of labels such as 'exclusive' and 'special investigation'. Journalists and their employers have also adapted to the digital environment by developing their own online presence and social media profiles. This has enabled them to share stories beyond traditional platform and geographical boundaries, and to target a wider demographic. Another discernible change over time has been the increase in single-issue investigations of individual and corporate transgressions. In many cases, these stories, while worthy in their own right, are often less time-consuming and expensive to produce than systemic investigations.

Experimentation has revolved around funding models for investigative journalism and storytelling. As Chapter 7 highlighted, many newspapers have adopted digital paywall models. Some mastheads have experimented by switching between 'hard' and 'soft' paywalls, varying the numbers and types of stories offered to readers without charge. Some experimentation has led to abandoning the paywall altogether, as *The Sun* did in Britain in 2015. After a period of experimentation, most digital offerings of newspapers have settled on a metered model. This provides a balance between trying to establish a culture in which readers are happy to pay for online news, while also encouraging advertisers by maintaining online traffic flows of non-paying readers. Smaller digital-only outlets seem to have mostly settled on a diversified funding model without using paywalls to bring in revenue. This hybrid model might entail a combination of revenue streams including crowdsourcing donations and philanthropic support; native and other forms of digital advertising; sponsored media project work for clients; selling of readership data and access to databases; and organising paid events that complement the needs and wants of the core readership. The profitability of these models is mixed in a volatile time for digital media and raises concerns about the blurring of advertising with editorial, as the phenomenon of native advertising booms. However, as discussed in Chapter 7, the emergence and growth of several digital-only newsrooms in Australia suggests that the hybrid model can work for niche outlets, which are filling some of the gaps in reporting that resulted from legacy media's cutbacks.

Digital outlets have also experimented with how they tell their stories. Reporters working in digital-only newsrooms tend to be fewer in number but multi-skilled, with the versatility to tell stories variously using text, graphics, audio, and video. And in the modern era, unlike the 20th century, where newspaper stories were always told in text, the type of story influences how the story is presented. Also, stories are more likely to be released simultaneously on multiple platforms. The Panama Papers is an example of this phenomenon. Chapter 7 also highlighted changes in the way that journalists structure stories. Narrative storytelling has become more prevalent, and in many cases has replaced the traditional 'inverted pyramid' formula of news reporting, where facts were presented in descending order of perceived importance, answering questions of 'who', 'what', 'where' and 'when', in the first few paragraphs. There is also less adherence to the objective of impartiality, and more activism and attitude in some contemporary reporting.

Finally, the digital age has opened up new opportunities for experimentation in the practice of investigative journalism with the rise of data mega leaks. These leaks have resulted in multi-newsroom collaborations in various configurations, and new approaches to disclosing data ranging from radical transparency (*WikiLeaks*) to a more traditional journalist-source relationship (Snowden and the NSA leaks) through to large-scale networks of 'equal partners' working together in a diffuse power structure (ICIJ). As newsrooms adapt to their changed financial circumstances, investigations are becoming more national and transnational in focus. This shift, however, might come at the expense of more local investigations.

3. Collaboration and the Emergent Global Digital Public Sphere

To overcome time and financial constraints, traditional newsrooms have adapted by sharing their resources and fieldwork efforts with others, including former media rivals. In Australia one of the earliest forms of collaboration involved the syndication of stories within commercial media groups, such as *The Age* and *The Sydney Morning Herald*, then owned by Fairfax Media. Towards the end of the millennium's first decade, journalists from mastheads within the same news groups started working together on the same investigations. Through simultaneous cross publication, the impact and reach of stories, jointly produced by newsroom stablemates, benefitted from exposure to Australia's two largest capital city markets (Sydney and Melbourne). As newsroom cuts deepened and more editorial redundancies occurred, collaborations extended beyond stablemates to rival media organisations. In the United States, award-winning cross-media investigation took off in 2004 when *The New York Times* worked with PBS *Frontline* and the Canadian Broadcasting Corporation (CBC) on an investigation into workplace fatalities (see Chapter 5). In Britain, award-winning collaborations appeared several years later when *WikiLeaks* partnered with *The Guardian* in 2010. In Australia, the ABC and Fairfax began working together at about this time. A negative aspect of this is that as resources have been squeezed, joint media operations might limit news diversity for the public. But diversity has arguably been enriched in other ways, including by traditional newsrooms teaming up with non-media partners such as academics and even the general public to crowdsource information for investigations. One example was *The Guardian*'s investigation into British politicians' abuses of their work expense claims. The newspaper relied on members of the public across 650 electoral districts to detect and report unusual expense claims belonging to their political representative.

This shift in journalistic practice to embrace collaboration is significant because it allows journalists to expose misuse of power on a potentially global scale. Thus, journalists can now more readily and effectively investigate issues such as economic inequality and political and electoral corruption beyond their own borders. The connective journalism model using hundreds of reporters from scores of countries coordinated by non-profits (such as the ICIJ) also returns agency to journalists and enables them to leverage their employers' remaining institutional power to gain

global attention. The spread and impact of these global collaborative stories is supported through digital technologies such as social media, under-
scoring the importance of new media in tackling the fragmented news
environment to facilitate a global public sphere. A diffuse power structure within a reporter network and the development of trust between
the network partners to abide by agreed publishing dates and a uniform
approach to redaction appear to be key features of successful collaboration, as evidenced in the ICIJ examples. In the *WikiLeaks* example, however, trust broke down between *WikiLeaks* founder Julian Assange and
some media partners, eventually leading to the collapse of collaboration
under this model.

For investigative reporters, Manuel Castells' (2013) network communication theory highlights how digital technologies and networks of the
21st century assist journalistic collaboration by bringing together reporters from different newsrooms and locations and linking them to a global
audience. Castells' theory posited that the internet was playing a democratising role, enabling citizens to come together to overcome traditional
and limited 'flows of power', replacing these with flows of information or
the 'power of flows'. In this way, journalists can inform local audiences
about global problems, such as tax avoidance and environmental harms,
in new ways. This local/global reporting nexus shows how some investigative stories can reinvigorate Habermas' normative conception of the
public sphere on a global scale, enabling the same conversations across
the world about massive global problems. For example, the reporting
of the Panama and Paradise papers brought unprecedented worldwide
focus on the cost to ordinary citizens of tax evasion by elites, with revelations of an estimated US$8.7 trillion, or 11.5 per cent of the world's GDP,
held in offshore tax havens (Zucman 2017).

4. The Rise of Data Journalism

Another remarkable trend in investigative journalism this century has
been the rise in data journalism, involving the use of digital technologies
and often social science methods to produce evidence-based reporting.
Data journalism, particularly when combined with collaborative investigative reporting, can be a democratising force that dissolves spatial and
time boundaries by enabling journalists to simultaneously analyse and
report the same mass dataset regardless of where they live in the world.
The result is an emergent and powerful public information sphere highlighting global problems to an international audience. Large-scale collaborative investigative reporting has shown the power of numbers to tell
human stories of global significance in innovative ways.

Data use in journalism also enables the audience to participate in
reporting. *ProPublica* crowdsourced information for its 'Electionland'
stories, while *The Guardian* engaged citizen volunteers to analyse data to

expose British politicians' expense claims. The engagement of audiences in the researching of stories is a new development in investigative journalism this century that offers another potential way forward in an era of tight editorial budgets. Sharing stories through social media networks has also dramatically lowered the cost of reaching an audience compared to just a few decades ago, when the only distribution options involved the considerable expense of printing and distributing newspapers or, in the case of radio and TV, broadcast licenses. The digital era has also helped to bring together audiences from different physical places and online spaces, thus extending the reach and impact of investigations. Technology enables a story's impact with a digital audience to be measured, which provides newsrooms with the opportunity to refine and relaunch a story that is failing to find an audience. 'Data is a huge part of what we do', said *Junkee*'s Tim Duggan. 'Almost every piece of content we look at, we figure out why it's working or why if it's not working, how can we do it better. It is not perfect for prediction, that still requires a "journalist's hunch"' (2017, interview with the author, July 12).

The uptake of data journalism in newsrooms across the globe is uneven. While the Global Editors Network (GEN) annual data journalism awards are receiving more entries (about 700 in 2018) from more countries (57 nations in 2018) than when they began in 2012, data skill levels of journalists vary between nations. Compared to the United States and Britain, Australia has far fewer examples of data journalism coming from its major newsrooms (Wright and Doyle 2018). And, as Chapter 7 showed, few newsrooms have experimented with data journalism due to cost and training constraints. This is likely to change with the announcement in late 2018 that Google has partnered with Australia's national Walkley Foundation, which oversees the Walkley Awards, with the goal of training 4,000 journalists and journalism students in the use of digital technologies within the next few years (Mason 2018). This financial support comes from the Google News Initiative, which promised US$300 million in 2018 to invest in a range of different journalism projects across the globe (Mason 2018). Other media organisations' websites such as GEN, and the Global Investigative Journalists Network (GIJN), provide free access to online data journalism tools, and tips and lessons to encourage reporters to experiment with data journalism. The GIJN predicted in 2019 that data journalism would be a growth area, with more journalists utilising artificial intelligence and machine learning, as well as working more closely with computer programmers and coders to find stories through pattern recognition algorithms (GIJN 2019). Head of Google Labs and former *Guardian* journalist Simon Rogers (2018) predicted data journalism 'will become a truly global field of work' with more cross-border collaborations, globally and regionally, to draw attention to global problems such as environment degradation, international crime, mass migration, and illegal money flows. American University's data editor, Jennifer

LaFleur (GIJN 2019), expected that data research would be used more extensively in investigative reporting in coming years, especially the use of 'artificial intelligence and machine learning . . . [to] process huge document dumps, identify doctored photos and videos, and draw connections between people and organizations'. Investigative journalist and academic Brant Houston (GIJN 2019) said journalists would 'construct better ways of visual storytelling when reporting on the complex transactions and networks involved in global corruption'.

The use of scientific methods to verify information holds the prospect of restoring public trust in media organisations in an era blighted by the spread of 'fake news', curtailed media freedom, and the surveillance of journalists' activities by both liberal and illiberal governments. As the next section will discuss, the co-founder of *Veri Gazeteciliği Türkiye* (Data Journalism Turkey), Pinar Dag (GIJN 2019), argues that data reporting that is transparent about its methods and datasets will become 'increasingly important'.

5. Unresolved Challenges to Investigative Journalism Practice

This final chapter began with a review of how technological and economic disruptions this century have altered the operating environment for organisations undertaking investigative journalism. Media outlets have responded to these economic challenges through experimentation, adaptation, collaboration, and use of data to support the continued production of investigative reporting. Concurrently, media audiences have become active participants in the processes of newsgathering and story dissemination. And the online sharing of stories has provided new opportunities to reach previously disparate audiences and achieve a wider impact for stories, in some cases through global collaborative investigative reporting.

But political and technological challenges to investigative journalism's practices and viability discussed in this book cannot be ignored. Trust in the news media has been falling in many Western democracies in recent decades (Edelman 2018). Studies indicate how political elites' use of the term 'fake news' to try to discredit media criticism of themselves or their organisations negatively affects individuals' trust in news media (Brummette et al. 2018; Van Duyn and Collier 2018). As discussed in Chapters 5 and 6, politicians (most notably US President Donald Trump) have embraced the term 'fake news' as a verbal weapon to delegitimise journalism that paints them in a negative light (Wardle and Derakhshan 2017, p. 5; McNair 2018). By contrast, the rise of actual 'fake news'— whereby individuals or organisations wilfully spread misinformation on social media platforms to influence public opinion—undermines the quality of information available to citizens, particularly during election campaigns. To the extent that its messages resonate with the general public, the fake news phenomenon is problematic in democracies because trust in journalism holds together the ideal of the public sphere, providing citizens with accurate information that informs political discourse and can influence voting intention (McNair 2017). Without trusted information, 'rational choice' and potentially 'participation'—two central tenets of a well-functioning democracy—are lost (see Chapter 3). As examined in Chapter 6, investigative journalism provides a counter-narrative to fake news because it is evidence-based reporting that can be verified, often through the use of publicly accessible data.

When functioning effectively, trusted news organisations that practice investigative journalism can provide an indispensable aid and refuge for people trying to establish objective facts in an era when technology has provided unprecedented reach and influence for self-interested peddlers of misinformation. The 'Trump bump', which describes a rise in some mastheads' subscriptions and donations after Donald Trump's election (including for *ProPublica*, *The New York Times*, and *The Washington Post*), is considered an example of the value citizens place on quality journalism. In this case, a victorious circle was created because increased funding has enabled these newsrooms to continue to produce quality investigative reporting.

Another political challenge to journalism has emerged with the development of surveillance technologies and amendments to national security laws in response to terrorist acts in the post-9/11 world. As noted in Chapter 6, global indices show that media freedom has fallen this century, including in liberal democracies, since countries have tightened their security measures (Freedom House 2017) and in some cases enacted laws that could lead to journalists in receipt of state secrets being imprisoned (Lidberg and Muller 2018). In spite of this more restrictive environment, there has been a rise in mass radical disclosures of state and corporate secrets in the media. As noted by the ICIJ's data and research unit head, Mar Cabra (2016) (see Chapter 6), mega leaks as a source for investigative journalism is a 'new normal'.

A third challenge is the absence of a dependable and proven new funding model for commercial media companies in the digital era. Legacy media companies that previously relied principally on advertising revenue to fund their journalism have lost much of this revenue to multinational online giants, most notably Google and Facebook. The closure of local media outlets and the curtailment of newsrooms due to falling advertising revenue and acquisitions and mergers has left some communities with dramatically reduced local news coverage, or in some cases none at all (Carson et al. 2016). Hayes and Lawless (2015) found that communities with fewer local news options had higher numbers of citizens with diminished political engagement and participation in US House of Representatives elections. Media companies have responded to their financial predicament both with editorial budget cuts and attempts at building other revenue streams, including the erection of paywalls to encourage paid subscriptions and direct appeals to readers for donations. Individual journalists, meanwhile, have addressed the challenge through collaboration and building personal online presence and social media profiles.

Some Western democratic institutions and governments have acted to help commercial media survive the various digital age challenges. The European Union has changed the regulatory environment for news media to address anti-competitive activity from the technological giants. Europe has also instructed digital platforms and the advertising industry to abide by a code of practice to tackle disinformation, including the spread of fake news. The code is also designed to promote transparency in political advertising (European Commission 2018).

The United States provides tax incentives to encourage third-party funding of investigative journalism. The Spanish government chose a different policy approach to pay for journalism when it changed copyright laws in 2015. It applied a compulsory fee to news aggregators like Google that use 'snippets' of news content from media outlets to be paid to the outlets. It backfired. Google News, Yahoo News, and Bing News responded by terminating their Spanish news services. The European Parliament at the time of writing was negotiating changes to copyright laws with these examples in mind (Athey et al. 2017).

In Australia, its competition watchdog, the Australian Competition and Consumer Commission inquiry into the impact of digital platforms on media and advertising markets was underway at the time of writing. Its interim report released in December 2018 considered various tax changes to act as incentives to produce journalism. Meanwhile, the Australian government was considering strengthening whistleblower protections to address inconsistencies between its states and between the public and private sectors (Parliamentary Joint Committee on Corporations and Financial Services 2017). While a full investigation into political remedies to increase media trust, ensure media freedom and sustain public interest journalism offers avenues for future research, democracies need to heed these challenges if the media's watchdog role is as valued by their citizens as past surveys suggest.

This chapter has drawn upon the major findings within this book to evaluate the future of investigative reporting and democratic accountability in the digital age. The case studies, content analyses, and interviews conducted for the study provide strong evidence that investigative journalism, despite its contemporary challenges, continues to play an essential watchdog role in the life of Western democracies. The study presents positive evidence of how technology and collaboration are sustaining and invigorating the practice of investigative journalism, allowing journalists to expose abuses of power and injustices in ways that would not have been possible in the supposed golden era of the craft during the 1980s. I have argued that the endurance of investigative journalism in the digital age is best understood by returning to mass media theories of dominance and pluralism, and rethinking these as existing on a continuum with capacity for overlap to explain media outlets' incentives for pursuing investigative journalism. While motivations might vary, it is within this space that newsrooms of different types, commercial and otherwise, are inclined to pursue investigative reporting. This chapter finds that while digital disruption has led to formidable challenges for newsrooms, particularly in the form of revenue losses and the erosion of public trust exacerbated through the phenomenon of 'fake news', predictions about watchdog journalism's demise in democracies are unfounded. Rather, this study provides strong cause for optimism about the future of investigative journalism. This matters because, in the words of Brant Houston (2016, interview with the author, 23 September), when all other means of redressing injustice fail, investigative journalism is the 'court of last resort'.

References

Athey, S, Mobious, M & Pal, J 2017, 'The impact of aggregators on internet news consumption', *Graduate School of Stanford Business*, working paper No. 3353, 11 January, accessed 15 February 2019, from www.gsb.stanford.edu/faculty-research/working-papers/impact-news-aggregators-internet-news-consumption-case-localization.

Birnbauer, B 2018, *The Rise of Nonprofit Investigative Journalism in the United States*, Routledge, New York.

Brummette, J, DiStaso, M, Vafeiadis, M & Messner, M 2018, 'Read all about it: The politicization of "fake news" on Twitter. *Journalism & Mass Communication Quarterly*, 95(2), 497–517.

Cabra, M 2016, 'The Panama Papers: Lessons learned and the road ahead', *Uncovering Asia*, 23 September, Global Investigative Journalism Network Conference, Kathmandu, Nepal.

Castells, M 2013, *Networks of Outrage and Hope*, Polity Press, Cambridge.

Carson, A, Muller, D, Martin, J & Simons, M 2016, 'A new symbiosis? Opportunities and challenges to hyperlocal journalism in the digital age', *Media International Australia*, 161(1), 132–46.

Doctor, K 2018, 'Newsonomics: 18 lessons for the news business from 2018', *Nieman Lab*, accessed 19 December 2018, from www.niemanlab.org/2018/12/newsonomics-18-lessons-for-the-news-business-from-2018/.

Dodd, A, Carson, A & Ricketson, M 2018, 'Media files: Covering trump, funding news and the rise of impunity: The Guardian's Kath Viner on the big media stories of 2018', *The Conversation*, accessed 6 December 2018, from https://theconversation.com/media-files-covering-trump-funding-news-and-the-rise-of-impunity-the-guardians-kath-viner-on-the-big-media-stories-of-2018–106540.

Edelman, R 2018, *Trust Barometer: Global Report*, Edelman, accessed 5 January 2019, from www.edelman.com/sites/g/files/aatuss191/files/2018-10/2018_Edelman_Trust_Barometer_Global_Report_FEB.pdf.

European Commission 2018, 'Code of practice on disinformation', *European Commission*, 26 September 2018, accessed 5 January 2019, from https://ec.europa.eu/digital-single-market/en/news/code-practice-disinformation.

Freedom House 2017, *Freedom of the Press*, accessed 12 March 2018, from https://freedomhouse.org/report/freedom-press/freedom-press-2017.

Global Investigative Journalists Network [GIJN] 2019, 'What the experts expect for data journalism in 2016', *Global Investigative journalism Network*, 18 January, accessed 18 January, from https://gijn.org/2019/01/18/what-the-experts-expect-for-data-journalism-in-2019/.

Halliday, J 2010, 'Investigative journalism "dying a death"', *The Guardian*, 5 November, accessed 1 May 2018, from www.theguardian.com/media/2010/nov/04/investigative-reporting-sheffield-docfest.

Hamilton, J 2016, *Democracy's Detectives: The Economics of Investigative Journalism*, Harvard University Press, Cambridge.

Hayes, D & Lawless, JL 2015, 'As local news goes, so goes citizen engagement: Media, knowledge, and participation in US house elections', *The Journal of Politics*, 77(2), 447–62.

Kelley, S 2009, 'Investigative Reporting, Democracy, and the Crisis in Journalism', in *Centre Blog*, 21 May. The Canadian Centre for Investigative Reporting, Ottawa.

Knobel, B 2018, *The Watchdog Still Barks: How Accountability Reporting Evolved for the Digital Age: How Accountability Reporting Evolved for the Digital Age*, Fordham University Press, New York.

Lidberg, J & Muller, D 2018, *In the Name of Security: Secrecy, Surveillance and Journalism*, Anthem Press, London.

Mason, M 2018, 'Google provides funds for new AAP factchecking division ahead of 2019 elections', *Australian Financial Review*, 21 December, assessed 31 December 2018, from www.afr.com/business/media-and-marketing/publishing/google-provides-funds-for-new-aap-factchecking-division-ahead-of-2019-elections-20181217-h197me.

McNair, B 2017, *An Introduction to Political Communication*, Routledge, London.

McNair, B 2018, *Fake News: Falsehood, Fabrication and Fantasy in Journalism*, Routledge, Oxon.

Media, Entertainment and Arts Alliance [MEAA] 2017, 'Submission to the senate select committee inquiry into the future of public interest journalism', *Media Entertainment and arts Alliance*, 14 July 2017, accessed 10 February 2018, from www.meaa.org/download/meaa-submission-to-public-interest-journalism-inquiry-170714/.

Parliamentary Joint Committee on Corporations and Financial Services 2017, 'Whistleblower protections in the corporate, public and not-for-profit sectors', *Parliament of Australia*, 14 September, accessed 5 January 2018, from www.aph.gov.au.

Rogers, S 2018, 'Data journalism becomes a global field', *NiemanLab*, December 2018, accessed 15 January 2019, from, www.niemanlab.org/2018/12/data-journalism-becomes-a-global-field/.

Schiffrin, A 2014, *100 Years of Investigative Journalism from Around the World: Global Muckraking*. The New Press, New York, 60–1.

Van Duyn, E & Collier, J 2018, 'Priming and fake news: The effects of elite discourse on evaluations of news media', *Mass Communication and Society*, doi: 10.1080/15205436.2018.1511807.

Wardle, C & Derakhshan, H 2017, 'Information disorder: Toward an interdisciplinary framework for research and policymaking', *The Council of Europe*, 27 September, accessed 5 December 2017, from https://shorensteincenter.org/wp-content/uploads/2017/10/PREMS-162317-GBR-2018-Report-de%CC%81sinformation.pdf?x78124.

Wright, S & Doyle K 2018, 'The evolution of data journalism: A case study of Australia', *Journalism Studies*, doi:10.1080/146167OX.2018.1539343.

Zucman, G 2017, *The Hidden Wealth of Nations*, University of Chicago Press, Chicago.

Appendix
Tools for Defining Investigative Journalism (Operative Definition)

Nine story elements	Considerations	Satisfied by fulfilling any of the following	Pts
1. *Does the article set the public agenda and/or is it exclusive to that publication?	• It is genuinely identified as an exclusive, 'special report', or 'investigation' of the publication • It does not need to be branded 'exclusive' to be exclusive/revelatory, but: • The article sets the news agenda, delivering readers information outside the daily news cycle • A journalist is specifically commissioned to investigate the story that is not covered elsewhere • It may include collaborations • The story is non-scheduled, in that it is less reliant on a timed event	• Marked 'exclusive' or 'special report' (deservedly); no other media carries the same story (except if syndicated or part of a coordinated collaboration) • Information is genuinely new and revelatory • May be a news tip that comes from a journalist's networking capabilities or contacts that takes time and effort to get	1
2. *Does the story provide evidence of skills, and techniques of active reporting?	• Unique sources are sought out and mentioned (don't have to be named) • Passive elements of reporting are excluded: e.g. the story results from press release, observational journalism; i.e. parliamentary question time, courts, other hearings with no follow-up reporting	• More than a reliance on passive reporting • Uses original sources and/or content • The story would not have made the public sphere at this time if it were not for the journalist's investigative efforts	1
3. *Is there evidence of time, research, and effort in the story, or series of stories?	• Evidence of time or effort—looking for any mention of resources/number of interviews/travel/FOI requests/reference to documents, etc. • More information and detail than what are expected from a daily news report	• May be evidenced through, or reference to case studies, interviews, documents, witnesses, time to travel to location, which are included in article(s). Or, time taken to get important, exclusive interview. Or, part of an ongoing series that demonstrates the above	1

4. *Does the story investigate (and verify 'facts'), rather than rely on a compilation of opposing viewpoints?	• There are serious attempts to verify the information, and not just report it, involving: • Story goes beyond duelling anecdotes of allegation and denial by competing sources • It does not rely only on 'official' sources • Evidence that time was involved in researching and producing the story • Leaves the audience clearer about where the 'truth' lies because of the investigative efforts of the reporter • Weighs different information source and seeks to use quality evidence such as Ettema and Glasser's hierarchy of evidence' model (see Chapter 2)	• Verifies allegations with supporting documents/video evidence, witness accounts, i.e. not just he said/she said • Uses information beyond quoted protagonists • Journalist's time and effort is evident in the story (trying to contact a target for comment and not succeeding is not sufficient)	1
5. *Does the revelatory information belong in the public rather than private sphere (e.g. is it in the public interest)?	• Identifies a political dimension important for the public to know in the story, and makes apparent why it belongs in the public sphere • Attempts to hold public figures or institutions to account on behalf of the public by interviewing them or relevant authorities; may interrogate private companies that have impacted on public well-being in some way • The story has relevance beyond mere voyeurism (i.e. scandalous journalism) • Methods for collecting information can be justified because of the public interest in the revelations • The general public benefit of the story outweighs any negatives; journalist attempts to minimise harms because of the story	• The story involves a target of at least one of following political figures: politician, public entity (i.e. government, statutory authority), public servant • Or, a private figure or company using public resources, or a private figure whose actions have harmed the public (i.e. public funds required for reconstitution) in some way • The story's longer-term outcomes lead to social, political, legal, or economic reforms that benefit society and can be attributed to the investigation	1
6. Does it identify victims and villains?	• Does the reporting in some way give the powerless a voice to provide their version of events against those of the powerful? Or, enable an injustice or unfairness to be addressed?	• Powerless/powerful dichotomy present in the story, or 'victim(s)' mentioned (not necessarily personally identified) or quoted, but their viewpoint given	1

(Continued)

(Continued)

Nine story elements	Considerations	Satisfied by fulfilling any of the following	Pts
7. Does the story investigate a breach of public trust?	• The story shows that the public have been misled; rules/laws have been transgressed, or evidence that a public official has acted with impropriety in some way that adversely affects the public's trust invested in the transgressor • A breach of trust between a principal and agent within an organisation is demonstrated • May expose double standards of a public figure that bear in some way or contradict their public duties or utterances (stated ideologies) that damage public trust	• Reveals information that shows a transgression of rules/laws/social norms that is, in some way harmful to the public and/or the trust invested in the public figure or private institution with public impacts	1
8. Does it expose hidden information or pursue a suppressed truth, and is it in the public interest to do so?	• Uncovers important information that someone has suppressed for reasons of self-benefit at the expense of others • Unveils new information about an 'old' story such as a cold case crime • Provides new context that sheds light on an 'old' story	• The unearthing of 'new' information benefits the public in some way (e.g. justice for an unresolved crime), and it is information not previously disclosed • The hidden information is revealed in the story • It takes time and effort to reveal the 'truth' because of active suppression; or neglect of available information or its context; or, new information comes to light	1
9. Is a moral standard implied?	• Story operates within a moral framework. It upholds or identifies a normative value, i.e. it polices public order and identifies the boundaries of societies' accepted norms, and reveals actions outside of those boundaries	• It says why the story is important to the public • It assumes a societal standard and indicates how that has been breached • Explicitly identifies a perversion of societal values	1
Total points 9			

Source: Author.

*Denotes mandatory elements that must be present for a story to be considered investigative.

Notes: Each story, whether part of a story series or not, was assessed on its merits, and then on its merits as part of a collective. The series of stories needed to contain the mandatory elements to be considered investigative. The outcomes of stories were followed using academic news databases LexisNexis and Factiva. This sometimes involved following a story across several years.

Index

Note: Page numbers bold indicate a table and page numbers in italics indicate a figure on the corresponding page.

AB demographic 29
accountability 87, 98
adaptation 227
Adelaide Advertiser 125
Adorno, Theodor 9, 88
advertising 4; 'clickbait' 40; and the hybrid business model 205, 206; native 206, 207, 208; partnerships 208; revenue, comparing between Australian and American newspapers 34, 35; *see also* marketing
'Afghan War Diary, 2004–2010, The' 182; *see also WikiLeaks*
Age, The 22, 26, 29, 30, 37, 60, 76, 112, 122, 132, 229; circulation 40; collaboration with *The Sydney Morning Herald* 158; follow-up stories 128; investigative reporting 124; peak circulation 26
agenda-building 6
Al Jazeera 173
anti-terrorism measures, freedom of the press impact on 173
Assange, Julian 178, 179, 180, 181, 182, 183, 230
Aucoin, James 60, 68; *The Evolution of American Investigative Journalism* 6
audience: crowdsourcing stories 166, 167; news audience compared to the citizen 86–8; for online advertising platforms 37; of online stories, measuring 116, 117; reaching through social media 205
Australia: advertising market share by platform 36, **36**; broadsheets 22, 25; Channel Nine 24;

circulation of print newspapers in 39, 40, 41, 42; commercial newspaper attacks on public broadcasting 44, 45; concentration of newspaper ownership in 24, 25; consolidation of newspapers in 44; counter-terrorism legislation 172, 173; cross-media ownership laws 91; crowdsourcing stories 166; data journalism in 177; decline of print ad revenue in 35, 36, 37, 38, 39; decline of print newspapers in 32, 33, 34, 35, 36, 37–9, 40, 41, 42; Freedom House ranking 174; history of the newspaper market 22, 23, 24, 25; investigative journalism in the 1950s 119, 120; investigative journalism in the 1960s 120, 121, 122; investigative journalism in the 1970s 122; investigative journalism in the 1980s 111, 122; investigative journalism in the 1990s 123, 124, 125; investigative journalism in the 2000s 125; job cuts in its newspaper industry 43; multiple-newsroom investigations 158; narrowing of story targets in 154, 155; National Security Legislation Amendment Bill (2014) 174; paywall models 198; philanthropic journalism 212, 213, 214; platform neutrality in 165; print ad revenue, comparing with United States 34, 35; print media in 21; Public Interest Journalism

Foundation 213; second-wave of investigative journalism 140n1; single-issue investigations in 155, 156, 168; subsidising of investigative journalism in 117, 118; Walkley Awards 30, 109; *see also* broadsheets; Walkley Awards
Australian, The 25, 26, 27, 28, 29, 30, 71, 97; circulation 40
Australian Broadcaster Corporation (ABC) 28, 44–7, 61, 117, 118, 126, 136, 145, 157; 'Money Makers, The' 130
Australian Communications and Media Authority (ACMA) 113
Australian Financial Review 29, 76, 112, 125, 134; corporate investigative reporting 126
Australian Law Reform Commission 72
Australian Press Council 73
autocracies, and democracies 12
award-winning investigative reporting 151; collaborations 157, 158, 161; correlation with decline of print's circulation 112, 113; GEN awards 231; single-issue versus systemic-issue 155, 156, 157; Walkley Awards 231; *see also* Press Awards; Pulitzer Prizes; Walkley Awards

Baer, Julius 180
Bagdikian, Ben 93
Baker, Mark 103, 126
Baker, Richard 126, 130, 158
Ball, James 183
Barry, Paul 61
Barstow, David 61, 62, 63, 66, 77, 163
Baughman, James 59
'beat' reporting 155, 227
Beecher, Eric 179, 194
Bell, Emily 34, 64, 71
Belsham, Bruce 111
Bengtsson, Helena 63, 157, 166
Berglez, Peter 101
Bergman, Lowell 69
Berners-Lee, Tim 171
Bernstein, Carl 5, 85
Berridge, Virginia 83
Besser, Linton 136, 155, 175
big data 5, 7, 103, 172, 189, 190; access to 171; *see also* NSA leaks; WikiLeaks
Birnbauer, Bill 73; *The Rise of Nonprofit Investigative Journalism in the United States* 6, 212

Blumer, Jay 72, 73
Bly, Nellie 56
Bobbio, Norberto 12
Boland-Rudder, Hamish 162, 163, 164, 166
Bolles, Don 6
Bond, Alan 61
Boston Globe 60, 154; investigation of alleged child sex abuse in the Catholic Church 87, 144
Bray, Theodor 58, 59
breaches in the public trust 74, 75, 115
Britain: Centre for Investigative Journalism 176; 'Climategate' 180; counter-terrorism initiatives 173; crowdsourcing stories 166; data journalism in 176; Freedom House ranking 174; Investigatory Powers Act (2016) 174; local reporting 157; narrowing of story targets in 154, 155; paywall models 198; *see also* Press Awards
'broadloid' 94
broadsheets 22, 29, 30; *The Age* 22, 26; *The Australian* 25, 27, 28; and award-winning investigative journalism 139; circulation of in Australia 39, 40, 41, 42; conversion to tabloids 41, 42; follow-up stories 127, 128, 129, 130; green zone stories 114, 115; and investigative journalism 30; naming of sources 133, 134; *The National Times* 28, 29, 30; 'quality' 226; self-promotion of investigative journalism 131, 132; *Sydney Morning Herald* 22, 26; and tabloids 29; Walkley Award winners 134, 135
Brown, Robert 31
budgets: balancing with reporting 116, 117; of newsrooms, cuts in 145
Burke, Edmund 10
Burns, Creighton 26
Burrowes, Tim 200, 201, 205, 209, 210, 225
Bush (George W.) administration, war with Iraq 61, 62
Business Spectator 76, 116, 117
BuzzFeed 38, 204, 209
bylines 131

Cablegate 178
Cabra, Mar 188, 233
Calvert, Jonathan 67
Cameron, David 91, 187

Carlyle, Thomas 10
Carson, Andrea: *Journalism Studies* 7;
    Media, Culture & Society 7
Castells, Manuel 100, 230
Center for Public Integrity 89
Chadwick, Paul 91
challenges: of investigative journalism
    153, 190; to investigative
    journalism practice 232, 233,
    234, 235; to the media's right to
    know 172, 173, 174, 175, 176; for
    paywall models 199, 200
Chandler, Sol 121
Channel Nine 2, 24, 91, 118
chaos theory 9, 83, 84, 88, 89, 96,
    96, 97, 98, 99, 100, 148; and
    cultural chaos 187, 188, 189;
    reconceptualising 225, 226, 227
chaos-and-control theory 13, 15
checking the facts 67, 68, 69
Chicago Tribune 60
Chomsky, Noam 83, 188;
    *Manufacturing Consent: The Political
    Economy of the Mass Media* 92
'churnalism' 94, 97
circulation, of Australian print
    newspapers 39, 40, 41, 42
Citizenfour 70
citizens, comparison with news
    audience 86–8
classified advertising 4, 194, 195
Clegg, Brett 197
'clickbait' 2, 40, 94, 97
Clinton, Hillary 183
Clurman, Richard 59
Cold War 120; and the 'dark ages' of
    investigative journalism 58
collaborative investigative journalism
    145, 167, 230, 231, 232; award-
    winning collaborators 157, 158,
    161; and the chaos model 226;
    costs of 167, 168; cross-media
    161; between discrete media
    organisations 126; Fairfax and
    public broadcasters 118, 119; and
    GEN awards 177; and the global
    digital public sphere 229, 230; 'The
    Money Makers' 130; multiple-
    newsroom investigations 147, 148,
    149; Panama Papers 144, 148,
    149; *ProPublica* 162; in watchdog
    reporting 101, 102; *WikiLeaks*
    181, 182; *WikiLeaks'* breakdown
    in 182, 183, 184; *see also* cross-
    newsroom collaborations

commercial newspaper attacks on
    public broadcasting 44, 45
computer-assisted reporting (CAR) 15,
    172, 176
conglomerate media businesses 93
connective publishing 178, 179,
    229, 230
constitutionality 12
constructivist media theories 87, 88
content aggregation 38, 39
control theory 9, 11, 13, 15, 83,
    84, 96, 96, 97, 98, 99, 100, 148;
    reconceptualising 225, 226, 227
Conversation, The 212, 213
Cooke, Henry 26
Cooke, John 26
Coronel, Sheila 63; on investigative
    journalism 64
corporate investigative reporting: in
    Australia during the 1990s 124,
    125; decline in 61; GFC impact on
    153, 154
cost-cutting, job cuts 43
Coulthart, Ross 175, 176, 180, 181
counter-terrorism legislation, in
    Australia 172, 173
Courier Mail, The 125
Craigslist 4
Crikey 211
crime stories 124
Critical Theory 9
critiquing the liberal media system 88
cross-media collaborations 161
cross-national collaborations 63, 64,
    80, 167
cross-newsroom collaborations: *The
    Age* and *The Sydney Morning Herald*
    158; in the United States 158, 161
crowdfunding 211, 310
cultural chaos 9, 88, 187, 188, 189
Curran, James 3, 83, 94, 96, 97;
    Media and Power 88
Cushion, Stephen 128
custom native advertising 207

Dag, Pinar 232
Dahlgren, Peter 94, 134
Daily Mail, The 38, 185
daily news reporting 75, 76
Daily Review 204, 207
Daily Telegraph 166
'dark ages' of investigative journalism 58
data journalism 165, 166, 171; CAR
    176; evolution of 176, 177; GEN
    awards 177; rise of 230, 231, 232

data reporters 164
databases 209
Davie, Michael 26
Davies, Nick 12
Dawson, Lynette 27
Day, Benjamin H. 145
DC Leaks 183
de Burgh, Hugo 54, 70, 75, 76;
　*Investigative Journalism: Context
　and Practice* 6
declaring native advertising 208, 209
decline of print newspapers in
　Australia 32, 33, 34, 35, 36, 37–9,
　40, 41, 42
degeneration of the public sphere 11
democracy: and accountability 87;
　constitutionality 12; direct 12;
　investigative journalism, role of 5;
　liberal democratic theory 11–12;
　normative functions of the press in
　85; representative 17n2
'depth' of a story 127; follow-up
　stories 127, 128, 129, 130; and
　naming of sources 133, 134; and
　placement of stories 132, 133;
　self-promotion of investigative
　journalism 131, 132
deregulation, and the public sphere
　90, 91
detective reporting 56, 57; *see also*
　watchdog reporting
developed countries, print ad revenue
　in 37
digital age 3, 4, 5, 12, 21, 80; arrival
　of in Australia 21; avenues of
　experimentation in 228, 229;
　examples of philanthropic funding
　of journalism in 213; impact on
　Australian newspapers 23; impact on
　investigative journalism 62, 63, 64,
　65; legacy media responses to 43, 44;
　and newspaper consolidation 44; rise
　in syndication of news stories 125,
　126, 127
digital-only newsrooms, paywalls for
　200, 201
digital public sphere 100, 101, 102, 103
digital tools for investigative journalists
　163, 164, 177, 178
direct democracy 12
Disney's acquisition of 21st Century
　Fox 93
Doctor, Ken 194
Doig, Alan 94

Domain 44
dominance theories 9, 95, 96, 97
donations 210, 211
Dowler, Milly 71
Duggan, Tim 200, 204, 206, 210, 231
'dumbing down' of news 94

eBay 4
editors: and budget constraints 116;
　and investigative journalism 31;
　IRE 65
'ElectionLand' 178, 225
Epstein, Rafael 128
Ettema, James S. 54, 59, 65, 66, 67, 70,
　71, 76; *Custodians of Conscience* 6
Eun, David 195
Evans, Harold 60
evening newspapers 23, 24; demise of 4
events, hosting 209, 210
evidence-based reporting 68, 69, 98,
　145; and 'fake news' 147
evolution of data journalism 176, 177
exclusivity of investigative journalism
　75, 76
experimentation: in digital newsrooms
　228; in funding models 227, 228;
　opportunities for 228, 229
exposés 97
'exposure journalism': and reporting
　in the public's interest 72; and
　'routine reporting' 66

Facebook 23, 38, 100, 131, 195, 202,
　234; 'Journalism Project' 203
fact checking 67, 68, 69
Fairfax, John 26
Fairfax, Warwick 26
Fairfax Media 24, 31, 39, 91, 97, 103,
　229; award-winning investigative
　reporting 111; decline in stock
　price 32, 33, 34; *Domain* 44;
　'Money Makers, The' 130, 132;
　MyCareer 44; *The National Times*
　28, 29; paywalls 200; role as media
　watchdog 46; syndication 125, 126;
　Walkley Awards 135, 136
'fake news' 15, 46, 89, 146, 190, 232,
　233, 235; and Donald Trump 147;
　inaccurate reporting 147; 'Moon
　Hoax' 145; from the political
　economy perspective 148; rise of 145
false news 146, 173
Farrell, Paul 174
Feldstein, Mark 6, 57, 58

Fields, Robin 164; on investigative journalism 54
financial tabloids 29
Five Eyes group 173
Flew, Terry 180
follow-up stories 127, 128, 129, 130
Forrest, Andrew 158
Four Corners 66, 67, 136; 'Moonlight State' 137
four-step process of investigative journalism 68
fourth estate 10, 83, 84, 101
Franklin, Bob 94, 112, 133, 134
Freedom House, press freedom rankings 174
freedom of the press: anti-terrorism measures impact on 173; in Britain 174; Freedom House rankings 174; in the United States 173, 174; *see also* NSA leaks; *WikiLeaks*
free-to-air television 4, 37; Channel Nine 24
funding investigative journalism in Australia: through philanthropy 119, 212, 213; through subsidies 117, 118
future of investigative journalism 224
'Future of Journalism' 7

Gawenda, Michael 124
Gearing, Amanda 101
Gerard, Robert 126
'Gilded Age' 56
Gill, Raymond 209
Glasser, Theodore L. 54, 59, 65, 66, 67, 70, 71, 76; *Custodians of Conscience* 6
global digital public sphere 229, 230
Global Editors Network (GEN) 177, 231
Global Entertainment & Media Outlook 8
Global Financial Crisis (GFC) 61, 138, 139; and decline in newspaper stock prices 32, 33, 34; and decline of Australian print newspaper circulation 41, 42; impact on corporate investigative reporting 153, 154; and print ad revenue 34, 35; print ad revenue in Australia, decline of 35, 36, 37, 38, 39
Global Investigative Journalism Network (GIJN) 101, 231
global journalism 187, 188, 189

Global Mail 119
global media watchdog model 172
'golden age' of investigative journalism 56
'golden era' of investigative journalism 58, 59, 60, 61
Google 1, 23, 38, 195, 202, 233; iKiosk 203
Gottliebsen, Robert 123
'greater good,' vs. the public interest 73
green zone stories 115
Greenwald, Glenn 70, 173, 184, 185
Greste, Peter 173
gross domestic product (GDP), comparing with changes in print ad revenue 34, 35
Guardian, The 12, 38, 72, 119, 151, 165, 166, 174, 176, 204, 225, 229; NSA leaks 184; revenue model 214; *see also WikiLeaks*
Guardian Labs 207, 208
Gunnlaugsson, Sigmundur Davíð 75, 188
Guthrie, Bruce 30, 122

Habermas, Jürgen 14, 230; on the internet 100; public sphere 9, 10, 11; *The Structural Transformation of the Public Sphere* 9, 84; *see also* public sphere
Hamilton, Alexander 57
Hamilton, James T. 97, 99, 148; *Democracy's Detectives* 6, 74, 98
Haneef, Mohamed 27
Harding, Luke 183
hard news 76
hard paywalls 196, 197, 198
Harmer, Wendy 204
Harwood, Simon 166
'hate media' 27
Herald, The 119, 120
Herald Sun 30
Herman, Edward S. 83, 188; *Manufacturing Consent: The Political Economy of the Mass Media* 92
Hicks, David 127
Hills, Ben 28
history of the Australian newspaper market 22, 23, 24, 25
Hogg, Lionel 120
Hohenberg, John 66
Holmes, Jonathan 61, 66, 136, 137
Horkheimer, Max 9, 88
Houston, Brant 54, 63, 68, 102, 232

HuffPost 38, 204
hybrid business model 203, 204,
    205, 218; advertising 205, 206;
    databases 209; declaring native
    advertising 208, 209; hosting events
    209, 210; native advertising 206,
    207, 208; new media products 210
hyper-commercialism 93, 94
Hywood, Greg 41

Independent Press Standards
    Organisation (IPSO) 75
in-feed ads 207
information drops 76
injustice, and investigative journalism 59
Insider, The 69, 70
Institute for Nonprofit News 161
International Consortium of
    Investigative Journalists (ICIJ)
    63, 164, 165, 185, 225, 226;
    collaborations 162; data analysts
    164; Panama Papers 15, 144, 148,
    149, 161, 172, 178, 179, 185, 186,
    187, 189, 230; Paradise Papers 161
international news media 38
internet, the 5, 99, 100, 194;
    democratizing role of 100, 101;
    Habermas on 100; as news source
    45; online advertising 23
investigative journalism 2, 12, 14,
    15, 53, 55; applying a slide scale
    to 79; assembling the story 68;
    in Australia during the 1950s
    119, 120; in Australia during the
    1960s 120, 121, 122; in Australia
    during the 1970s 122; in Australia
    during the 1980s 122; in Australia
    during the 1990s 123, 124, 125;
    in Australia during the 2000s 125;
    and broadsheets 22, 30; budgets
    116, 117; challenges of 153, 190,
    232, 233, 234, 235; comparative
    analysis 9; Coronel on 64; and daily
    news reporting 75, 76; 'dark ages'
    of 58; data reporters 164; decline
    in corporate investigative reporting
    61; decline of 3; 'depth' of a story
    127; detective reporting 56, 57;
    and the digital age 62, 63, 64, 65;
    digital tools for 163, 164, 177, 178;
    evidence-based 68, 69; follow-up
    stories 127, 128, 129, 130; four-
    step process of 68; funding through
    philanthropy 119; future of 224;

future of in developed countries 21;
    in the 'Gilded Age' 56; 'golden age'
    of 56; 'golden era' of 58, 59, 60,
    61; lack of scrutiny of the doctrine
    of war 61, 62; legal costs of 67;
    limits of 66, 67; media's pursuit of,
    reasons for 99; media's signaling
    the value of 97; muckraking 55,
    57, 58; naming of sources 133,
    134; narrowing of story targets
    153, 154, 155; non-profit 101,
    102; operative definition 149, 150;
    operative definition of 78, 79;
    opportunities for experimentation
    228, 229; peak times for 111;
    peaks for in Australia 28; penny
    press 55; personal skills needed
    for 76, 77; placement of stories
    132, 133; platform, correlation
    with Walkley awards 136, 137,
    138; platform neutrality of 164,
    165, 166; in print newspapers 31;
    promotion of *133*; protection of
    sources 175; qualitative features of
    113, 114, 115, 116, 117, 118, 119;
    'quality' 76, 140; quantity of 108,
    109, 110; reasons for studying 5,
    6, 7; resourcing 155; return benefit
    from 129; rise of data journalism
    230, 231, 232; Robin Fields on 54;
    self-promotion of 131, 132; single-
    issue investigations 87, 139; 'special
    reports' 129, 130; subsidising of in
    Australia 117, 118; systemic issue
    investigations 139; technology's
    impact on 60; and television 59;
    and transnational consolidation 93;
    'Trump bump' 89; Walter Robinson
    on 53, 54; *WikiLeaks* as 180, 181;
    see also collaborative investigative
    journalism; data journalism; traits
    of investigative journalism
investigative journalists, role of 85
Investigative Reporters and Editors
    (IRE) 6
'Iraq War logs' 182; *see also*
    WikiLeaks
Isikoff, Michael 53, 76, 225

Jefferson, Thomas 57
job cuts 43
John Fairfax Holdings 1, 2
journalism: data-driven 171; decline
    in 2; global 187, 188, 189; job cuts

43; public trust in 89; 'yellow' 29; *see also* data journalism; evidence-based reporting; revenue models for journalism
Junkee 38, 200, 204, 206, 207, 231

Kaplan, David 101, 149
Keane, John 12
Kemp, Charles 26
Khashoggi, Jamal 173
Kitchener, Jennifer 61
Knightley, Phillip 60
Knight Ridder 2
Knobel, Beth, *The Watchdog Still Barks* 6
Koang-Hyub, Kim 13
Kohler, Alan 76, 116, 117, 129
Krautreporter 211

LaFleur, Jennifer 231, 232
leaked information 76
Leen, Jeff 62, 63, 67, 70, 71, 76, 80, 152
legal costs of investigative journalism 67
legislation, impact on freedom of the press 174
Leigh, David 183
Lewis, Charles 56, 59, 61, 148, 161; *935 Lies* 62
Lewis, Paul 166
Lewis, Terry 137
liberal democratic theory 9, 11–12, 14, 89, 90; anti-terrorism measures 173; chaos paradigm 83, 84; critiquing 88; and marketing 152; *see also* political economy theories of the media
limits of investigative journalism 66, 67
Lippmann, Walter 86, 92, 146; *Public Opinion* 90
local reporting 157; correlation with resourcing of investigative journalism 155
local/global nexus 95

MacFadyen, Gavin 176
mandatory fields in the operative definition of investigative journalism 78, 79
Manne, Robert 27, 179
Manning, Chelsea 182
manufactured consent 90
Marinda, David 184
marketing: and liberal democratic theory 152; new media products
210; self-promotion of investigative journalism 131, 132
Martin, Catherine 123
Masters, Chris 77, 111, 116, 117, 136, 137
mastheads: closures 153; job cuts in 43; *The National Times* 28, 29
Mayman, Jan 124
McCarthy, Joanne 24
McChesney, James 83
McClymont, Kate 53, 63, 68, 76, 165, 195, 202
'McDonaldisation' of print media 133
McGregor, Craig 123
McKenzie, Nick 126, 158
McKnight, David 6, 28, 59, 119, 133, 134
McLuhan, Marshall 194
McNair, Brian 12, 83, 86, 96, 100; chaos theory 88, 89
McQuail, Denis 73, 83
measuring, audience of online stories 116, 117
measuring quality 114
media: business model of 195; chaos-and-control theory 13; criteria of the public interest 73; Habermas on 11; and liberal democratic theory 11–12; power of 72; power of in the 21st century 92, 93, 94; propaganda model 92; reasons for pursuing investigative reporting 99; and the state 92; state influence over 90
Media, Entertainment and Arts Alliance (MEAA) 31, 32
media's right to know 172; NSA leaks 184, 185; Panama Papers 185, 186, 187; whistleblowing, cost of 184, 185; *WikiLeaks* 178, 179, 180, 181, 182, 183, 184
methodology, interviews 7, 8
Meyer, Philip 13, 98, 104; *Precision Journalism* 176
Miami Herald 2
micropayments 215, 216, 217
Mill, John Stuart 86
Mitchell, Chris 27
Mitford, Jessica 58; *The American Way of Death* 6; *The Making of a Muckraker* 5
'Money Makers, The' 130, 132
'Moon Hoax' of 1835 145
morality, as trait of investigative journalism 69, 70, 71

muckraking 55, 57, 58, 59, 119
Muller, Denis 73, 75
multiple-newsroom investigations 147, 148, 149; in the United States 158
Mumbrella 200, 207, 209, 210, 225
Murdoch, Dame Elizabeth 27
Murdoch, James 44
Murdoch, Rupert 24, 26, 27, 39, 44, 197; Disney's acquisition of 21st Century Fox 93; media assets 91, 92
MyCareer 44
MySpace, News Corp's acquisition of 39

naming of sources 133, 134
narrative storytelling 228
narrowing of story targets 153, 154, 155
National Times, The 28, 29, 30, 109; investigative reporting 123; Walkley Awards 122
native advertising 206, 207, 208; declaring 208, 209
network theory of communication 100, 101
Newcastle Herald 24, 87, 125
News.com 38
News Corp: acquisition of MySpace 39; paywalls 200; Walkley Awards 135, 136
News Corp Australia 24, 37, 91; decline in stock price 32, 33, 33, 34; News.com 38
Newsday 60
news organisations, and content aggregation 38, 39
newspapers: closures 153; penny press 55; 'profit controversy' 104; size of, tabloid versus broadsheet award winners 134, 135; tabloidisation of 94; 'Trump bump' 89
newsrooms: budget cuts in 145; multiple-newsroom investigations 147, 148, 149
news stories, increase in syndication in the digital age 125, 126, 127
News of the World 71
New York Sun, 'Moon Hoax' of 1835 145
New York Times, The 61, 77, 95, 151, 229; collaboration with *ProPublica* 158; paywall model 198, 199; Tweed Ring investigation 56, 57
Nixon, Richard 5
noble paywalls 196, 197, 199

non-profit newsrooms 102, 161; philanthropy model for revenue 212, 213, 214, 215; Reporters without Borders 173; in the United States 214, 215
non-scheduled reporting 76
normative functions of the press in a democracy 85
Norris, Pippa 87, 88
NSA leaks 178, 179, 184; *see also* Snowden, Edward; *WikiLeaks*

Obama, Barack 175, 182
Obermayer, Bastian 185
O'Donnell, Penny 113
OECD countries, print ad revenue in 42
O'Neill, Eamonn 31
online advertising 23; share of all advertising expenditure 37
operative definition of investigative journalism 78, 149, 150; mandatory fields of 78, 79
'other, the' 92
overlap between chaos and control theory 96
ownership: of Australian newspapers 24, 25; correlation with Walkley Awards 135, 136; cross-media, Australian laws on 91; and digitisation of physical goods 202

Packer, Kerry 118
paid search units 207
Paine, Thomas, *Common Sense* 10
Panama Papers 63, 144, 148, 149, 161, 172, 179, 185, 186, 187, 189, 230; and cultural chaos 187, 188, 189
Paradise Papers 161, 230
Paranyuk, Nina 120
participation 12
paywalls 201, 217, 218; challenges for 199, 200; consumer attitudes toward 202; for digital-only newsrooms 200, 201; 'freemium' model 197, 198; hard 196, 197; hybrid business model 203, 204, 205; for legacy newspapers 198; one size does not fit all 197, 198, 199; for quality news 202; for smaller newspapers 199, 200; 'sweet spot' 198, 199; for tabloids 197, 198; *see also* evidence-based reporting
Pell, George 87
penny press 55, 145

Perkin, Graham 26, 28, 60, 122
philanthropy 196; funding investigative
  journalism through 119; as revenue
  model 212, 213, 214, 215
Philby, Kim 60, 147
Pitkin, Hana F. 86
placement of stories 132, 133
platform neutrality 164, 165, 166
platform of investigative journalism,
  correlation with Walkley Awards
  136, 137, 138
pluralist media theories 83, 84, 95, 96;
  versus constructivist theories 87, 88
Poitras, Laura 70, 161
political economy theories of the
  media 89, 90; and 'fake news' 148;
  manufactured consent 90; media
  power and the state 90, 91, 92;
  propaganda 90
power: 21st-century media 92, 93,
  94; chaos theory 83, 84, 88, 89;
  'of flows' 101; liberal democratic
  theory 89, 90; media and the state
  92; and the public interest 72
Press Awards 150; digital journalism
  awards 163
press barons 215
Pringle, John D. 26
print newspapers 1, 9; in Australia, ad
  revenue decline in 35, 36, 37, 38,
  39; in Australia, circulation 39, 40,
  41, 42; in Australia, history of 22,
  23, 24, 25; in Australia, ownership
  concentration 24, 25; consolidation
  of 44; decline in circulation 3, 4, 21;
  and international news media 38;
  job cuts in 43; reader demographics
  32; revenue decline in 31, 32; stock
  price 32, 33, 34, 35, 36, 37–9, 40,
  41, 42; *see also* broadsheets
'profit controversy' 13, 104
promotion of investigative stories
  133
propaganda 90
propaganda model 92
ProPublica 64, 97, 98, 119, 212;
  collaboration with *The New York
  Times* 158; 'ElectionLand' 178, 225,
  230; other collaborations 162
protection of sources 175
Protess, David 87; *Journalism of
  Outrage* 74
public broadcasting 88; collaboration
  with Fairfax media 118, 119;

commercial newspaper attacks on
  44, 45
public interest: and the 'greater good'
  73; as trait of investigative journalism
  71, 72, 73, 74
Public Interest Journalism Foundation
  213
public opinion: and manufactured
  consent 90; trust in the media 89
public sphere 9, 10, 84; degeneration
  of 11; and deregulation 91; global
  229, 230; news audience compared
  to the citizen 86–8; *see also* digital
  public sphere
public trust, breaches in 74, 75
Pulitzer, Joseph 56
Pulitzer Prizes 150; digital
  investigative projects 165; digital
  journalism awards 163

qualitative features of investigative
  journalism 113, 114, 115, 116, 117,
  118, 119
'quality' journalism 76, 98, 113, 114,
  140, 226; correlation with decline
  of print's circulation 112, 113;
  cutbacks, impact on 104; measuring
  114; and paywalls 202, 203
quantity: of investigative journalism 108,
  109, 110; of print investigations 111

radical sharing 188
radical transparency 178, 179, 189
rationality 12
reader demographics 32
recommendation widgets 207
reconceptualising chaos and control
  theories 225, 226, 227
Reporters without Borders 173
representative democracy 11–12, 17n2
resourcing of investigative journalism
  155
revenue: comparing between
  Australian and American
  newspapers 34, 35; print ad
  revenue in Australia, decline of 35,
  36, 37, 38, 39; of print newspapers,
  decline in 31, 32; *see also* revenue
  models for journalism
revenue models for journalism 196;
  crowdfunding and donations 210,
  211; experimentation 227, 228;
  hybrid business model 203, 204,
  205; micropayments 215, 216, 217;

paywalls 196, 197; philanthropy
212, 213, 214, 215; *see also* paywalls
rise of 'fake news' 145, 146, 147;
inaccurate reporting 147
Robinson, Paul 122
Robinson, Walter 154, 157, 203;
on 'beat' reporting 155; on
investigative journalism 53, 54
Rockefeller, John D. 57
Rogers, Simon 231
Roosevelt, Theodore 57
'routine reporting,' and 'exposure
journalism' 66
Rusbridger, Alan 72
Ryle, Gerard 69, 75, 186, 189

Sanders, Bernie 183
scheduled reporting 76
Schiffrin, Anya 61
Schudson, Michael 6, 11, 85, 124,
147, 182; on watchdog reporting 86
Schultz, Julianne 6, 28, 60
Schumpeter, Joseph 86
Scott, Mark 117, 119, 152; on
Twitter 132
second-wave of investigative
journalism in Australia 140n1
'serious' papers, tabloidisation of 94
Seven West Media 24
Sheridan Burns, Lynette,
Understanding Journalism 72
Shirky, Clay 195
Sinclair, Upton, *The Jungle* 57
single-issue investigations 87, 139, 227;
in the 1960s 121, 122; in Australia
155, 156, 168
size of newspapers, tabloid versus
broadsheet award winners 134, 135
Smith, Mike 27
Smith's Weekly 58
Snooper's Charter 174
Snowden, Edward 15, 63, 70, 161, 172,
174, 175, 185, 189; NSA leaks 184
social media 100, 163; crowdfunding
210, 211; as news source 45;
reaching bigger audiences with 205;
shareability of news stories 131, 132;
third-party promotion through 132
social network analysis (SNA) 177, 178
soft news 76
soft paywalls 196, 197, 217
Spain, compulsory fees for 'snippets' 234
Sparks, Colin 94, 134

Sparrow, Jay 72, 73
'special reports' 129, 130
Speight, Selwyn 127
Stapenhurst, Rick 74
state, the: danger of disclosing secret
information 175; and media power
90, 91, 92; and surveillance 184, 185
State of the News Media report 39
Steffens, Lincoln, *The Shame of the
Cities* 57
Stiglitz, Joseph 61
stock price, of newspaper companies
3, 32, 34, 35, 36, 37–9, 40, 41, 42
Stokes, Kerry 24
Street, John 94
subscriptions 197; *see also* paywalls
subsidising of investigative journalism
in Australia 117, 118
Süddeutsche Zeitung 185
Summers, Anne 123
Sunday Age, The 125
Sunday Telegraph, award-winning
investigative journalism of 121
Sunday Times, The 30, 60, 122, 151
'sunshine journalism' 179
surveillance: and NSA leaks 184; as
threat to investigative journalists
174, 175, 233
'sweet spot' 13
*Sydney Gazette and NSW Advertiser,
The* 22, 26
Sydney Herald 22
Sydney Morning Herald 26, 29, 30,
37, 112, 194, 229; circulation 40;
collaboration with *The Age* 158;
'Report on Migration' series 127
Sykes, Trevor 61
syndication of news stories, increase in
during the digital age 125, 126, 127
systemic issue investigations 87, 101,
139; in the 1960s 121, 122; in
Australia 119, 120

tabloidisation 94; crime stories 124
tabloid newspapers 27, 29; and
broadsheets 29; conversion of
broadsheets to 41, 42; financial
tabloids 29; moral panic about
94; paywalls 197, 198; *Truth* 121;
Walkley Award winners 134, 135
Tarbell, Ida 57
Taylor, Lenore 165
Teacher's Pet, The 27

technology: and access to big data
171; data technologies and methods
177, 178; digital public sphere 100,
101, 102, 103; as hindrance to
investigative journalists 175; impact
on investigative journalism 60, 95;
internet, the 99, 100
television, and investigative
journalism 59
theories 9; 'chaos' 13, 88, 89, 96,
97, 98, 99, 100; 'control' 11, 96,
97, 98, 99, 100; Critical Theory 9;
dominance 95, 96, 96, 97; liberal
democratic theory of the media
11–12; pluralist versus constructivist
88; political economy theories of the
media 89, 90; *see also* chaos theory;
control theory
third-party promotion through social
media 132
third wave of watchdog reporting 59, 60
Thomas, Hedley 27, 69, 71
Thomson, Mortimer 55
Thyer, Danielle 56
Tiffen, Rodney 39, 54, 69, 91
Till, Emmett 59
Times, The 26, 29, 97, 151
tips 68
Tomlinson, Ian 166
Toohey, Brian 61
traits of investigative journalism:
agenda-setting 75, 76; checking the
facts 67, 68, 69; exclusivity 75, 76;
exposing hidden information 69;
morality 69, 70, 71; public interest
71, 72, 73, 74; time and resources
65, 66; victims and villains 71
transnational consolidation 93
Trump, Donald 62, 212, 232; and
'fake news' 146, 147
'Trump bump' 89, 233
trust 234; and 'fake news' 146; and
inaccurate reporting 147; in the
media 89; in the news media 46;
public, breaches in 74, 75
Truth 121
truth-telling, as trait of investigative
journalism 69
Turner, Graeme 61
Twain, Mark 56
Tweed, William M. 56
Twitter 100, 131, 132; crowdsourcing
stories 166

UK Joint Committee on Privacy and
Injunctions 72
United States: corporate media
ownership in 93; cross-newsroom
collaborations 158, 161;
crowdsourcing stories 166; data
journalism in 176; freedom of the
press in 173, 174; GEN awards
177; local reporting 157; multiple-
newsroom investigations 158;
narrowing of story targets in 154,
155; non-profit newsrooms 214,
215; NSA document leaks 174, 175;
paywall models 198; philanthropy
model 212, 213; platform neutrality
in 165; print ad revenue, comparing
with Australia 34, 35; *ProPublica*
97, 98; Rupert Murdoch's media
assets in 91, 92; war with Iraq, lack
of media scrutiny of 62; *see also*
Pulitzer Prizes
unscheduled reporting 76
US Constitution, First Amendment 10
US Investigative Reporters and Editors
(IRE) 65

van Niekerk, Mike 31
verification, as trait of investigative
journalism 67, 68, 69
Veri Gazeteciligi Türkiye (Data
Journalism Turkey) 232
Vice 38
victims and villains, in investigative
journalism 71
Viner, Katharine 214, 225

Wainer, Dr Bertram 121
Walker, Bret 172
Walkley Awards 109, **150**, 151,
231; in the 1950s 119, 120;
in the 1960s 120, 121; in the
1970s 122; in the 1980s 122; in
the 1990s 123, 124, 125; in the
2000s 125; criteria for 'quality'
114; digital journalism awards
163; ownership, correlation with
135, 136; platform of journalism,
correlation with 136, 137, 138;
tabloid versus broadsheet award
winners 134, 135; to *WikiLeaks*
180; winners of 30
Wall Street Journal, The 97, 151, 206
Warner, Charles Dudley 56

Washington Post, The 5, 26, 30, 63, 95, 98, 151, 199; Watergate investigation 122
watchdog reporting 5, 9, 53, 84, 95, 225, 2214; collaborative 101, 102; decline in corporate investigative reporting 61; and the digital age 62, 63, 64, 65, 80; Fairfax Media 46; muckraking 57, 58; Nellie Bly 56; news audience compared to the citizen 86, 87, 88; penny press 55; 'quality' 115, 140; Schudson on 86; sustainable funding 104; and television 59; third wave of 59, 60; Tweed Ring investigation 56; *see also* traits of investigative journalism
Watergate scandal 5, 6, 122, 147; role of the investigative journalist in 85
West Australian 24; investigative reporting 123
whistleblowing: cost of 184, 185; NSA leaks 184, 185; Panama

Papers 185, 186, 187; *WikiLeaks* 178, 179, 180, 181, 182, 183, 184
Whitton, Evan 53, 58, 120, 121, 123, 180; 'Life on the Pension' 124
WikiLeaks 76, 126, 127, 161, 172, 176, 188, 189, 225, 229, 230; 'The Afghan War Diary, 2004–2010' 182; breakdown of collaborations 182, 183, 184; Cablegate 178; 'Collateral Murder' 181, 182; connective publishing 178, 179; as investigative journalism 180, 181; involvement of the mainstream media 179, 180; 'Iraq War logs' 182; radical transparency 178, 179, 183; Walkley Award to 180
Wilson, Jason 180
Woodward, Bob 5, 85

'yellow' journalism 29
Young, Sally 27, 29, 30, 86, 127
YouTube 38, 100

Printed in the United States
by Baker & Taylor Publisher Services